MENTORING TO EMPOWER RESEARCHERS

SUCCESS
IN RESEARCH

MENTORING TO EMPOWER RESEARCHERS

SAM HOPKINS
SUSAN A. BROOKS
ALISON YEUNG

$SAGE

Los Angeles I London I New Delhi
Singapore I Washington DC I Melbourne

$\circledS$SAGE

Los Angeles | London | New Delhi
Singapore | Washington DC | Melbourne

SAGE Publications Ltd
1 Oliver's Yard
55 City Road
London EC1Y 1SP

SAGE Publications Inc.
2455 Teller Road
Thousand Oaks, California 91320

SAGE Publications India Pvt Ltd
B 1/I 1 Mohan Cooperative Industrial Area
Mathura Road
New Delhi 110 044

SAGE Publications Asia-Pacific Pte Ltd
3 Church Street
#10-04 Samsung Hub
Singapore 049483

Editor: Jai Seaman
Editorial Assistant: Lauren Jacobs
Production Editor: Manmeet Kaur Tura
Copyeditor: Sarah Bury
Proofreader: Jill Birch
Marketing Manager: Susheel Gokarakonda
Cover Design: Shaun Mercier
Typeset by: C&M Digitals (P) Ltd, Chennai, India

Library of Congress Control Number: 2019944398

British Library Cataloguing in Publication data

A catalogue record for this book is available from
the British Library

ISBN 978-1-5264-6512-2
ISBN 978-1-5264-6511-5 (pbk)

Dedication

This book is dedicated to all the mentors and mentees in our lives: past, current and future. It is also dedicated to:

The memory of **Miriam Brooks**,

The **Deeres, Hopkins and Haveropkins**,

The **Yeungs – Sitkow, Peter and David**.

Contents

List of further resources

Activities

Case studies

Checklist

Examples

Figure

Reflection points

Tables

Top tips

Voices of experience

Acronyms and abbreviations

3MT – Three-minute thesis
AFHEA – Associate Fellowship of the Higher Education Academy
BBC – British Broadcasting Corporation
BME – Black and minority and ethnic
CEO – Chief executive officer
CV – Curriculum vitae
ECR – Early career researcher
FHEA – Fellowship of the Higher Education Academy
GDPR – General Data Protection Regulation
HE – Higher education
HEI – Higher education institution
HR – Human resources
IT – information technology
LGBTQ+ – Lesbian, Gay, Bisexual, Transgender, Queer plus
NSS – National Student Survey
PI – Principal investigator
PRES – Postgraduate researcher experience survey
REF – Research Excellence Framework
STEMM – Science, Technology, Engineering, Maths and Medicine
SWOT – Strengths, weaknesses, opportunities, threats
TEF – Teaching Excellence Framework
USP – Unique selling point

About the authors

Sam Hopkins is now the teaching fellow in learning development on the biosciences foundation year programme at the University of Surrey. Before this she worked in the Researcher Development Programme at the University of Surrey. She has designed a range of training and support activities for researchers at doctoral and postdoctoral level and lead on the mentoring programmes. The mentoring programmes cover four main transition points in the academic career: for final-year undergraduates thinking about moving into academia; for new doctoral researchers; for early career researchers making the move towards funding or a permanent academic position; and for those making the transition out of academia and into other areas of work. Sam studied BSc Zoology in the UK and then completed her MSc and PhD in South Africa. Following completion of her doctorate, she held positions as tutor and then lecturer at the University of the Western Cape. She then continued her postdoctoral research career in biological sciences at the University of Surrey and spent a short time at the Zoological Society of London creating a course for fellows on the EDGE Programme. Sam met Alison through their work at the University of Surrey and Susan at various researcher support conferences.

Susan A. Brooks is Director of Researcher Development at Oxford Brookes University where she develops, oversees and delivers the professional development and skills training programmes for research students and research-active staff at all levels across the university. She began her academic career by completing a doctorate, in pathology, at University College London Medical School in 1990. She continued with postdoctoral cancer research at the same institution until 1995 when she joined Oxford Brookes University, initially as a Senior Lecturer in Cell Biology, and later as Reader. Her interest in researcher development began in 2006 when she took what was originally planned to be a three-year half-time secondment that eventually turned into an ongoing passion – fuelled by her own experience of the joys and challenges of attempting to build a career from the starting point of being a researcher. She continues to teach biomedical sciences to undergraduates and heads a small cancer research team alongside her researcher development role. She was promoted to Professor in 2016, partly based on her researcher development work. Susan has a deep interest in mentoring, having established a university-wide research staff mentoring scheme in 2015 and, over the course of her career so far, having benefited from the wisdom, experience and friendship of many formal and informal mentors. She first met Sam when they were thrown together with the task of delivering a workshop on mentoring at a researcher development conference, and met Alison through Sam.

Alison Yeung is an independent academic writing consultant. She has substantial experience of designing and delivering writing training to academics in various research institutions in the South East of England. Prior to working independently, Alison had been Writing Skills Teaching Fellow at the University of Surrey for seven years, where she had responsibility for the design and delivery of writing training for doctoral researchers. While her professional career of over 30 years has been in the teaching of English and the design of teaching materials, her doctoral research, which she completed in 2004, was in Systematic Christian Theology and Chinese Philosophy. This deep interest in understanding the differences, and indeed similarities, between cultures has served her well in her work to support doctoral researchers in today's international academic environment. She continues to be passionate about the importance of intercultural understanding in our higher education institutions. Alison first met Sam at the University of Surrey, and since then they have worked together on a number of projects. It was through Sam that Alison met Susan at the start of this book project.

Acknowledgements

We wish to thank all those who have helped to bring this book to fruition, some of whom have offered anonymous Voices of Experience, for which we are extremely grateful.

We also owe a debt of gratitude to the following, who have offered their voices of experience, advice and feedback:

Dr Adam Bingham-Scales, Learning Development adviser (Outreach), University of Surrey

Gemma Connell, doctoral researcher, University of Surrey

Sam Connolly, doctoral researcher, Oxford Brookes University

Dr Tom Crook, Senior Lecturer in Modern British History, Oxford Brookes University

Claudia Davidson, doctoral researcher, University of Surrey

Dr Jacques Deere, Postdoctoral researcher, University of Amsterdam

Dr Peter Dukes, Deputy Director, Africa Research Excellence Fund

Jos Finer, Co-Director, Centre for Academic, Professional and Organisational Development, University of St Andrews

Dr Elena Forasacco, Teaching Fellow, Imperial College London

Rajat Gupta, Professor of Sustainable Architecture and Climate Change, Oxford Brookes University

Dr Alexander Harden, Students' Union President, University of Surrey

Gillian Johnstone, Organisational & Staff Development Adviser, University of Strathclyde

Nigel King, Professor of Applied Psychology, University of Huddersfield

Dr Jacquetta Lee, Reader in Sustainable Systems Analysis, University of Surrey

Alistair McGregor, Professor of Evolutionary Developmental Biology, Oxford Brookes University

Dr Tim Mitchell, CEO, Sareum Ltd

Jason Okwuonu, Undergraduate in Medical Science, Oxford Brookes University

John Runions, Professor of Biological and Medical Sciences, Oxford Brookes University

Dr Nadya Yakovchuk, Teaching Fellow, University of Surrey

Finally, we wish to extend our sincere thanks for all the help, feedback and support we have received from the team at SAGE and, of course, from our collaborative authors in the *Success in Research* series: Pam Denicolo, Dawn Duke, Marcela Acuña-Rivera, Julie Reeves, Sue Starbuck and Carol Spencely.

1

Introduction

Who is this book for and what is it about?

Those of us who write and edit for the *Success in Research* series believe that those who engage with research will do it better and will enjoy it more if they know more about it. Knowledge is power! We also subscribe to, and live by, the notion that we all improve our practice and delight further in our work if we share our ideas, challenges and successes with others. This book exemplifies that and is intended for doctoral researchers and professionals in higher education institutions (HEIs) at any stage of career with an interest in mentoring in an academic context. Your interest may be in running mentoring programmes within your institution, being mentored for a particular career-related reason, or being a mentor to support the career development of someone else. We have aimed to create a practical guide on mentoring within the academic context that feels as if we, the authors, are speaking directly to you, the reader. To create that feel, throughout the book, we use 'you' when referring to the readership, and 'we' when referring to the authors. Obviously, because a mentoring partnership consists of mentor and mentee, we sometimes use 'you' to refer to mentor and 'you' to refer to the mentee, but we hope we make it clear within the text as to which readership we are addressing at the time.

To intensify the personal feel throughout the book, in each chapter, we invite you to reflect on the topic under discussion, either in the form of an Activity or Reflection Point. You will also find various other boxes in the chapters, including Top Tips, Voices of Experience and Case Studies, which we hope you will find inspiring, thought-provoking and engaging.

The book is split into three parts. Part I covers mentoring at transitions and explores key transitions in the path from the journey into the doctorate all the way to academic progression and beyond academia. It also includes a chapter on cultural awareness. Part II covers mentoring for skills development, where chapters focus on key aspects of an academic career and how mentoring can be used in each one. For example, there are chapters on publishing and writing funding bids, as well as networking and speaking skills. Part III covers mentoring in everyday practice within higher education. Here, we touch on doctoral supervisors and principal investigators as mentors as well as the newer concept of reverse mentoring.

What is mentoring?

Mentoring, in essence, is simply a conversation with a purpose. You might then wonder why there is so much written about mentoring when it is such a simple concept. The abundant amount written on the subject lays bare how complex it can be, how useful it is and in how many situations it is seen as being advantageous.

Mentoring in the modern sense has its roots in the business world, from which it has filtered through to education, the health service and charities. As such, much of the literature so far has come from the business world and only recently has the mentoring taking place in academia been put under the spotlight and researched.

In this introduction, we touch lightly on the definition of mentoring and on some theory behind it, but do not go too deeply into either because this book is intended as a practical guide rather than as a tome about the theory. If you are interested in the theory behind mentoring, we have provided a Further Reading section at the end of this chapter that includes several good publications on the theory.

The definition of mentoring

Mentoring is not well defined in a large proportion of the literature; indeed, there is even discussion about whether a true definition is actually required (Garvey, 2011). For the purpose of this book, we loosely define what mentoring is in our context, and what it is not.

A mentor is usually more skilled or experienced than their mentee in a particular topic or situation (Murray, 2002). Shea (2002) defines a mentor as a 'trusted counselor [sic] or guide', and we agree that there must be trust between mentor and mentee because the advice given by the mentor is unlikely to be adopted if there is little trust between the pair (Monti et al., 2014). The mentoring process is based around a relationship between two people, and is therefore different for every pairing, which may help to explain why it is such an intangible concept to define and describe. At the same time, this individual, directed and entirely bespoke support is what makes mentoring so effective and empowering. After reading many definitions of mentoring and coaching we have come to agree with Hamilton (1993: 3):

> It can seem that one has slipped into Lewis Caroll's world of Humpty Dumpty where a word can mean '…just what I choose it to mean – neither more nor less'.

In essence, we define mentoring as a developmental activity. The relationship is built on trust and the mentor has experience of a specific skill or background. It is a relationship between a more experienced (mentor) and less experienced (mentee) person with the goal of developing the mentee by conversations between the pair.

How is mentoring distinct from other one-to-one developmental activities?

The distinctions between mentoring, coaching, tutoring and even supervising are notoriously ambiguous, and often the terms are used interchangeably. We certainly recognise the blurred boundaries between each of these terms but prefer not to regard them as synonymous. Instead, we view them as part of a broad spectrum of developmental activities, ranging from those that tend to be non-directive to those that are more directive in nature (Thomson, 2013). The emphasis here is very much on 'tend to', as it would be wrong to assume that those activities at one end of the spectrum are completely devoid of the features characteristic of activities at the other end.

Tutoring and supervising are more directive actitivities, due to their emphasis on providing guidance for a specific outcome and learning. Mentoring and coaching, with their emphasis on personal development of mentee or coachee, are frequently less directive. What tends to distinguish mentoring from coaching is specific non-directive techniques employed by coaches to enable the coachee to find their own solution to a problem, while mentors bring their wider knowledge, experience or skill to help the mentee achieve their aims.

We emphasise throughout this book that good mentoring relationships are highly reflective and are often driven by the mentee, the effect of which is to foster fewer directive elements in the relationship. Below, Tünde Erdös, an experienced coach, explains her understanding of the difference between coaching and mentoring.

Voice of Experience 1.1

The difference between coaching and mentoring

Coaching may be viewed as an umbrella term for various forms of facilitation, including mentoring. In contrast to mentoring, coaching may be regarded as a vehicle that 'contains' coachees. The *Encyclopedia Britannica* defines coach as a 'horse-drawn carriage [...] an enclosed body [...] carrying passengers' from where they were to where they want to be. Unlike mentoring, coaching represents an instrument on the coachee's journey from A to B rather than a person who is familiar with the coachee's field of work, imparts expert knowledge, contributes experience or gives instructions – a mentor.

In Homer's *Odyssey*, we learn how Mentor is put in charge of Odysseus's son Telemachus when Odysseus leaves for the Trojan War. As an old friend of the family, Mentor advises Telemachus on, and assists him with, how to find his father. From the *Odyssey*, we can gain deep insight into mentoring as we understand and practise it today: a **dyadic** informal approach to dealing with dilemmas adopted by a more experienced professional who imparts wisdom to and shares knowledge with a less-experienced individual in a workplace setting. While both the coaching and mentoring relationship are bounded by time and characterised by trust and benevolence, mentoring's primary goal is to promote the mentee's knowledge-based development.

Tünde Erdös, Executive Coach and Coaching Process Researcher,
Owner and Director of PTC Coaching

The theory behind mentoring

Academics have attempted to apply theory to why and how mentoring works. Research has considered the function of the mentoring relationship, how the mentoring relationship grows and progresses, and the characteristics of mentor, mentee and situation that make the relationship successful. This has resulted in no one clear overarching theory, but several well-established schools of thought being applied to mentoring.

We will not dwell on the theory in this introduction because other authors have done it better than we could in the short space permitted here. For this reason, in the 'Further Reading' section of this book we reference other texts that you can consult for a deeper understanding of mentoring theory. For a wonderful review, look at the critique written by Bozeman and Feeney (2007), where they despair at the large number of mentoring programmes in relation to the small amount of useful theory developed, and conclude that the issue lies with the multi-disciplinarity of any sort of mentoring research and therefore the natural splitting of any theory developed.

Benefits of mentoring

Due to the broad range of activities falling under the umbrella of mentoring, the benefits are considerable. For that reason, in each chapter, we highlight the benefits specific to the mentoring context focused on in the chapter. In this intro-duction, we wish simply to summarise the general benefits for the mentee and the mentor. We start by summarising the benefits to the mentee using the three categories that Crisp and Cruz (2009) highlight as areas where mentoring tends to operate effectively: professional and career development, role modelling and psychological support. We then focus on benefits to the mentor, by using the categories proposed by Dolan and Johnson (2009).

Professional and career development

Mentoring is effective in supporting professional and career development. Among the many facets of this support is the role a mentor plays in introducing a mentee to the 'rules of the game'. An example of this is seen in academia when new members of a faculty have a mentor to help them understand the values of the department they have joined, the way the department works and what is expected of them as new members of staff. People often seek mentors who are one step ahead of themselves in terms of career progression. This strategy can aid the career development of the mentee because the mentoring pair are able to have conversations about what will be expected of the mentee at the next level and what they need to do to get there. Mentoring for professional and career develop-ment is discussed throughout this book and is particularly focused on in Chapter 2, 'Mentoring for those entering doctoral education', Chapter 3, 'Mentoring for early career researchers', Chapter 4, 'Mentoring for academic progression and promo-tion' and Chapter 6, 'Mentoring for the transition out of academia'.

People also seek mentors to develop professionally in one area of their work. For example, an individual who is good at speaking at conferences may mentor someone less confident in public speaking with the goal of passing on their experience in this one skill. We consider this in Chapter 10, 'Mentoring to support development of spoken communication skills'. Alternatively, an academic who has had grant or publication success might mentor a junior colleague in these endeavours, which we cover in Chapters 7, 'Mentoring to support publication', and Chapter 8, 'Mentoring to support grant success'.

Role modelling

Mentors frequently act as a role model to their mentees because they are often in a position to which a mentee is seeking to aspire. Academia uses mentoring for role modelling in many of its schemes, where mentors are assigned to mentees with a similar profile, such as the same gender, ethnic group, background or culture, to have conversations about strategies to optimise progress and maximise success. An example of this is the popularity of **women** mentors in Science, Technology, Engineering, Maths and Medicine (STEMM) subjects, where they have been traditionally under-represented in more senior positions. We touch on the topic of role modelling within mentoring throughout this book, especially in Part I, where we discuss mentoring at transitions, Chapter 9, 'Mentoring to support networking', and Chapter 5, 'Mentoring to promote cultural awareness'.

Psychological support

Mentoring works best when there are no line management responsibilities between mentor and mentee, and so conversations can be very open and honest. We cover the tension between line management responsibilities and mentoring in Chapter 11, 'Incorporating good mentoring principles into doctoral supervision', and Chapter 12, 'Incorporating good mentoring principles as a **principal investigator**'. With this openness comes psychological support that often cannot be given within line management. Evidence suggests that when a student has a mentor, their chances of staying at the institution, graduating and being comfortable within higher education increase (Budge, 2006; Crisp and Cruz, 2009). These outcomes must be in part due to the support that a mentor provides and that they may not get from elsewhere.

Benefits to the mentor were categorised by Dolan and Johnson (2009) in a study of postgraduate students. In the study, mentors reported 14 different gains or benefits, grouped by the authors into five different categories: 'instrumental' benefits, covering employability and productivity; 'socio-emotional' benefits, involving aspects such as confidence, satisfaction and enjoyment; 'interpersonal' benefits, consisting of skills such as communication and mentoring; 'cognitive' benefits, covering intellectual growth; and 'professional' benefits, referring to the better understanding of the workings of the faculty that mentors gained. Each of these broad groups covers a wide range of benefits, which are repeated in the following studies by different authors.

Understandably, given the nature of the mentoring relationship, mentors report feeling fulfilled and developing better interpersonal and communication skills, as well as personal skills such as compassion and patience, while carrying out the role of mentor (Budge, 2006; Dolan and Johnson, 2009; Hudson, 2013). Others highlight very tangible benefits: for example, in Horowitz and Christopher's (2013) report on a mentoring project designed to train postgraduate students in mentoring skills, the mentors reported tangible outputs of the relationships, such as posters, conference papers and publications. Other reported benefits for mentors include greater commitment to and renewed enthusiasm for their work (Clinard and Ariav, 1998), and more time to reflect on personal work practices, which is often not possible in a busy work environment (Lopez-Real and Kwan, 2005; Hudson, 2013).

Another more unusual benefit is the transferability of coaching and listening techniques used in mentoring to other non-mentoring relationships. For example, in Clinard and Ariav's (1998) study, mentors reported using these techniques in their private lives. There are other, more unexpected, outcomes reported, such as mentors of student teachers learning new skills and technologies from their mentee and using some of the skills they had learnt to mentor with the students in their classrooms (Clinard and Ariav, 1998), an aspect of reverse mentoring that is the focus of Chapter 13, 'Reverse mentoring'.

Final word

We hope that in this introduction you have gained a taste of at least some of the many flavours of mentoring present in higher education institutions today. We also hope that this book inspires you sufficiently to find out more about the mentoring avenues open to you at your institution and provides you with enough mentoring tools for you to be able to propose mentoring initiatives if they are currently lacking in your institution.

Further reading

Bozeman, B. and Feeney, M.K. (2007) Toward a useful theory of mentoring: a conceptual analysis and critique. *Administration & Society*, 39(6): 719–739. doi: 10.1177/0095399707304119.

Budge, S. (2006) Peer mentoring in postsecondary education: implications for research and practice. *Journal of College Reading and Learning*, 37(1): 71–85. doi: 10.1080/10790195.2006.10850194.

Clinard, L.M. and Ariav, T. (1998) What mentoring does for mentors: a cross-cultural perspective. *European Journal of Teacher Education*, 21(1): 91–108. doi: 10.1080/0261976980210109.

Crisp, G. and Cruz, I. (2009) Mentoring college students: a critical review of the literature between 1990 and 2007. *Research in Higher Education*, 50(6): 525–545. doi: 10.1007/s11162-009-9130-2.

Dolan, E. and Johnson, D. (2009) Toward a Holistic view of undergraduate research experiences: an exploratory study of impact on graduate/postdoctoral mentors. *Journal of Science Education and Technology*, 18(6): 487–500. doi: 10.1007/s10956-009-9165-3.

Garvey, R. (2011) *A Very Short, Fairly Interesting and Reasonably Cheap Book About Coaching and Mentoring*. London: SAGE. Available at: http://worc.summon. serialssolutions.com/.

Hamilton, R. (1993) *Mentoring: A Practical Guide to the Skills of Mentoring*. London: Industrial Society.

Horowitz, J. and Christopher, K. (2013) The Research Mentoring Program: serving the needs of graduate and undergraduate researchers. *Innovative Higher Education*, 38(2): 105–116.

Hudson, P. (2013) Mentoring as professional development: 'growth for both' mentor and mentee. *Professional Development in Education*, 39(5): 771–783. doi: 10.1080/19415257.2012.749415.

Lopez-Real, F. and Kwan, T. (2005) Mentors' perceptions of their own professional development during mentoring. *Journal of Education for Teaching*, 31(1): 15–24. doi: 10.1080/02607470500043532.

Monti, M. et al. (2014) Retail investors and financial advisors: new evidence on trust and advice taking heuristics. *Journal of Business Research*, 67(8): 1749–1757. doi: 10.1016/j.jbusres.2014.02.022.

Murray, M. (2002) *Beyond the Myths and Magic of Mentoring: How to Facilitate an Effective Mentoring Process*. Chichester: John Wiley & Sons.

Shea, G.F. (2002) *Mentoring: How to Develop Successful Mentor Behaviors*. Menlo Park, CA: Crisp Publications. Available at: http://site.ebrary.com/id/10058896 (accessed 29/09/2017).

Thomson, B. (2013) *Non-Directive Coaching: Attitudes, Approaches and Applications*. Northwich: Critical Publishing. Available at: http://worc. summon.serialssolutions.com.

PART I

Mentoring at transition points

Overview

In any long-term academic career, and indeed in any career, there are major turning points that mark some form of transition. Whether the transition relates to career progression, a change of work focus or work status, or a change of work location, they often mark the point when careers are at their most exciting, but also at their most ambiguous. One reason for the ambiguity, as with any experience that is new, is the element of the unknown – the element of discovery – that underlies the transition. Transition points require us to consider our options and to make decisions and so are the time when we might need the guidance of someone who has already been through a similar transition, for example, the guidance and insights of a mentor.

In Part I we explore different aspects of transition commonly experienced by professionals in higher education institutions (HEIs), following the sequence in which these transitions are likely to happen in a career. For example, Chapter 2 focuses on the initial stage of an academic career, the doctoral researcher stage. Here, we explore how mentoring partnerships can support those considering undertaking a doctorate but who are not yet fully committed to an institution, and those who have committed and are adapting to doctoral research.

We then move on, in Chapter 3, to examine the value and types of mentoring that can help those in the early stages of their postdoctoral academic career, such as an **early career researcher** (ECR) or a postdoc. Here, we acknowledge the often temporary nature of these positions and highlight the ways that a mentoring partnership can help individuals at this stage to manage their current role as well as to make vital preparation for their next position. We emphasise the importance, at the institutional level, of providing mentoring support for this career stage, which so often tends to be rather limited or, in some institutions, even non-existent.

In Chapter 4, focus shifts to the value of mentoring partnerships in supporting academic progression. We consider how mentoring can support those applying for promotion or wishing to build the visibility of their research, for example, by extending their professional network or developing their online presence. We also address issues such as ways that mentoring can help those who form part of an under-represented group in academia, or those wishing to find a workable balance between career and personal life.

In Chapter 5, we address a phenomenon that applies equally to anyone pursuing a career in academia irrespective of their stage: the need for cultural awareness in the HEIs of today with their emphasis on internationalisation. We explore how mentoring can provide valuable support for those transitioning from one culture to another. At the same time, we acknowledge the value to institutions of mentoring that helps all professionals in HEIs, irrespective of cultural background, become more aware of their own culturally-derived assumptions, values and expectations.

Finally, in Chapter 6, we examine the role that mentoring can play in helping those professionals wishing to make the transition out of academia. Here, we focus on mentoring that draws on the expertise and experience of mentors external to academia, and the ways they can help the professional within academia who is considering stepping out to make an informed decision about their move.

At the end of each chapter, we provide specific guidance and suggestions for those responsible for mentoring provision on how to best facilitate and support mentoring partnerships at each of these transition points.

2

Mentoring for those entering doctoral education

In this chapter, we consider:

- Mentoring as an effective support for those deciding whether to undertake a doctorate
- Benefits to doctoral researchers of being supported and guided by a mentor
- Common topics that arise during mentoring at this transition
- The value of mentoring for the mentor, mentee and institution
- Advice for those establishing a mentoring programme for individuals making the transition to doctoral research

Introduction

The transition to doctoral research is exciting and challenging. When considering undertaking this type of study, it is often difficult to know precisely what will be involved in terms of time commitment as well as emotional and financial investment. A mentoring partnership at this pre-commitment stage can play an important role in ensuring that the candidate, should they decide to commit to a doctoral project, does so with clear understanding of what they are committing to. This clarity, in turn, will increase the likelihood that the project is successful and is a rewarding experience.

Once the commitment to a doctoral programme has been made, the next challenge facing the new researcher is not knowing the best way to be productive or what is expected of them at the beginning of the project. This is natural as a doctorate is unlike any other mode of academic study, requiring autonomy and self-direction. Again, mentoring partnerships at this stage can help the researcher to tackle some of these initial stumbling blocks that might impede productivity. Such support is also beneficial for the institution with the current emphasis on ensuring that doctoral researchers move through their programmes in a timely manner.

For those deciding whether to undertake doctoral research, the conventional forms of support offered at HEIs tend to be information-giving events, careers support, open days and information webinars. Those already within an HEI in the final stages of taught education will also have access to academics and careers advisors, from whom they can seek information about doctoral research; however, this type of support will not be available to those considering a doctorate who are in employment outside academia. To help people make an informed choice about entering doctoral education, a mentor who has doctoral experience can be beneficial.

For new doctoral researchers, HEIs will often offer some introductory material sent out before arrival, and may offer an induction for each new cohort or a workshop to introduce doctoral researchers to the task ahead and what is expected of them. All these forms of support can introduce the student to the doctorate; however, many of them assume that the new doctoral researcher will take the information away and use it when they need it, which is not necessarily the case. Too much initial information is likely to lead to information overload and will be lost. Doctoral researchers will gain most from information about the transition if it is given at the right time and so a more bespoke approach to the type of support offered can be useful. This is where mentoring by later-stage doctoral researchers and ECRs can be a useful tool.

A mentoring relationship has considerable value in helping individuals to transition to doctoral research. First, the one-to-one support that a mentor offers provides bespoke and tailored assistance, giving information when it is needed. As this support is less hierarchical than that of an academic or another member of staff, mentoring can feel more comfortable if you are the mentee, allowing you to be more open and candid in your questions to your mentor without fear of judgement or assessment. Second, as all doctoral programmes are different, having a mentor who responds as issues and questions arise will provide more timely support and advice.

Another valuable aspect of mentoring at this transitional stage is the support it provides to help the new researcher integrate into their new research community. For example, as a mentor, you will be able to help your mentee to understand the culture of the new institution, namely the norms, values and expectations that are shared in the institution. If your mentee has never undertaken any form of research before, you can also help them to adapt to the culture of research, which is quite distinct from that of taught programmes. As a mentee, one way that you can help yourself to make this adaptation is by taking cues from your mentor with respect to how to behave, communicate and act in this new culture.

Mentoring to support the two stages of transition to doctoral research can have considerable benefits not just for the mentee, but also for the mentor and the institution. These benefits can often extend beyond the immediate issues relating to the doctorate to personal and social concerns that are common around the periphery of the research. For example, mentees in a 'Starting doc' programme designed for new women doctoral researchers (Stroude et al., 2015) reported benefits including getting information about the process, guidance, counselling, sharing, discussing expectations and networking. Mentees stated that the scheme enhanced their productivity and alleviated isolation and loneliness. Supporting those more personal concerns relating to doctoral research, including how to manage the work and life balance, can make a considerable difference to the doctoral researcher's experience of the transition.

In Table 2.1, below, we outline the potential value of mentoring at the transition to doctoral research for the mentee, mentor and institution.

Table 2.1 Benefits of mentoring at the transition to doctoral research

Benefits of mentoring to final-stage undergraduates and new doctoral researchers	Benefits to the mentors	Benefits to the institution
You will get a feel for what will be expected of you as a doctoral researcher at the outset of your project. Being clear about these expectations will help to ensure that you make the most of your relationship with your supervisors and peers.	As a doctoral researcher or early career researcher (ECR), the time you spend as a mentor will allow you to reflect on how far you have come as a researcher.	Undergraduate mentees discover what a doctorate is actually about and can make an informed choice. This can create a pool of engaged potential doctoral researchers within the institution which may well help to reduce doctorate drop-out rates.
With your mentor you can discuss the unwritten rules of doing a doctorate such as working hours and strategies for effective networking (explored more in Chapter 9).	Talking about your work with a mentee will allow you to reflect on how others perceive your research, which will help you to hone your skill at speaking about your research to those outside your discipline.	New doctoral researchers settle into their project quickly, which will promote greater productivity and more timely completion of the project.

(Continued)

Table 2.1   (Continued)

Benefits of mentoring to final-stage undergraduates and new doctoral researchers	Benefits to the mentors	Benefits to the institution
Your mentor can help you understand the expectations and processes of doing a doctorate.	In mentoring you will enhance your communication skills, which can be applied to other areas of your work, such as working with peers and communicating with your supervisor or principal investigator (PI).	The mentor network can be a good source of early information for the institution on problems, such as a supervisory relationship issue, allowing interventions to be put in place before the problems become critical. (In Appendix B we consider the importance of not guaranteeing confidentiality within a mentoring relationship in situations where the well-being or safety of the mentee or mentor is at risk.)
Your mentor can help you network with other researchers and act as a signpost to other support on campus.	In acting as a signpost for your mentee, you will learn about the services offered at your HEI that you may not have previously been aware of.	Promoting mentoring support at induction events and in marketing material for potential doctoral candidates may attract higher calibre candidates.

The Voices of Experience below touch on some of the benefits to mentoring at this early stage of the doctoral journey. Both people were involved in a programme that matches new doctoral researchers with later-stage doctoral researchers. In this programme, partnerships are not made within departments, but mentoring pairs have common ground in other aspects of their lives, such as their home country or family situation.

Voice of Experience 2.1

New doctoral researcher (mentored for the first six months of her doctorate)

Before my PhD, I was running my own dance company and working as a freelance choreographer and dance workshop facilitator. In the first few months of my doctorate, I really enjoyed doing a literature search and embedding myself more in my field of study. Soaking up knowledge was something that I found really fulfilling. However, there were times where it felt like I was flailing around in the dark, not quite knowing what to do with all this knowledge. That is where my mentor was so important – to have someone to talk to who had been through the same process and the same feelings, and who was able to help me make sense of my thoughts.

I like to have a clear plan of where I am going from the outset. This is quite difficult to sustain in a PhD because your research can take so many twists and turns. I found this quite challenging at first, sometimes feeling like I was always getting things wrong because I had tried one path and found that it did not work, so then had to search for another path. It takes time to realise that this journey is what a PhD is all about; how you respond to new challenges along the way.

Having a mentor made me feel like I was not alone, and also that I was not going crazy! When you are so close to your research, you sometimes cannot see issues and their solutions very clearly. Having a mentor who was also in an artistic discipline, but a very different one to my own, was instrumental in helping me figure out solutions to problems, and sometimes even helped establish that something I thought was a problem was actually an opportunity.

Gemma Connell, second-year doctoral researcher

The benefits of mentoring extend beyond the mentee to the mentor, as illustrated in Voice of Experience 2.2.

Voice of Experience 2.2

A mentor to new doctoral researchers

Being a mentor has been a very worthwhile experience for me in that it has meant I have had to reflect on my own journey – to find what worked well, where the challenges lay and what the effective strategies were for overcoming them. Being able to share these insights with someone else was the cherry on the cake. It also gave me increased confidence when dealing with the new challenges that arose as I entered the final phase of my PhD. These are very different from those that one encounters at the beginning but hearing myself tell these new researchers to take a deep breath and trust the process, meant I did just that myself.

While my first mentee has found her feet and her wings and moved on confidently to other things, we do cross paths and these meetings are always joyous, celebratory ones. She knows that if she does need someone to talk to, I would happily agree to meet with her. My other mentee and I are now exploring a joint initiative for possible presentation next year.

Claudia Davidson, final-year doctoral researcher

How to find a mentoring partnership

The easiest way to get involved with mentoring, whether you are considering a doctorate or just embarking upon one, is to join a mentoring programme already available to you at your institution. These programmes may be called 'peer mentoring' or a 'buddy scheme'. If there is no institution-wide scheme, there may be a local one organised within your department or faculty. These programmes can be particularly valuable if you are an international researcher who is adapting to a new country as they can often match you with a mentor from your own culture, to help you to settle into your new environment. We discuss the value of mentoring to support cultural adaption in Chapter 5.

If you are considering a doctorate and there is no mentoring scheme established at your HEI, you will need to find the necessary support in a less official way. One way to find a suitable person is to seek opportunities to talk to researchers currently undertaking their doctorate. For example, you could contact your institution's Researcher Development Team, Graduate School or Doctoral College and ask if there is a social event, such as a researcher café, that you could visit to meet researchers. Alternatively, you could speak to peers, postdocs or academics, who are often only too happy to introduce you to someone who may be a good match. Another way is to get to know people by joining clubs and societies at the students' union, or by attending events, seminars and training where there will be a broad mix of people at different stages in their academic career.

As a new doctoral researcher, if there is no official mentoring scheme, then you could approach later-stage doctoral researchers whom you meet in your first few weeks at the university. It is a good idea to find someone who is not in your research group or does not share your office to give you a different perspective because this will give you the opportunity to have open and honest conversations with your mentor about your experience of the transition to the institution and research programme. Remember, you do not have to define it as mentoring if that would make it easier for you to approach people. If you do not feel able to source your own mentor, then speak to someone you feel comfortable with, whether that is your supervisor, an administrator or researcher developer, and ask them to help you find a mentor.

Topics that may be covered in transitions to doctoral research mentoring

Mentoring conversations at this transition often cover common themes, which we outline below. Having a sense of these themes can help you as mentor or as mentee to gauge the parameters of your mentoring partnership and prepare for some of these conversations.

Uncovering what a doctorate is

If the mentoring pairing is between someone who is considering a doctorate and someone with doctoral experience, then the conversations are likely to focus on the ability of the mentee to take on the work and what day-to-day life is like. Underlying questions might be 'Am I clever enough?' or 'Do you have to be a boffin to do a doctorate?' Often the step from undergraduate, master's level study or work outside academia to the doctorate can feel quite intimidating. Discussions about the reality of that step and what to expect will help you, as the mentee, make an informed choice.

In mentoring between a new doctoral researcher and their mentor, there will still be conversations about what a doctorate is. Part of the process of doctoral research is becoming an independent researcher. When you are new to this level of study, you cannot inherently know what this means, and it can take some time to find out. Initially, when the research topic is relatively unknown, you may not realise that you are expected to drive the process of the research and almost project manage your project. As a mentor, you can guide your mentee to become more assertive and take their own initiative. You can approach this using gentle but probing questioning. For example, if your mentee comes to you saying that their supervisor has asked them to read around topic X and they do not know where to start, then you can ask them questions to help them to reflect on what they might do to 'read around a topic'. Question asking in this way, which is a common feature of mentoring conversations, empowers the mentee to find solutions to their own issues within the safety of the mentoring partnership.

Discovering how the process of applying for a doctorate works

Again, if the mentoring partnership is between a mentee who is considering a doctorate and someone with doctoral experience, conversations are likely to focus on the process, such as how to find a supervisor, how to decide on a research topic and how to find funding for the programme. If you want to undertake a doctorate, there are two broad options. First, you can find and apply for a funded studentship, and second, you can develop your own research idea and talk to a potential supervisor. As a mentee, if you are in the institution that you wish to remain in, then approaching a supervisor is a matter of talking to academics within the department.

If you are outside the institution, then within the mentoring sessions you can both do some research into which academics to approach. As a mentor, you might also signpost your mentee to websites such as 'find a PhD' (www.findaphd.com) and 'jobs.ac.uk', and as a mentee, you could do some research on these sites before you meet your mentor, so you go into the meeting prepared with some ideas to discuss.

The relationship between doctoral researcher and supervisor

The relationship between doctoral researcher and supervisor is different from the manager–employee or student–teacher relationship. Supervisory relationships are often based on the expectation that, first, as a doctoral researcher, you will discuss ideas and plan your project with guidance from your supervisor, and, second, that you will manage the relationship. This includes setting the agenda for meetings and suggesting goals and targets for upcoming work. However, unless this is pointed out, you may not be aware of these expectations and may expect a far more directive approach. These differences in expectations sometimes lead to communication problems and can be safely discussed with a mentor outside the supervisory team. Setting clear expectations at the outset of the doctorate helps to promote a harmonious and positive working relationship between supervisor and supervisee, which we discuss more in Chapter 11. This forward planning and expectation setting can be around a diverse range of topics, such as holiday entitlement, working hours, feedback and the working relationship.

In your mentoring discussions, the topic of managing the supervisory relationship may arise. As a mentee, it is useful to know what is expected of you and how challenging it can be for a new doctoral researcher at the start of the programme. As a mentor, reflecting on your own experience at the start of your doctorate can help show your mentee one way of managing this crucial relationship and helping them to find their way.

The topics above are highlighted in Voice of Experience 2.3, where an experienced mentor discusses the main topics that arise in her conversations with mentees.

Voice of Experience 2.3

An experienced mentor talks about common topics in transitions mentoring

During the first meeting, I encourage mentees to tell me a little about themselves – how they came to be doing a PhD, and their research area, and I share a little of my own journey. Thereafter, each meeting begins with me asking the mentee how they are doing and what has happened since our last meeting. The conversation that follows is shaped by their response.

Some topics we cover:

- **Settling in** – where to find help/information (on and off campus). This is of particular concern for the international mentee who, like me, has to grapple with the demands of settling in a new country as well as embarking on their studies.
- **Training and development** – this is the only topic I deliberately engineer, urging mentees to attend the training on offer to doctoral researchers. I share my own experience, explaining what I gained from those I attended.
- **Research skills** – this topic only arises when it becomes a concern for the mentee. I share what worked for me and I point them to workshops and highlight the valuable resource they have in specialist librarians.
- **Supervisor relationship** – conversations on this topic are mainly about how to 'interpret' some of the comments made by the supervisors, understand supervisor obligations and manage their own expectations. For me, it is important that the mentees see their supervisors as being on their team, to ensure each candidate delivers their best work, while honouring the fact that the research ultimately belongs to the researcher. I speak out of my own experience because for me the shift in dynamic from teacher–student to co-researchers was quite significant.
- More generally speaking, conversations I have with the mentees are about **supporting them** – cheering their successes, encouraging them in their initiatives and giving them space to reflect on their own journey in a non-judgemental interaction.

Experienced transitions mentor

Advice for institutions and those establishing mentoring at the transition to doctoral research

In Appendix A we cover the basic aspects of setting up a generic mentoring programme. Below, we focus on two areas that are directly relevant to this specific type of mentoring programme.

Training mentors

It is important to offer mentors at this stage some basic training as they are likely to be doctoral researchers and unlikely to have taken on the role of mentor before.

Within the training, there should be some expectation setting. A key feature of training should focus on what a mentor is and does. For example, in the training and in the guidelines, the boundaries between mentor, tutor and counsellor should be discussed. It is important that mentors know what they can be asked to do and what they should pass on to other services.

There should be a strong emphasis on the other services available, such as student finance, accommodation, well-being, etc., and how to signpost the mentee to the appropriate help. To protect the mentor from feeling that they must shoulder all the mentee's problems, it is important to have a safeguarding statement that requires mentors and mentees to discuss the nature of the relationship, how much can be confidential and what will happen if the mentor is ever concerned about the health or well-being of the mentee. Most HEIs will have a safeguarding policy which you should refer to. A generic safeguarding statement may look like this:

> The conversations we have will be confidential and information will only be disclosed with your consent or in exceptional circumstances where your health, safety and well-being or the health, safety and well-being of others is a concern.

In Chapter 1 we highlighted some differences between coaching and mentoring. However, within the training it is useful to include some coaching models which allow the mentor to see that to be a good mentor does not require them to have answers for all issues; rather, they should focus more on asking questions to help the mentee develop their own answer. Any coaching model that suits the trainer will work, but our preference is the GROW model (Whitmore, 2009) for its simplicity.

Matching

There is no easy rule that will guarantee a good match every time. Our advice is to get to know your mentors so that when you have an application from a mentee, you will be able to match not just on the information provided on the application form, but also based on your personal knowledge of the mentor. When the mentors apply, you might include a question on the form about their background, hobbies, academic and work history. This will give you the insight to make matches on more than simply their current academic situation.

When mentees apply, they should be asked to outline what they would like in a mentor and any specific requirements that would help you match their needs to one of the individuals in your pool of mentors.

Chapter summary

The transition to doctoral research is one of the major steps in higher education. As a mentee, it is essential before embarking upon a doctorate to be aware of what to expect so you can decide if it is right for you, and mentoring can assist with that. When beginning a doctorate, the support of a mentor at the transition can help you to settle into the new environment and the way of working so that you can make the best start possible. Clearly, this benefits the institution as well as the mentors and mentees, and this is a good reason for institutions to initiate and support mentoring programmes for people at this stage. We have also provided guidance to potential mentees on strategies for finding a mentor and making the most of the mentoring partnership. Further, we have offered suggestions to mentors on how to be effective in the mentoring partnership and how to get the most from the experience. Having explored mentoring for those entering doctoral research, in the next chapter, we consider mentoring for early career researchers.

Further reading

Collings, R., Swanson, V. and Watkins, R. (2014) The impact of peer mentoring on levels of student wellbeing, integration and retention: a controlled comparative evaluation of residential students in UK higher education. *Higher Education*, 68(6): 927–942. doi: 10.1007/s10734-014-9752-y.

Golde, C.M. (1998) Beginning graduate school: explaining first-year doctoral attrition. *New Directions for Higher Education*, 1998(101): 55.

Lunsford, L. (2012) Doctoral advising or mentoring? Effects on student outcomes. *Mentoring & Tutoring: Partnership in Learning*, 20(2): 251–270. doi: 10.1080/13611267.2012.678974.

Stroude, A. et al. (2015) Mentoring for women starting a PhD: a 'free zone' into academic identity. *International Journal of Mentoring and Coaching in Education*, 4(1): 37 52. doi: 10.1108/IJMCE-06-2014-0019.

de Valero, Y.F. (2001) Departmental factors affecting time-to-degree and completion rates of doctoral students at one land-grant research institution. *Journal of Higher Education*, 72(3): 341–367.

Waye, F. (2017) *Safeguarding Students and Changing the Culture*. Available at: www.universitiesuk.ac.uk/blog/Pages/Safeguarding-students-and-changing-the-culture.aspx

Whitmore, J. (2009) *Coaching for Performance: GROWing Human Potential and Purpose. The Principles and Practice of Coaching and Leadership* (4th edition). London: Nicholas Brealey.

3

Mentoring for early career researchers

In this chapter, we consider:

- A definition of early career researcher (ECR)
- How mentoring is useful for researchers at this stage
- How to establish a beneficial mentoring relationship
- Common topics covered in mentoring conversations
- How to establish a mentoring programme in a department or HEI

What is an early career researcher?

There is no general agreement on the definition of an ECR. You might be perceived as one if you are in a postdoctoral position where you have taken a job funded through a research grant and where the research is guided by the grant-holding principal investigator (PI). Alternatively, you could hold a fellowship grant having been awarded the funding to do your own research. In a few, very specific, situations you may, as defined in the **UK Research Excellence Framework (REF)** 2014 exercise, be a new member of academic staff within the standard probationary period but on a permanent contract (Research Excellence Framework, 2017).

In this chapter we will only concentrate on the former two definitions (see Chapter 4 for mentoring for probationary academics). Common to the first two definitions is the research-only focus of the fixed-term contract. This means that to move onto your next position, which might be an academic post (see Chapter 4) or a move outside academia (see Chapter 6), you must actively find opportunities in your current post to acquire the skills that you are likely to need in your next position. Thus, temporary contracts for ECRs sometimes lead to a conflict of interest between you the researcher and your line manager, especially if you are in a postdoctoral position, because the line manager will have employed you to do a specific piece of research while you are concerned about your next step and how to improve your chances of gaining employment beyond your current contract.

Why do ECRs need support?

Often ECRs are a forgotten group because their voices are not present in national metrics and league tables, such as the UK National Student Survey (NSS) or Teaching Excellence Framework (TEF). This makes the case for supporting ECRs difficult, but also essential, as Dr Carol Spencely explains in Voice of Experience 3.1.

Voice of Experience 3.1

A researcher developer's view of ECRs' support needs

Rather than asking 'Why do ECRs need support?', I think we should be asking 'Why are we not supporting our ECRs more?' ECRs are often at a pivotal career stage. They are frequently on fixed-term contracts with a dedication to their research projects that overrides their own best interests to focus on securing the next position.

The next stage in their careers is not clear and straightforward (in contrast to what others may perceive). An academic position is not guaranteed, but many will have no experience beyond the academic world and will be unsure of any other career possibilities. This group of staff is the 'hinge' in the scissor plots when we monitor the gender balance in our university research staff profiles. They are dedicated, fabulous and inspiring people with a wealth of skills that can be used in a multitude of future career options. However, they are not officially 'academic' staff and they are not students, so they may fall between the established development provision and careers support provided for these groups.

Our ECRs are a valuable group of staff for universities; they are usually the main drivers of research outputs within research teams and are the future of the academy, who will bring in research funding and attract students and other researchers into their teams. Coupled with this is the fact that they are often at a life-stage when starting a family or other life-decisions will be prominent. Thus, the questions should be 'Why are we not supporting ECRs more?' and 'How can we support them more?'

Dr Carol Spencely, lead in the development of ECRs, University of Surrey

Mentoring is an empowering activity for ECRs because the support is personal and tailored to the needs of the mentee. As an ECR, the fixed-term nature of your contract is likely to mean that you have multiple foci in your work: conducting research to the highest standard, getting involved in developmental activities and thinking about your next position. You may have a line manager who will provide good advice and guidance about your current role (see Chapter 12). However, as you are also likely to be focused on your next career step, your line manager may not be best placed to have a candid conversation about future plans as your priorities may not be totally aligned; specifically, your line manager's primary goal is to complete the project, while for you this goal is only one of many. Having a mentor from outside the group or department can be a step towards you developing research independence from your line manager, because a mentor will provide you with a different perspective to help you reflect on your research and options for future directions, while introducing you to their own research network.

Apart from those general benefits, there are numerous specific benefits for mentee, mentor and the institution, which are summarised in Table 3.1.

Table 3.1 Benefits of mentoring ECRs to the mentee, mentor and institution

Benefits to the ECR	Benefits to the mentor	Benefits to the institution
Talking to someone outside your research group offers a safe space to discuss personal challenges away from your line manager.	You will increase your researcher network and discover research being done in other departments, kindling fresh ideas for your own research.	Successful research staff will go on to form networks that benefit the institution.
You will get an opinion on your plans, achievements and current work that is likely to be less focused on your current project.	You may meet potential collaborators for the future.	Providing this type of support contributes towards the metrics that win external recognition, e.g., Athena SWAN and HR Excellence in Research award submissions.
Talking to someone outside your research group will broaden your network across your current institution. (See the benefits of having a broad professional network in Chapter 9.)	Mentoring counts towards your continuing professional development. Mentoring of junior colleagues is often a criterion for promotion to senior positions.	Successful ECRs are likely to be more productive in terms of research outputs, publications and/or impact during their time at the HEI.
You may be exposed to opportunities about which you would not have otherwise heard.	Being a mentor will enhance your communication skills with other ECRs. This can help your relationships with your own ECRs, leading to a more productive research team.	Mentoring is good for staff well-being for both mentors and mentees, which may contribute to higher levels of staff satisfaction with their work and workplace.

(Continued)

Table 3.1 (Continued)

Benefits to the ECR	Benefits to the mentor	Benefits to the institution
If you are aiming for a lectureship and your mentor has already taken the next step in that direction, you will gain insight into what you must do to make that step yourself.		
If your mentor is a senior academic, they will be able to provide insight into how HEI departments work and the types of strategy to use to further your career.		

How to get involved with ECR mentoring

Mentoring is part of everyday life in academia whether we recognise it as mentoring or not. In their review of the mentoring literature, Crisp and Cruz (2009) consider a number of mentoring functions, including role modelling, encouraging, counselling, consulting and sponsoring, which we mentioned in Chapter 1. As an ECR, the type of role you want your mentor to play will depend on the stage you are at in your career and the mentoring goals you have. Reflection Point 3.1 may help you to find an appropriate person.

Reflection Point 3.1

What to consider as an ECR when searching for a mentor

As an ECR, there are many goals that a mentor can help you with. It is useful to identify precisely what you need your mentor for so that you can identify a suitable person. Answer each of the questions below as honestly as possible:

- What goal are you aiming to achieve through mentoring? For example, are you looking for someone with whom to discuss a fellowship bid, or someone who can help you negotiate departmental politics?
- Are there particular characteristics or experience you want them to have? For instance, experience with a specific funding body or of managing work and a young family, or a researcher who has just made the step to a permanent position?

- Would you like them to come from a particular department or research field? As an ECR, it is important to develop your research independence from your PI to broaden your research network as much as possible. You could use this mentoring opportunity to network with researchers from other disciplines with whom you could collaborate later.

Know that the answers to these questions will change as your progress through your career, and so you are likely to need various mentors at different times.

Once you are clear precisely what you want your mentor for, the next stage is to investigate if there is a mentoring programme at your institution. The scheme may be run from a staff development department or a Doctoral College or Graduate School. The scheme might be a general staff scheme rather than one specifically for ECRs. If there is no dedicated mentoring programme, you may be able to join a course such as Springboard, Navigator or Aurora (see Further Reading), which is likely to have an aspect of mentoring embedded within it, such as mentoring with a senior academic or a buddy scheme. There may be cost implications for these courses and so it is sensible to talk to your PI if you would like to join one.

As a mentee, if your HEI does not offer dedicated programmes, then there are some steps you can take to find a mentor yourself. You could use the mentor profile that you identified in Reflection Point 3.1 to help you find the right person. You may already know someone with a suitable profile within your department, but a better idea is to have a mentor outside your department who will be detached from your current project. This may also help you to be open and honest about your concerns, aspirations and plans. If you do not know anyone, ask around. Colleagues may know an academic who has the experience you are interested in or you can get information from institutional and web-based online profiles about academic experience. Join institution-wide events and network at training and seminars to see if there is anyone suitable. A final source of mentors may be funding bodies or professional bodies which may offer their own schemes or at least allow networking so you can meet your future mentor. Once you have identified a potential mentor, email them outlining what you are asking of them and why.

As a potential mentor of an ECR, if you are approached by a prospective mentee, find out what they want a mentor for. Assess if you can provide that support and if you have the knowledge. Remember that it is not your role to know all the answers but to know how to guide your mentee to their own answers. It is also important as a potential mentor to:

- find out from your mentee what kind of time commitment they are looking for from you
- be confident before committing that you can afford that time for a mentoring relationship
- reflect on any potential conflicts of interest with other relationships you have within the department or institution that might arise if you take on this specific mentee.

If you are both happy to establish a mentoring partnership, then you can use the proforma in Appendix A to help guide the first conversation and set the expectations for future meetings

The mentoring relationship

Mentoring between an ECR and a member of academic staff can take many forms and cover many topics. A key priority of this particular type of mentoring partnership is ensuring that it is carried out in a psychologically safe place. As a mentor, creating a confidential environment where your mentee feels that they can broach any topic and feel listened to will allow you to support your mentee appropriately. Voice of Experience 3.2 offers a mentor's thoughts on the relationship.

Voice of Experience 3.2

Being a mentor for an ECR

Being a mentor to an ECR is a challenge and a privilege. You need to build a relationship in which they can be honest about how things are (or are not) working, where they want to go next and what they need to be able to get there. It can be tempting to tell them 'do it this way', but you need to remember that they are not you, so only give examples and support, and work with them to understand the likely outcomes of any course of action on their part.

Importantly, you need to recognise when your role as a mentor has reached a natural end, and to make that transition smooth and harmonious. That does not necessarily mean you cease contact, but it changes the dynamic between you. Watching a mentee outgrow the mentee/mentor relationship is a wonderful thing – it means it has worked!

Dr Jacquetta Lee, University of Surrey

Reasons for establishing an ECR mentoring relationship

Generally, the reasons that ECRs seek a mentor fall into eight broad themes: developmental activities, managing current relationships, future career steps, role model, champion, signpost, unwritten rules and personal aspects of life. We explore each of these next.

Conversations are likely to be about developmental activities that can be undertaken by members of research staff. If you are an ECR, it is often not easy to discuss these aspects of your work with a line manager because their advice may be skewed towards the need for you to produce outputs for the current grant. A mentor, however, will have no conflict and so can provide unbiased advice about what is right for you. For example, you may wish to attend a course on writing a fellowship application, but that course will take up several hours. Since writing a fellowship application is not part of your current role, your line manager may not see the value in you attending. As a mentor, however, you will be able to weigh up the usefulness of the course with your mentee, discuss whether it is a good use of their time and help them make a case to their line manager that they should find time to attend the course.

At this stage, mentoring may also be about negotiating the relationships and politics of the research group, department or school. With a line manager, these relationships may be too close to have an honest conversation; it might even be that the challenging relationship is that with the line manager. As an ECR, you may have come from a relatively solitary existence as a doctoral researcher and are now expected to manage relationships with your colleagues and line managers. As a mentor in this situation, ensuring that the mentoring space is safe and confidential for these conversations is clearly of utmost importance.

If your mentee is trying to manage a difficult relationship, the conversation could focus on the other party's possible point of view, or how to behave with particular people to make the relationship smoother. When the mentee feels they need to have an open conversation with the other party, then you can help by taking the role of the other person or by helping them prepare what they want to say. As the mentee, you may wish to take some time to reflect before your mentoring meeting to uncover the particular aspects of the relationship or situation that you are finding challenging.

Mentoring conversations at this level are also often about future career steps, given the uncertain nature of short-term contracts common for ECRs. This conversation will be slightly different depending on whether you, as mentee, are in a postdoctoral position or have a fellowship. If on a fellowship, then your next career steps could be a permanent academic position or something outside academia. If you are in a postdoc position, then there is a third option of applying for a fellowship for an individual research project. Be aware, though, that PIs can sometimes talk to their ECR about funding they are applying for and how they will be able to extend their ECR's contract but without any concrete assurance that this is possible. As a mentor, you are in a good position to consider the situation objectively and give your suggestions based on what you believe is best for the mentee without being concerned about the project or institution. An example of this would be if your mentee has been offered a permanent position six months into an 18-month contract: their line manager may have a different viewpoint from you about whether it is in your mentee's best interests to take the new position. Hearing your viewpoint as well as that of their PI will allow your mentee to reflect on their options from different angles, which will help them to make an informed decision. When considering career planning, you may find Activity 3.1 useful.

Activity 3.1

Career planning in a mentoring conversation

As part of the mentoring conversation, carry out the following activity together to explore career options and planning.

- Together, investigate the types of future careers possible. Discuss the sorts of jobs available in your discipline and do some online research together about the availability of these roles. If you are the mentor in this conversation, you could help your mentee identify the aspects of their current role and previous jobs that they have enjoyed or found fulfilling. You could then look at different jobs that include these aspects. However, it is important for both you and your mentee to be aware that you are not a career coach; rather, your function is to act as a signpost for additional professional support if you feel your mentee needs it. For example, you could suggest that they visit your institution's careers service, if you have one.
- Look together at job adverts and the requirements for different roles and positions. As a mentee, you could do some online research and take a print-out of the types of position you are looking at to your mentoring meeting. As a mentor, you will be well placed to signpost your mentee to places they may not have looked.
- Together use the gap analysis activity in Chapter 4 with an example job advert for the next career step the mentee wants to take (see Activity 4.2 on p. 49). This analysis considers what is required for the role and how far the mentee's current skills and experience match those needed for the role. That activity focuses on academic progression but the principles will apply for any job. For example, if your mentee

wishes to move away from academia to become a medical writer, you can identify the lists of skills and experience required of a medical writer and work together on how your mentee can gain these skills and experience.

Role modelling in ECR mentoring can be valuable in various aspects of academic life. It can be a useful vehicle for learning how to function as an academic, for example, how to interact with colleagues both within and outside the institution or how to manage a heavy workload. Role modelling can also be about how to manage a certain situation. For example, we are often asked by ECRs for a mentor who has a young family to learn strategies for successfully managing work and family responsibilities.

A mentoring partnership that includes an element of role modelling can also be beneficial for individuals from groups that may be under-represented in academic positions (Green et al., 2017), such as ethnic minorities or those with particular disabilities. A mentor who has first-hand experience of the challenges that mentees face in this respect will be a valuable role model from whom strategies to address such issues can be learnt. For example, if you feel an outsider in your academic community, which is sometimes the case if you are a member of an under-represented group, your mentor's role modelling might help you to learn strategies to integrate into the community (see Chapter 11). You might also be able to follow their example of building their research network and making influential connections to further career opportunities, which are discussed in Chapters 4 and 9.

Mentors may act as the champions or sponsors for their ECR mentees by taking active steps to advance their mentee's career. As a mentor, you may introduce your mentee to certain influential individuals, such as successful grant writers for conversations about ways to approach writing a grant proposal (considered further in Chapter 8), or an academic with a strong publication record for advice on writing convincing journal papers (discussed in Chapter 7). Alternatively, you can put your mentee's name forward for particular activities that will enhance their career prospects or reputation. For more detailed discussion of the championing role of a mentor, see Chapter 4, p. 47.

We have already noted that ECR contracts tend to be short-term, and consequently ECRs often need a mentor who can help them adapt to a new environment quickly. To support this settling-in process, as a mentor, you may consider pointing your mentee to people and departments that can help them in their current work or their future plans. You can also talk about the unwritten rules of your institution that you have learnt about over the years. This type of conversation is particularly helpful to mentees who have no previous experience of moving institutions, and so assume that new work environments are like previous ones. Mentors with experience of numerous academic institutions will be only too aware that each work environment has its own implicit rules and idiosyncrasies that employees only discover slowly.

It may be that the mentoring partnership does not focus solely on the next career step but more on personal circumstances and how to balance the role as ECR with life outside the institution. As a mentor, if you feel happy to discuss these aspects, then it can be helpful for the ECR to hear about how you dealt with similar experiences. If, however, you feel that this is beyond your role or ability, then make sure you know which staff members, often in Human Resources (HR) departments, to refer them to in order for them to get the support they need.

How to care for the relationship

As with any worthwhile relationship, the quality of your mentoring partnership will be determined by the amount of time and energy that both parties invest in it. You are both likely to have considerable work pressures, so it is easy for your mentoring relationship, a personal development activity, to be pushed to the bottom of the list. However, to make the most of the benefits that both can gain from the partnership, you each need to invest the same level of commitment and energy to maintaining it. The relationship will have a natural life-span, and it is important at regular points to reassess the goals of the relationship and check if the mentoring remains useful. When it has come to an end, it is important to formally terminate the relationship rather than letting it peter out. One way to do this is to discuss future steps. It may be that you have gained a future collaborator, contact or champion.

Not all mentors will have had training in how to be a good mentor, nor will all mentees have had any guidance on how to be a good mentee. This may lead to situations where guidance offered by the mentor does not feel right for the mentee. For example, as a mentee, you may find that your mentor strongly suggests something which you do not feel would work for you. Then, as a mentee in this situation, it is important to highlight to your mentor in a tactful way that you are not sure the option is right for you. Using open questions is a useful strategy to encourage your mentor to help you explore all of the options open to you, so that you can pick one option and make a solid action plan around it.

As a mentor, it helps to be aware that you are not expected to have answers to every question or problem that your mentee presents, but to know how to guide your mentee to their own answers. Being aware of this will free you from feeling the need to direct your mentee on the 'correct' course of action or solution. Instead, help the mentee to reflect on the advantages and drawbacks of each potential course so that they can make their own informed decision. Once that decision is made, you can then offer support in helping to create a plan of action, outlining the steps to take, people to talk to and final goals.

Information for the institution and those wishing to establish a mentoring programme to support ECRs

In Appendix A we outline the basic guidelines for establishing a mentoring programme. Below we cover the aspects that are unique to a mentoring programme for ECRs.

Recruiting mentors

Academic members of staff are usually very generous with their time to support newer colleagues. It is a good idea to have a pool of willing mentors whom you can call on but you may have to search for mentors with specific skills and experience. At this level, is it useful to have some recognition of the programme from senior staff members, for example, an endorsement from the Vice-Chancellor or heads of department. Such endorsement helps potential mentors to feel that the time they offer is permissible and viewed as valuable by the institution.

Training mentors

You may decide to train your mentors before they begin their mentoring. If so, see Appendix A for more guidance. The advantages of this are that your mentors will have an idea of what is expected of them and gain some skills in mentoring. However, be aware that academics may be reluctant to become mentors if they are required to attend training that takes time out of their busy schedule, and which they may view – rightly or wrongly – that they do not need. At this level, it may be enough to talk to the potential mentee, as an experienced professional, about how to approach the relationship. If you do plan to train your mentors, you might wish to use Checklist 3.1 to begin to develop your training.

Checklist 3.1

Training plan

- Decide what your mentors need to know.
- Collect a directory of all of the services that your ECRs can access.
- Pick a few coaching techniques. This allows the mentors to see that they do not have to have all of the answers and that they can be non-directive.
- Create a set of guidelines about what mentors can and cannot do. For example, it may be important to highlight that a mentor is not a counsellor or a proofreader.
- Show the mentors the process of how the programme works.

Matching

At ECR level, the needs of the mentee are quite specific, as indicated above, and mentees may also ask for very specific characteristics in their mentor, such as a woman mentor or a mentor who has a young family. It is worth developing an extensive contact list for this purpose.

Administration and tracking

Both academics and ECRs are busy people. One way to encourage the mentoring partners to meet regularly is to ensure that they schedule the first meeting. Once the pair have met, they are much more likely to keep up the meetings. To facilitate this, you can offer to arrange that first meeting. It is then the responsibility of the mentoring pair to decide how to take the relationship forward, but tracking the relationship, perhaps an email every three months, to monitor that the pairs are still meeting can help. If they are not, the mentor can be returned to your pool.

Feedback

As with all developmental activities, it is important to gain feedback to make sure that the time you are investing in the programme is worthwhile. The type of feedback you collect will depend on who needs the information and what you wish to use the feedback for. For example, you might wish to collect feedback to evidence the impact of the programme, to improve it, to find out what the ECRs in your institution need, or to gain some understanding of what mentees get from mentoring. So, first, clarify your purpose in collecting feedback and then structure the form appropriately.

Chapter summary

As an ECR, having a mentor can be extremely beneficial because it is a bespoke developmental opportunity. ECRs are a special group for whom mentoring can be especially valuable in preparing them for their next career step due to the liminality of their position. This chapter has indicated the numerous benefits of a mentoring relationship for the mentor and the mentee and has covered how to care for the relationship when both parties are busy working professionals. It has also offered guidance on the types of topic that are commonly covered within these mentoring partnerships and some advice on how to tackle them if they arise. Whatever your role, we hope that this chapter has helped you to see that giving a little time to mentoring at this stage can make a considerable difference to the success of the ECR in their future endeavours.

Further reading

Clarke, H.E. (n.d.) *Aurora, Advance HE*. Available at: www.lfhe.ac.uk/en/programmes-events/equality-and-diversity/aurora/index.cfm (accessed 18/12/2018).

Crisp, G. and Cruz, I. (2009) Mentoring college students: a critical review of the literature between 1990 and 2007. *Research in Higher Education*, 50(6): 525–545. doi: 10.1007/s11162-009-9130-2.

Green, T.D. et al. (2017) African–American Mentoring Program (AAMP): addressing the cracks in the graduate education pipeline. *Mentoring & Tutoring: Partnership in Learning*, 25(5): 528–547. doi: 10.1080/13611267.2017.1415807.

Innovation and Skills Group (2016) *Academic Career Mentoring and Best Practice for Formal Mentoring Programmes*. Biotechnology and biological sciences research council (BBSRC) https://bbsrc.ukri.org/documents/1609-bbsrc-review-mentoring-best-practice/

Research Excellence Framework (REF) (2017) *What is the REF? REF 2021*. Available at: www.ref.ac.uk/about/what-is-the-ref/ (accessed 14/12/2018).

Springboard Consultancy (2018) www.springboardconsultancy.com/ (accessed 18/12/2018).

4

Mentoring for academic progression and promotion

In this chapter, we consider:

- The benefits to mentee, mentor and the institution of engaging in mentoring programmes for academic progression and promotion, including for those groups who may be under-represented in senior roles, such as women and Black and Minority Ethnic (BME) staff
- The ways that individuals can get involved in this type of mentoring, and how institutions can best support them in their endeavours
- How mentors and mentees can work most effectively together to support the academic progression of the mentee

Introduction

In the previous chapter, we considered mentoring for ECRs. In the early stages of their professional careers, this group of staff face specific challenges in making the transition from research-only roles within universities or research institutes to either their first academic post, or out of academia and into other fields. Now, for those who have successfully established their first permanent academic job, the academic career journey is just beginning, so in this chapter we will consider how mentoring can support their development through it. We consider engagement with formal mentoring programmes specifically designed to support academic career progression. This includes schemes to support staff wishing to apply for promotion exclusively, and other mentoring schemes directed at academic progression more broadly, for example, addressing building a strong professional profile, publishing, winning grants, coping with the stresses and conflicts of balancing an academic career with a personal and family life.

A mentor for academic progression and promotion is distinct from, and plays a different role to, a line manager, who may also provide career progression and promotion advice (considered in Chapter 12). The mentor in this context is an individual who is outside the mentee's line management structure and, in order to be distant from local 'politics', outside their immediate academic circle of departmental colleagues as well. They are also clearly separate from the many informal mentors whom, over their career, successful academics acquire through their broader professional network.

The case for mentoring to support academic progression and promotion

Clear evidence of the value of mentoring for career development has emerged from the business world, where this type of mentoring was first established. Consequently, it is embedded in many large organisations. In the USA, for example, 70% of the top companies (the 'Fortune 500') have a mentoring programme. An example of a study demonstrating that career-focused mentoring benefits mentors, mentees and the company, and therefore makes sound business sense, is that of Sun Microsystems (Bellevue University, n.d.). They analysed a range of career progression outcomes, including promotions, salary increases, performance-related bonuses, and retention in around 1,000 employees who had received mentoring compared to colleagues who had not. The results were striking. For example, only 5% of the non-mentored controls achieved a salary increase during the study period, compared to 25% of the mentees and 28% of the mentors. Interestingly, the mentors also enjoyed increased career success, and this finding is borne out in many other studies. Also, the retention rate for the control group over the study period was 49%, compared to 72% for mentees and 69% for mentors, suggesting that both mentors and mentees experienced improved job satisfaction. While the cost of the programme was around $1 million for this large company, the improvement in retention rates alone represented a saving of $6.7 million in avoidable staff replacement costs.

Having taken their lead from the business world, many HEIs now have mentoring schemes to support academic progression. If you are a member of academic staff, engagement with this type of mentoring can be a tailored and effective way to develop the skills, competencies, institutional know-how, strategic thinking and networking necessary to build a successful academic career. As in business, there is ample evidence that these types of mentoring schemes can be effective. For example, Morrison et al. (2014) carried out an evaluation of the impact of formal mentoring on, specifically, promotion rates of academic staff in the Faculty of Medicine, University of Toronto, Canada. They showed that staff who engaged with mentoring were promoted on average a year earlier than those who chose not to.

For HEIs, there are clear benefits to the institution in staff having access to mentoring to support them in developing the skills and attributes necessary to achieve advancement and promotion. They are more likely to feel well supported and valued; consequently, as an employer, you will not only reap the rewards of investment in training and skills development of those staff, but will make financial savings in staff replacement costs. You are also more likely to retain your most talented individuals and see an improvement in staff morale and well-being, which will have a positive indirect effect on student recruitment and satisfaction.

As a potential applicant for an advertised academic post, you may look for evidence that mentoring will be available to support your career progression and, rightly, view such provision as a sign of a good employer. Thus, for HEIs, providing such support maximises your chances of attracting and retaining the best people, which will inevitably impact on metrics such as grant income and publication success, benefiting both those involved in mentoring and the institution they work for. This is part of a 'virtuous circle' of well-supported staff contributing to a positive working environment, which in turn is viewed externally as a good place to work. Below, Gillian Johnstone, who established and runs a mentoring scheme at the University of Strathclyde, reflects on the benefits of mentoring for academic progression and promotion to the mentors, mentees and her institution.

Voice of Experience 4.1

The benefits of mentoring for academic progression/promotion for mentors and mentees and the institution

It makes for a healthy institution, where people are actively engaged in supporting others throughout the organisation to progress. Also, working with someone outside your immediate area in a helping relationship shares knowledge, builds networks and creates opportunities. Universities offer many development opportunities and most people can gain advice within their own department; however, if someone is looking for tailored support from someone who understands their context, who's been there and done that, yet is able to be a little more objective, that's really valuable. Mentoring also builds capacity within the institution for supporting others.

> Our mentees tell us how helpful it has been to them and want to give back by becoming a mentor in the future.
>
> *Gillian Johnstone, Organisational & Staff Development Adviser, University of Strathclyde*

Many mentoring schemes to support academic progression and promotion are equally open to all research/academic staff. In comparison, targeted programmes designed to meet the needs of a particular staff group in their career progression, such as supporting women academics, those who were brought up in a different culture from the one in which they are currently working (discussed more in Chapter 5), or those from ethnic minority backgrounds, can help address issues specifically experienced by these individuals. As an institution, being able to evidence that you are actively supporting the career progression of all your staff will contribute to positive statistics that are increasingly being scrutinised and made public, for example, as part of submissions for **Athena SWAN** and **HR Excellence in Research awards**.

The reasons for these staff facing less favourable career progression experiences are very complex. However, if you are a member of one of these staff groups, it is easy to appreciate that a contributory factor is that, traditionally, the informal mentoring relationships that effectively enhance career progression often form spontaneously between individuals who recognise common ground and can relate easily to each other. Forming such informal partnerships is more challenging if you find that those in senior positions in your institution, who are best placed to support you, have had different life experiences and faced a different range of professional and personal challenges. Engaging in a targeted mentoring programme can, at least, be part of the solution to this issue.

The evidence indicates that these targeted schemes can have powerful effects in empowering the individuals who engage with them to achieve greater academic success. The Equality Challenge Unit (2012) reported on the benefits of several UK university mentoring schemes aimed specifically at supporting women (academic and sometimes also support) staff. They make the point that it is impossible to establish whether positive effects (for example, in terms of career progression) are a direct result of mentoring or due to a combination of factors. However, they report, for example, that at the University of St Andrews, since their programme began in 2005, the proportion of women senior lecturers has increased from 15% to 27%; readers from 15% to 20%, and professors from 11% to 16%. In some cases, success in supporting women staff has led to the programmes being expanded to welcome men mentees too.

The benefits of mentoring for academic progression and promotion to both mentoring partners

As with all types of mentoring, there are clear benefits for both partners in being involved in mentoring for academic progression and promotion. Some of these are generic to any type of mentoring and are covered in Chapter 1. If you are a mentee, for example, benefits include the opportunity for you to honestly discuss and evaluate your current status, strengths and weaknesses, plans and ambitions with a neutral individual from outside your normal line management structure. If you are a mentor, they incorporate feeling a sense of personal fulfilment in knowing that you are helping a colleague to progress in their career, which can be especially profound when you are mentoring someone with whom you feel a specific affinity, for example, someone from a similar social background or ethnic group to yourself. In addition to the generic benefits outlined above, there are benefits specific to this particular type of mentoring, for both partners, summarised in Table 4.1.

Table 4.1   Benefits of mentoring for academic progression and promotion

Benefits to mentee	Benefits to mentor
A greater likelihood of you remaining with your current institution and enjoying increased opportunities there.	Greater overall job satisfaction.
Better work–life balance and mental well-being.	Sharing your experience of balancing your work and home life and still achieving academic success may result in you honing your strategies further to achieve an even better balance.
Increased confidence and self-esteem.	Discussion about your mentee's career will inevitably make you think about, and discuss, your achievements in your own career, and how far you have already come, which may stimulate you to want to go further.
Improved time management linked to greater work productivity.	Discussion of time management strategies within your mentoring discussions may mean that you focus more effectively on your own time management and thereby increase your own productivity.
Greater success in winning external grant funding.	You may have the opportunity to act as a co-PI on your mentee's grant applications (also discussed in Chapter 8) or, through your mentoring discussions, discover new funding opportunities for yourself.
Improvement in your networking skills.	You will be making a new ally or friend, and possibly a new academic collaborator.
Having more ambitious career aspirations and feeling better prepared to achieve them.	Increased self-confidence from seeing yourself, and your achievements, through your mentee's eyes.

Benefits to mentee	Benefits to mentor
An opportunity to gain an insight into the promotion processes from someone who has successfully negotiated the next step in the career ladder and finding out what it will entail for you.	Focusing, with your mentee, on your institution's requirements for promotion/career progression may highlight what you need to do to take the next step yourself.
You are better equipped to develop a more strategic perspective on what your priorities and goals should be for you to make the next career step.	You may appreciate a fresh perspective on your own barriers to progression as you help your mentee to develop strategies to address theirs.
Improved career trajectory, including accelerated promotion and higher salary.	Being involved in mentorship of more junior staff is usually a criterion for promotion to senior academic positions, such as professor, which if you are not already there, you may aspire to.
Exposure, through your mentor, to opportunities that you would not have otherwise encountered.	All the above may contribute to your own improved career trajectory, including accelerated promotion and higher salary.

Source: Adapted in part from Equality Challenge Unit (2012)

Mentoring for academic progression and promotion can be especially empowering to you as a mentee if you initially feel reluctant to put yourself forward, or if you lack confidence in your abilities. This is highlighted by Voice of Experience 4.2, where a woman academic reflects on how her mentor encouraged her to overcome her reluctance to apply for promotion and offered her some very practical help.

Voice of Experience 4.2

Mentoring gave me the confidence to apply for promotion

I had been thinking about applying for promotion for a while and felt reluctant to do so. I think that this came mostly from a lack of confidence and fear of failure. I knew that it would take a lot of work and 'putting my head above the parapet' to go through the promotion application process, and I knew that I would feel crushed and embarrassed if I was not successful. I applied to my institutional academic mentoring scheme and was mentored by a woman academic who had herself been recently promoted. She clarified the whole process for me, gave me excellent suggestions for things I could, and should, get involved in to 'tick more boxes', and gave me brutally honest, and extremely helpful, feedback on drafts of my application. She was also immensely positive and reassuring, which really bolstered my confidence.

Woman academic, recently promoted to professor

Ways to get involved in mentoring for academic progression

If you wish to engage in mentoring for career progression or promotion as a mentor or mentee, you may find that there are formal or informal mechanisms to match you with a mentoring partner within your school or department, and you could ask your line manager for advice on this. Your annual appraisal or review interview, if you have one, is a good place to raise the issue. You could also engage with your institution's mentoring programme, which many HEIs provide as described previously.

If your workplace does not offer these options, it is worth suggesting to whoever oversees such initiatives, for example, the Director of Human Resources, the Head of your Research Office, your Academic Dean or Head of Department, that they should consider setting up a mentoring programme. You could cite some of the evidence as to why this is proven to be an effective strategy (reviewed on pp. 39–41). In the meantime, you may need to look for other ways to get involved. Ideas regarding how to go about this are given in Chapter 3 pp. 28–30. There we consider mentoring to support the career aspirations of ECRs specifically, but the advice applies equally to mentoring for academic staff at more senior career stages.

Top Tips 4.1

Seeking a mentoring partnership

1. Request a mentoring match from outside your immediate circle of colleagues. The mentoring partnership is likely to be more productive when it has a broader perspective free of local politics and you are likely to feel less inhibited about being completely open and honest in your discussions.
2. As a mentee, be very clear about your requirements – what *exactly* are you seeking from the mentoring relationship? What is your *goal*? This might be, for example, to successfully apply for promotion or to put into place the building blocks from which to advance your career over a slightly longer period of time, such as improving your publication record or grant success (each of which are addressed in more depth in Chapters 7 and 8, respectively).
3. As a mentor, be specific about what you can offer, for example, having had recent successful experience of the institution's promotions process, having a strong record of publication or grant success, having experience of successfully juggling your academic career with caring responsibilities.

Are you a good mentoring match?

For your mentoring partnership to be effective, it is essential at an early stage to define the mentee's goal and to confirm that the mentor really does have the relevant experience to support the mentee to achieve it. While this is true of mentoring for any purpose, we find that it is particularly important in mentoring for academic progression and promotion because of the diversity of issues that contribute towards building a successful academic career. Some of these issues are obvious, while some only come to light during mentoring conversations. For example, the mentee's stated goal may be highly focused, such as achieving promotion, publication or grant success, or more nebulous, such as developing greater assertiveness or confidence, managing work–life balance better or successfully keeping research going while raising a young family. If you have been matched by an institutional mentoring programme, then, based on the information that you both provided when you applied, theoretically at least, you should be well matched. However, in some instances, your appreciation of the situation may change as you begin to talk. An example of this is given in Voice of Experience 4.3, where a mentor explains how she realised that she was not a good match for the mentee that she had been paired with.

Voice of Experience 4.3

The importance of being the right match for your mentee

I was recently assigned a mentee through our university academic staff mentoring scheme. She had specifically requested a mentor who had a strong research profile while working part-time. While I match that profile exactly, when I met with her for the first time and we began to talk, we both realised that I was not who she needed. In effect, we are in very different positions. My part-time role is because I have a second part-time position elsewhere, and, critically, I am not a parent. My mentee, on the other hand, was struggling specifically because she was trying to keep her research going while being a mother to two young children and wanted advice on how to juggle her family responsibilities with work. I simply do not have that experience.

Woman mentor, Oxford Brookes University research staff mentoring scheme

Another example is where, as a mentee, you may have requested a mentor with recent experience of going through the institution's academic promotion procedure because you hope to apply for promotion yourself. During early mentoring discussions, you may both realise that some important groundwork needs to be done before you are ready to apply, and a mentor to support you specifically in raising your professional profile externally, strengthening your publication record or grant success record might be more useful at this stage. Your mentor may have that experience and knowledge to support these redefined goals. On the other hand, if you both feel that you are not the best match as a partnership, then you would be advised to refer back to the mentoring programme for an alternative pairing.

Making the most of your mentoring partnership

Of course, there are common aspects to good mentoring regardless of its purpose. These are described in Chapter 1. During your initial mentoring discussions, both parties should work together to clarify the parameters of your relationship, and you may find the 'generic mentoring contract proforma' in Appendix A a helpful guide in this.

There is a broad range of issues that you might focus on together in your mentoring discussions, dependent upon the mentee's needs. Some examples are given in Table 4.2, where we consider what types of experience the mentor might be able to contribute and how, as a partnership, mentor and mentee can go forward in working to achieve the mentee's goal.

Table 4.2 Examples of common mentoring goals and how the partnership can work towards achieving them

Mentee's goal	Mentor's experience	Working together
Raising your professional profile and improving the esteem measures that you may be required to evidence in any future promotion application.	You can share your own strategies for advancement or profile-raising within your department, school or faculty, and increase your mentee's awareness of local politics. You might be able to facilitate professional networking and collaborative opportunities for your mentee to raise their professional profile, within or outside your institution, or both. You may be able to give specific advice about applying for grants or publication.	You can jointly develop strategies to raise the mentee's professional profile, for example, expanding the mentee's professional network, developing their independent research and/ or scholarship profile through collaboration, publication and grant success, and developing, as well as documenting, their teaching excellence.

Mentee's goal	Mentor's experience	Working together
Applying for promotion.	If you have recently successfully negotiated this hurdle, you can bring a wealth of practical advice on the processes involved in promotion success. You can give invaluable feedback on written documents, such as draft CVs and promotion applications. You might suggest activities that your mentee can engage in to strengthen their application.	You can work together to ensure that the mentee understands, and can effectively address, the institutional promotion criteria and processes (further explored in Activity 4.1).
Addressing specific professional challenges that arise because of your background or life situation.	Sharing your experience, strategies and empathy can be both empowering and of great practical value to the mentee.	You can work together to develop strategies for the mentee to progress in their career and achieve the professional success that they desire, while addressing or working around the obstacles they face because of their specific situation.

In some cases, as a mentor, you may also be able to act as a sponsor or champion and to provide concrete opportunities for strategic career development for your mentee. This might include introducing your mentee to influential people, putting their name forward for a specific opening, nominating them for an award, and so forth. This is illustrated in Voice of Experience 4.4, where a mentee reflects on the opportunities that her mentor deliberately created for her.

Voice of Experience 4.4

Having a mentor as sponsor or champion

My promotion mentor was great. She is in a very powerful position within the university and is involved in organising, and speaking at, lots of events that involve external stakeholders. She asked me to deputise for her several times at big external meetings and put my name forward to be considered for membership of a prestigious external committee. Having these activities on my Curriculum Vitae (CV) really strengthened my promotion application.

Woman academic, recently promoted to professor

Designing a career plan

In mentoring for academic progression and promotion more generally, one common issue that may arise is the tension inherent between the need to take on greater responsibility in order to progress and the inevitable impact on work–life balance that taking on this responsibility will have. Your mentoring partnership is an excellent vehicle for considering these issues carefully. For example, your mentoring discussions could serve as a framework through which you might focus on the mentee's career goals and jointly plan a strategy to work towards them, while factoring in other non-career priorities, aims and ambitions. Working together on Activity 4.1 can act as a helpful structure for these conversations.

Activity 4.1

Designing a career plan

Working together, use the following framework to set strategic goals and draft a career plan. If you are the mentee, you can choose to answer the questions in terms of where you would like to be in, for example, a year, five years, 10 or 20 years, or at a range of time points looking forward, depending on your current position and your overarching goals.

1. Imagine yourself in XX years' time…
   - In terms of your career, where are you? What are you doing? How would you describe your life outside work?
   - What phrases do your colleagues or peers use to describe you? What terms do your family and friends use?
   - What are your major achievements or impacts professionally and personally?

2. In order to be there in XX years' time…
   - What specific strategic goals do you need to achieve in your professional and personal life?
   - At what time points do you, ideally, need to have achieved them?
   - Draw a timeline for when they will need to happen.

3. What competencies and skills will you need in order to do that?
   - List each one.
   - For each, how you will acquire them?
   - Who, or what, will you need to help you achieve them?

Considering promotion criteria

Ultimately, the goal of mentoring for academic progression is likely to be promotion, whether that be in the short term (for example, if you are a mentee who has specifically requested mentoring to support your application for promotion in the near future) or in the longer term (for example, where your immediate goals are to improve your publication record, grant success or profile with a view to promotion in due course). To that end, a very practical exercise you could carry out within your mentoring partnership is to carefully consider the institution's criteria for promotion to whatever the next academic grade would be for the mentee. This should be readily available through your HR department. You can then review together the mentee's current skills and experience against what is required for them to take the next step. A gap analysis, such as that outlined in Activity 4.2, may be a good way to do this. The mentee will need to be able to *evidence* that they meet the criteria. Once you can both identify the gaps in the mentee's skills and experience, you can work together to make an action plan, with a realistic time frame, to work towards filling those gaps.

As a mentee, even if you have requested to be mentored specifically for promotion, you may be unaware of promotion criteria and be surprised by how extensive and complex they sometimes are. This is especially true if you have come from a research-only background, where you may not be aware of the breadth of experience you will be expected to evidence. Here, frank discussion and planning with your mentor can be extremely valuable in going forward strategically.

Activity 4.2

Promotions gap analysis (example: promotion from lecturer to senior lecturer)

The criteria listed below, as an example, are a sample of those posted on the Oxford Brookes University HR webpages (www.brookes.ac.uk/services/hr/) for senior lecturer.

Set up a similar grid using the criteria advertised by your own institution for the grade that the mentee is working towards achieving. Work together to discuss which criteria you can already evidence that they meet, and where there are gaps. You can then begin to develop an action plan to address them.

(Continued)

Examples of criteria stated in role profile

Expected to lead on or have significant input to the design and implementation of written course materials and guides.

As a course leader, ensures that the planned quality of the teaching and learning experience is fully achieved.

Sets, marks and assesses coursework and examination material, and participates in awarding processes at faculty and university level.

Participates in university structures which are responsible for quality assurance, policy development and/or implementation, and enhancing the student experience.

Undertakes individual tutorial sessions, supervises projects and dissertations, manages external student activity which contributes to the student learning experience (e.g. fieldwork trips and work placements).

Engages in significant subject, professional and/or pedagogic research.

Disseminates research findings through publications (books, monographs, articles) and/or other appropriate methods.

Supervises the work of colleagues in a research team/project or PhD students.

Gives presentations, lectures, seminars (internal or external) based on personal scholarship and research, and/or exhibits work at appropriate events.

Identifies sources of research funding and contributes to the process of securing grants and/or other forms of research funding.

Information for the institution and those wishing to establish a mentoring programme to support academic progression

Demystifying promotion pathways

Promotion criteria and pathways are generally clearly posted on HR webpages. However, it is surprising how uninformed many staff, especially relatively junior research and academic staff, can be about promotion processes. To address this, if you are involved in supporting the career development of research/academic staff, it is good practice to run regular workshops or seminars to demystify the process. These can be illuminating for both mentors and mentees and inform their planning discussions. Typically, sessions should be aimed at a specific promotion route or level, for example, from junior to senior lecturer, or from reader to professor. Speakers – perhaps representatives from your HR Department or key players in promotion panels – can explain the promotions process and draw participants' attention to the promotion criteria, deadlines for applications and where they can find information online. This is an efficient way to ensure that important information to support career progression is delivered to all staff, including those groups, such as BME and women academic staff, who are often under-represented in senior positions.

There is a mentoring aspect in the sharing of experience by those who sit on promotion panels or those who have recently successfully negotiated the processes. If your institution has a specific issue with certain groups being under-represented in more senior positions, then role models representing that demographic can feature. This is also a good opportunity to promote mentoring schemes to support academic progression.

Setting up an institutional mentoring programme to support academic progression

If you are involved in researcher/academic staff development or are a senior academic who is interested in setting up a mentoring scheme within your department, you will find it helpful initially to consult the generic guidelines in Appendix A for setting up an institutional mentoring programme. We also provide some examples of established schemes and links to scheme resources that you might find helpful in Appendix B. In addition, below we highlight some specific issues that you might like to consider.

In planning your programme, it is particularly important to think about why it is needed and define its remit and aims. What is your evidence for there being a need? For example, is there a challenge in relation to the career progression of certain staff groups? Is there a staff retention problem at certain grades? Have staff commented in staff surveys that they would welcome mentoring for career progression? Do you wish specifically to support staff in academic promotion or in their academic progression more broadly, such as developing their research, publication, teaching excellence and/or grant success? Will it be open to all academic and research staff or targeted at a specific group, such as junior academic staff, women or BME staff? We provide some ideas for designing a programme in Top Tips 4.2.

Top Tips 4.2

Setting up a mentoring scheme for academic progression and promotion

1. Some information and support, for example, demystifying promotions processes and criteria, may be best delivered through a workshop or seminar format, as described above.

(Continued)

2. Start with an evidence base demonstrating a need from which to define the remit and aims of your programme.
3. Convince senior management of the need for, and the value of, mentoring for academic progression – for all staff or for selected staff groups, depending on the remit of the programme.
4. Hold a launch event, preferably with a high-profile and charismatic speaker.
5. Consider carefully on what basis you will match mentors with mentees.
6. Make matches between individuals outside their immediate department or school but within broad subject boundaries.
7. Provide guidelines, resources such as a handbook, and live or online training for mentors.
8. Consider providing a draft contract proforma that mentors and mentees can use as a framework for their initial interactions (an example is provided in Appendix A). This should include clear guidance on confidentiality.
9. Facilitate easy transition of mentees to a different mentor if initial pairings do not work out or once they have run their course.

We strongly advise that, from the outset, you consider how you will evaluate and evidence the impact of your programme. This is especially important because the organisation, administration and smooth running of such a programme requires considerable resources in terms of staff time as well as financial input, and to justify this it is necessary to be able to demonstrate its effectiveness. This is exemplified in Voice of Experience 4.5, where Jos Finer, who has many years' experience of running a very successful research staff mentoring programme, reflects on the challenges in effectively evaluating its impact.

Voice of Experience 4.5

Is a mentoring programme worth it?

I have no doubt that mentoring has the potential to deliver huge impact at individual level – I've seen it. But a good mentoring programme requires a significant investment of resources, so we really need to demonstrate that we are getting the expected benefits. Evaluating scheme processes and the quality of the mentor/mentee experience is pretty routine. The tricky part is understanding the longer-term impacts. This requires longitudinal studies, which get harder to do over time, as people leave the institution and become difficult to track down. However, persevere! Every three or four years, try to follow up with previous participants and ask them to answer a few key questions. For me it's about asking them to reflect on their mentoring experience and to consider what lasting benefit they gained from it. I would be asking them specifically what changes or achievements they would attribute in part, or in full, to their mentoring partnership.

Jos Finer, Co-Director, Centre for Academic, Professional and Organisational Development, University of St Andrews

Chapter summary

Mentoring for academic progression has proven benefits for the mentor, mentee and institution. Mentees and, perhaps surprisingly, their mentors both experience greater salary advances and promotion than their colleagues who have not been involved in such initiatives and are less likely to leave their employer. For the institution, this is clearly positive in terms of staff retention. Programmes directed specifically at supporting staff groups who are under-represented at senior levels, typically women and BME academic staff, for example, contribute to demonstrably equitable rewards for all talented and hard-working individuals within the institution. Staff engaged as mentees are more productive in terms of their pedagogy, scholarship, research, publication and grant success, as they are supported towards meeting promotion criteria and the focus on such criteria can stimulate mentors too to concentrate on their own career progression. Such successes also contribute to a positive working environment for staff and students, which translates into improved staff and student survey data, metrics, recruitment and achievement.

Further reading

Bellevue University (n.d.) *Case Study: Sun Microsystems University Mentoring Program*. www.hr.com/en/app/media/resource/_hcnvuvxk.deliver?s=tAtgXEal qEbPc0euy&layout=og.pdf&mode=download.

Dutta, R., Hawkes, S.L., Kuipers, E., Guest, D., Fear, N.T. and Iversen, A.C. (2011) One year outcomes of a mentoring scheme for female academics: a pilot study at the Institute of Psychiatry, King's College London. *BMC Medical Education*, 11: 13.

Equality Challenge Unit (2012) *Mentoring: Progressing Women's Careers in Higher Education*. www.ecu.ac.uk/wp-content/uploads/external/mentoring-progressing-womens-careers-in-higher-education.pdf

Fountain, J. and Newcomer, K.E. (2106) Developing and sustaining effective faculty mentoring programs. *Journal of Public Affairs Education*, 22(4): 483–506.

Iversen, A.C., Eady, N.A.J. and Wessely, S.C. (2014) The role of mentoring in academic career progression: a cross-sectional survey of the Academy of Medical Sciences mentoring scheme. *Journal of the Royal Society of Medicine*, 107(8): 308–317.

Morrison, L.J., Lorens, E., Bandiera, G., Lilies, W.C., Lee, L., Hyland, R., McDonald-Blumer, H., Allard, J.P., Panisko, D.M., Heathcote, E.J. and Levinson, W. (2014) Impact of a formal mentoring program on academic promotion of Department of Medicine faculty: a comparative study. *Medical Teacher*, 36(7): 608–614.

Oxford Brookes University Human Resources webpages. www.brookes.ac.uk/services/hr/. General criteria for promotion from lecturer to senior lecturer are given at www.brookes.ac.uk/services/hr/reward/academic/promotions/lecturer_to_senior_lecturer.html. The senior lecturer role profile is given at www.brookes.ac.uk/services/hr/reward/academic/sl_profile.html.

5

Mentoring to promote cultural awareness

In this chapter, we cover:

- How we define 'cultural awareness'
- The benefits of mentoring to support cultural awareness for mentee, mentor and institution
- Mentoring initiatives to support internationalisation in HEIs
- The value of mentoring partnerships in helping international HEI professionals adapt to a new culture and workplace
- Strategies for using peer networks to build informal mentoring initiatives

Introduction

In later chapters of this book, particularly in Chapters 7 and 10, we highlight the importance of effective communication skills – written and spoken – for researchers at all career stages, and the need to be able to adapt your communication style to the expectations of diverse audiences. Another aspect of communication skills development that is crucial for anyone pursuing an academic career in the 21st century, whether you are in your first year of doctoral research or in the final year of a life-long career in academia, is the ability to collaborate with colleagues from around the globe. The world of academia is precisely that – the world; it is now a global community that brings exciting opportunities through international collaborative projects. To make the most of these opportunities, it is important to understand that in whichever part of the world you have been educated and conduct your research, you are in just one of a multitude of research cultures. Internationalisation presents a wonderful opportunity to really reflect on your personal assumptions about research practice and ways of engaging with peers from cultures other than your own.

Culture is an extremely complex phenomenon that cannot be explored comprehensively in the space allowed in this chapter. For the purpose of this chapter, we refer to **academic culture** in terms of the expectations, attitudes to working and style of thinking, writing and speaking typical of individuals who have been educated in specific parts of the world. We focus on these particular aspects of culture because of their relevance to the current emphasis in HEIs on internationalisation. We acknowledge that researchers and academics raised and educated in different parts of the world may have diverse attitudes to working and styles of thinking, writing and speaking that result from the value systems underlying their respective geographical cultures (Deeks, 2004). We also acknowledge that the value of becoming aware of the diversity of academic culture around the world is not to focus on differences, but rather to allow each of us to become more aware of our own assumptions, prejudices and values upon which our attitudes are based. By becoming more self-reflective in this way, we can begin to forge a truly international research community that is respectful, imaginative and receptive to paradigms that we as individuals have not been exposed to before. The value of that is likely to be more international collaborations and ground-breaking research.

Incorporating mentoring initiatives that promote greater tolerance and understanding of cultural diversity within HEIs and that help international higher education (HE) professionals to adapt to a new culture have benefits for mentee, mentor and institution, as summarised in Table 5.1.

Table 5.1 Benefits of mentoring to support cultural awareness

For the mentee	For the mentor	For the institution
Having a smoother settling-in period to the new working environment is likely to boost your productivity and confidence levels.	Reflective conversations with your mentee on culture-related issues help you to reflect on your own assumptions, expectations and values. This, in turn, will help you to communicate more effectively with international colleagues.	Creating an environment that supports conversations and friendship across cultures will lead to greater opportunities for international collaborations.
Having a better understanding of your host culture will enable you to help your family adapt to their new environment.	Being sensitive to cultural differences between you and your junior colleague/doctoral researcher can stop misunderstandings which could hold the project back and delay completion time.	Working towards ensuring that international researchers socially integrate in the HEI will foster happier researchers and, consequently, higher completion rates among international doctoral researchers and more productive researchers at any level of career.

For the mentee	For the mentor	For the institution
Experience as a mentee will help you to be a good mentor for someone else, which will extend your peer network and increase your sense of belonging to the host culture.	Mentoring international HE professionals or PGRs gives you the opportunity to extend your own peer network and may also open more collaborative opportunities with international institutions.	Clearer communication from international HE professionals when teaching or lecturing is likely to result in higher student satisfaction levels.
Having a mentoring partnership to discuss differences and similarities between your culture and that of the host may increase your understanding and tolerance of cultural diversity.	Sensitivity to cultural differences in attitudes towards, for example, alcohol may help to ensure that social networking is inclusive.	Mentoring around culturally-derived differences in communication style will contribute to fewer breakdowns in communication between colleagues and a more harmonious work environment.
	Using your understanding and experience of your own culture to mentor someone else is confidence-boosting for you and helps you to feel a valued member of the academic community in your HEI.	Intercultural mentoring can help to foster a more truly international community.

Mentoring to support internationalisation

The truly international flavour of HEIs today means that researchers and staff at any career stage will work with colleagues, line managers, juniors or students whose expectations and values differ, sometimes quite significantly, from their own and indeed from those of the host institution. These differences can often lead to misunderstandings among colleagues or between supervisor and doctoral researcher and might also result in poor work performance or low levels of happiness when working in a different cultural environment.

Spencer-Oatey and Dauber (2015) have been strong proponents of the importance of the cultural component of university communities if those communities are to take seriously the internationalisation of their institutions. They argue that for an institution to be truly international, there need to be in place measures that assess not simply the number of international students, employees, etc. in an institution, but also the level of social integration between the international and host communities.

Cultural mentoring programmes provide an important step towards building a far more integrated international community in HEIs. For example, Albert Ludwigs Universität Freiburg in Germany offers international mentoring where students who are already at the university are paired as mentors with international students who are about to start their studies. One aim of the mentoring programme is to improve understanding across diverse cultures through mutual learning: the mentors provide guidance on aspects relating to studying at the university and, in return, the international students provide insights into their respective home cultures. Mentoring partners are matched according to study discipline and personal preferences. You can find more information about this mentoring initiative here: www.mentoring.uni-freiburg.de/intercultural

Mentoring partnerships such as those forged in the programme at Universität Freiburg help to foster a culture of self-reflection and tolerance within an institution. This is particularly important if working on international collaborative projects, where, for example, collaborative partners might have different perceptions about adhering to deadlines, or about how long a meeting should go on for, how long one colleague should speak in a meeting, or even whether there should be a hierarchy within the collaboration.

Self-reflection and tolerance can also develop outside formal institution-based mentoring programmes, for example, through reverse mentoring, discussed in detail in Chapter 13. As we explain, reverse mentoring refers to a mentoring partnership where the conventional model of mentoring, in which the mentor is typically either more experienced or older than the mentee, is turned on its head. Voice of Experience 5.1 illustrates how allowing a conventional mentoring partnership to also embrace a reverse mentoring element serves to intensify the benefits to both parties of that mentoring relationship and also to prompt greater reflection and awareness of diversity in cultural assumptions, expectations and norms.

Voice of Experience 5.1

The value of reverse mentoring to develop cultural awareness

I had been mentoring a doctoral researcher from China for several weeks. Jin-yi (pseudonym) had sought mentoring support for her writing skills as English was not her first language, and she had been given the opportunity to submit a paper in English to a prestigious conference. A few weeks into our mentoring partnership, I learned that my application for a secondment to a university in Beijing had been successful. However, I had never been to that part of the world, and I felt very much in need of some guidance on all sorts of matters, such as what would be expected of me as a teacher and lecturer there, etc.

I asked Jin-yi, who was from Beijing, if she could give me some advice, but I did not want to use our mentoring time to talk about my needs. So, we agreed to set up other mentoring meetings, where she would mentor me. As with our first mentoring partnership, we drew up a formal mentoring agreement, and I have to say, the arrangement worked incredibly well. I benefited hugely from it, and it helped me to better understand her. She told me that she also learned a lot about me from the questions I was asking, which all seemed to be connected to work-related tasks (e.g. how intensive study was over there; what kind of assignment tasks would be expected by students) and not so much to family and networking – something that surprised her. She realised though that perhaps that was a cultural difference between us.

Teaching Fellow in English Language

Mentoring to support cultural adaptation

A mentoring partnership to support cultural adaptation is particularly valuable for the mentee when taking up a new position or project in a culture that they are not familiar with. The settling-in period for any international move is hugely exciting, and daunting at the same time, because there is much to learn. This includes learning the requirements of the new role or project as well as adapting to the norms, value systems and protocols of the new environment. From an institutional and line-management perspective, supporting the international professional at this time of transition is important for productivity; a happy and settled employee is far more likely to be able to focus on the job at hand than one who is homesick or suffering from culture shock. Equally, for the individual themselves, settling in quickly is vital for personal well-being and for the welfare of their family if they have also made the move.

Supervisors and line managers as support for cultural adaptation

The most obvious mentor to support this cultural transition is a supervisor (discussed more in Chapter 11), line manager or PI (considered in depth in Chapter 12). Indeed, mentoring relationships often arise spontaneously with such people, particularly if you are a supervisor or line manager with considerable experience of overseeing employees or researchers from various cultures. When this does happen, it is often because of the chemistry between you and your junior or doctoral researcher, or it could be that you have worked abroad yourself. Such international experience will make you sensitive to some of the challenges they face when adapting to a different culture, such as culture shock and how to cope with it.

A line manager who is native to the host culture can also provide very valuable mentoring guidance if their junior is a newly-arrived international researcher. A particularly stressful aspect of adaptation when working in a different culture is the speed with which native-speaker colleagues seem to speak. As a line manager, if you are happy to act as a mentor in this respect, conversing with your mentee will help them to tune into the language. One way you can help your mentee here is, if your mentee does not understand what you have said, to repeat at the same speed, but to pause slightly longer at the end of each sentence or at a natural breathing point within a sentence before continuing. This will help your mentee to tune into the natural speed of delivery but will also give them time to process the words in manageable clusters.

While a supervisor or line manager is perhaps the natural first port of call, not all necessarily wish to act in a mentoring capacity because of potential conflicts of interest between their supervisory/managerial responsibilities and those of mentoring. For example, if you are in a managerial or supervisory position, you will have appraisal and assessment responsibilities, which may lead to conflict with the more nurturing function of a mentor. Similarly, in a mentoring relationship, as a mentee, you will need to feel free to reflect honestly on the mentoring experience. Having your line manager or supervisor as your mentor may mean that your freedom to express your feelings is stifled.

There is also a potential pitfall in allowing mentoring to evolve spontaneously within a line management or doctoral supervisory relationship. If there is no formal delineation between line management and mentoring conversations, misunderstandings can arise through differences in expectation between junior/researcher and line manager/supervisor. In some cultures, for example in the Middle East and parts of Africa, there is often a strongly hierarchical nature to the line manager/junior or supervisor/doctoral researcher relationship. The expectation of junior members of staff or doctoral researchers from those regions, therefore, may be for a line manager or supervisor to be hierarchically aloof from them. Other cultures, for example, China, are based on a blend of hierarchical and personal relationships that are characterised by strict and complex codes of behaviour between the two parties depending on the nature of the relationship. Allowing more personal, mentoring conversations to creep into a more formalised line management relationship without being sensitive to the expectations and the cultural norms of each person can lead to confusion, misunderstanding and possibly even a loss of trust, as Case Study 5.1 clearly illustrates.

Case Study 5.1

Communication breakdown between doctoral researcher and supervisor

Ahmed has extensive work experience in Africa and the Middle East. He has come for the first time to the UK for doctoral research. His supervisor is Chris, a young, dynamic academic from the UK, with no experience of supervising researchers from outside Europe.

The supervisory relationship between Chris and Ahmed has become strained. Chris feels that Ahmed relies too heavily on him for guidance and is not managing his project independently. Chris recalls that Ahmed often pops in for unscheduled meetings asking for direction on which body of literature to review next. Chris has had to point out that choosing which literature to review is part of the normal decision-making responsibilities of doctoral researchers.

Ahmed, however, feels lost in his project because he is not receiving the direction he expects of his superior. He does not wish to do any research that Chris might not approve of. He has been particularly thrown by Chris's recent response to his request for guidance on choosing literature: 'Only you can make that kind of decision, not me. Could you use your work experience to help you decide? I know you have much more work experience in that area than me.' For Ahmed, Chris admitting a lack of experience in his field of research is destabilising. In Ahmed's experience, supervisors have their position because of their authority, and their responsibility is to give clear direction.

Ahmed no longer pops in for unscheduled chats because he senses he is irritating Chris but does not know why. Chris is relieved that Ahmed seems to be working more independently. However, in the last meeting he was shocked at how little Ahmed had progressed in that month. Chris worries that Ahmed simply lacks the autonomy and drive necessary to manage his research project.

Case Study 5.1 illustrates how culturally-derived differences in expectation between a supervisor and researcher can lead to very real communication breakdowns and a confusing of the professional boundaries. Ahmed's educational background had been in cultures that are characteristically based on power distance and hierarchy, where the role of teacher or supervisor is to direct and the role of the student is to learn and implement the direction of their supervisor. In contrast, Chris's understanding of the supervisor–supervisee relationship was based much less on hierarchy and more on providing guidance and feedback to a peer responsible for their own project. Thus, there was mutual misunderstanding of the expectations and assumptions of the other party, leading to tension in their working relationship.

One way to resolve this type of issue is to ensure that, in initial supervisory meetings, there is the opportunity for an open and honest discussion about the expectations of the relationship. For example, as supervisor, you can encourage your researcher to talk about how they are adapting to their new environment and to their doctoral project with the aim of establishing what their, as well as your, expectations are of the supervisory relationship. We discuss strategies you can use to do this in Chapter 11 (see p. 165).

Formal mentoring programmes

If you decide that a mentoring partnership within the line management relationship is not appropriate, then another source of cultural adaptation support is through a formal mentoring programme, often known as a buddy scheme, offered at your HEI. You can also find mentoring support outside your institution. For example, EURAXESS, a virtual hub backed by the European Union, runs a buddy scheme that is open to all international researchers (https://euraxess. ec.europa.eu/).

Some institutions offer a mentoring programme which includes support for newly-arrived international students transitioning to doctoral research, which we mention in Chapter 2. In this type of programme, as a newly-arrived international doctoral researcher, you may well be paired with a doctoral researcher from your own culture who has already settled into the environment. This mentor can be tremendously supportive, especially in helping you to understand the unspoken rules of your new environment, such as departmental meeting etiquette. As a newly-arrived international academic, you may assume that the protocols used in your home culture will be the same as those in your new environment, but there can be considerable diversity in meeting protocols. Top Tips 5.1 may provide a useful focus for a mentoring conversation around the unspoken rules of meetings in your new institution.

Top Tips 5.1

Identifying the unspoken rules of meetings

1. Identify the unspoken rules relating to punctuality. For example, if the meeting is scheduled for 10.00, what time will people arrive? If it is scheduled to end at 12.00, how likely is it to end precisely at that time?
2. Ascertain whether participants wait for the Chair of the meeting to sit before they sit.
3. Check whether there are conventions about turn-taking in expressing opinions.

4. Clarify how long one participant can voice their opinion before colleagues become irritated at the amount of meeting time they are using.
5. Establish whether women participants would be offended by men colleagues shaking their hands or whether it is expected.
6. Find out whether it would be considered impolite to stand up and leave the meeting to take a phone call.
7. Enquire about the protocol relating to expressing agreement or disagreement with the Chair. For example, are there particular etiquette strategies that should be used? Would it considered rude to express disagreement in the meeting? Instead, is it considered polite to have discrete discussions with colleagues after the meeting to seek changes to a proposal made by the Chair?

Including business card and invitation protocols in mentoring to support cultural adaptation

We should also mention here the value of having a mentoring conversation about business card protocol in the host culture, as these protocols can vary around the world. For example, in some cultures, particularly in the Far East, if you are offered a business card, you should receive it with both hands, not just one, to show respect to the person giving it. It is also important to spend time looking at the card, and if there is print on both sides, to turn it over and study the reverse side too. In other cultures, making notes on someone's business card would be considered extremely rude. As mentor, being clear to your mentee about the protocols around business cards in their new environment will help them to make a good first impression at networking events, conferences and meetings. There is potential benefit for you too because you may well get insights into the protocol of your mentee's home culture in this respect, which may be useful for you in your own networking activities with international peers. We discuss networking strategies in more depth in Chapter 9.

Another potential minefield of misunderstandings that can arise when arranging meetings is expectations following an invitation to meet for lunch or refreshments for your discussions. In some cultures, such an invitation subsumes an assumption that the inviter will cover the costs so the invitee may not offer to share expenses, thinking it would be rude to do so. In contrast, the inviter might consider the other rude for not making that offer. It can be useful when arranging first meetings to suggest that one of the first things that can be addressed is the local customs about who pays for what when sharing refreshments or meals.

Ensuring a good mentoring match between mentee and mentor

Irrespective of the source of mentoring support, good mentoring partnerships form when there is a close match between the needs of the mentee and the skills, experience and/or background of the mentor. This means that if you are approached by someone to mentor them, it is important to know precisely what they are expecting from you. This also means that, as a mentee, you are very clear yourself about what your cultural adaptation needs are, which can sometimes be difficult to articulate.

Reflection Point 5.1 provides a useful focus for an early conversation between you and your potential mentor to clarify the need for the mentoring partnership and to determine whether your mentor has the skills and experience you are looking for to be an effective mentor for you. As a mentor, if you decide that you do not have the skills or experience your mentee is looking for, you will be able to use the third column 'possible sources of support' to signpost the mentee to further sources of help, which will have made this initial conversation worthwhile, even if it does not result in a mentoring partnership between you.

Reflection Point 5.1

Identifying your cultural adaptation needs

In the table below are common culturally-related issues that newly-arrived international doctoral researchers and HE professionals encounter when moving abroad. Which of the listed issues are relevant for you? Put a score for each issue in the right-hand column (*0 = not relevant at all; 1 = slightly relevant; 2 = moderately relevant; 3 = very relevant; 4 = urgent*). Then add any other issues that you feel you need to address at the bottom.

Culturally-related issue	How relevant for you? (0–4)	Possible sources of support
Ensuring that I have completed all the necessary stages of the formal registration process for new country and new workplace		• Embassy or Consulate • Institution's International Office
Finding a school for my children		• Institution's International Office • Induction programme • Staff Support services • Peer network • Work colleagues • Local Education Authority

Culturally-related issue	How relevant for you? (0–4)	Possible sources of support
Finding accommodation for my family		• Institution's Accommodation Office • Induction programme • Local estate agents • Work colleagues • Peer network
Finding a support network for my partner		• Institution's International Office • Institution's peer mentoring scheme • Peer network, especially international peers • Local interest groups • Social groups (within institution or local community)
Improving my communication skills		• Institution's language support unit • Language exchange programmes • Staff/doctoral researcher training department • Institution's peer mentoring programme
Understanding what is expected of me in my new role		• Supervisor/line manager • Staff/doctoral researcher training department • Work colleagues
Making friends		• Peer network • Institution's mentoring programme • Work colleagues • Local interest groups • Social groups (within institution or local community) • Other parents (if you have children) • Institution's sports parks • Training workshops/seminars • Departmental/faculty meetings
Gauging how formal to be; what topics of conversation are deemed acceptable		• Institution's mentoring programme • Institution's language support unit • Cultural awareness workshops

(Continued)

Culturally-related issue	How relevant for you? (0–4)	Possible sources of support
Knowing how to address and greet people		• Institution's mentoring programme • Institution's language support unit • Cultural awareness workshops • Supervisor/line manager
Other		

Initiating informal mentoring partnerships through peer networks

Another extremely useful mentoring resource is your peer network, whether you are seeking support or wishing to offer it to others. They can be valuable for a variety of cultural adaptation issues, such as learning about the unspoken rules of the institution. If you have already adapted from one culture to your current one, then you will have useful experience, skills and insight for supporting a peer from a similar culture to your own who has just arrived and who is perhaps ignorant of the differences.

Becoming a mentor to a peer early in their settling-in period may well help them to avoid any major embarrassments as they adapt to the new environment. Many of these relate to specific expected behaviours and/or communication styles. As well as differences in assumed protocols relating to meetings in various cultures, mentioned earlier, there are also unspoken rules relating to appropriate levels of formality in different working relationships, such as day-to-day communication, including appropriate body language, to use with peers, senior or junior colleagues, administrators, students, etc. For example, in some cultures physical contact, such as touching a colleague's arm repeatedly during a conversation or having direct eye contact with them throughout the conversation is conventional behaviour; however, in other cultures, this would be considered inappropriate behaviour, especially between colleagues of different gender.

Finding a mentoring partner through your peer network can also provide much needed support if adaptation issues relate to lecturing and/or teaching style or poor delivery of subject content when lecturing or teaching. Certainly, in our experience of our own institutions, we are aware of how poor communication by a teacher or lecturer sometimes leads to negative feedback from students, which can result in low scores in module evaluation and low levels of student satisfaction. If, as an international academic facing this specific issue, you have a peer who has encountered similar challenges, asking them to mentor you can be extremely supportive at a time when perhaps your confidence is low. Similarly, if you have already weathered that storm and have found strategies to develop your communication skills, you are probably an ideal candidate to be a mentor yourself. Sometimes it helps those who need a boost to their communication skills for you to be alert within your network to individuals who seem to be struggling. A hint that you have been in that situation yourself may be all that is needed to prompt them to ask you to mentor them, although they may use a different word to express that relationship.

Top Tips 5.2 offers useful strategies for creating an informal mentoring network if you have just started to work (or study if you are a doctoral researcher) in a new country. If you are already well established in the country and would like to support a newly-arrived international colleague who is uncertain how to build an informal peer network, you might wish to refer them to these tips.

Top Tips 5.2

Creating an informal mentoring network

1. Reflect on your personal needs, uncertainties or concerns, and actively seek opportunities to share those needs with others whom you think might have the same needs. Remember that if you are struggling to adapt to your new work culture, you need to talk about your difficulties. Staying quiet and hiding away are not helpful strategies.

2. Consider how you might engage with your peers. Possible ways are inviting peers for occasional informal coffee meetings to talk through culturally-related issues that may arise in the workplace; inviting peers to your home for a meal; or organising an international evening, where each person brings a dish from their home country to enjoy a 'bring and share feast'. Just be sure to be clear about customs related to invitations, such as who pays and whether a small gift is expected or would be embarrassing. (See Chapter 6 and Appendix 3 in our sister book, *Success in Research: Fulfilling the Potential of your Doctoral Experience* (Denicolo et al., 2017), for further examples of cultural issues, including those of research cultures and paradigms.)

3. Be the first to welcome new international researchers or visiting lecturers to your department. They will be appreciative, and there is nothing more confidence-building for you than showing a newcomer around your campus, faculty or department. You will then be the first point of reference for the new member of the department, which can lead to the beginnings of a mutual support network.

4. Look out for collaborative opportunities, perhaps authoring a joint paper or a joint conference presentation. This is a great way to get to know your peers. (See our sister book, *Success in Research: Inspiring Collaboration and Engagement*, Reeves et al., 2020)

Information for those wishing to set up a cultural awareness mentoring initiative

Throughout this chapter, we have highlighted the potential for miscommunication or even communication breakdowns in working, supervisory or staff–student relationships due to culturally derived differences in expectation, values and norms in the workplace. With today's emphasis on internationalisation in HEIs, cultural diversity is inevitable. Perhaps more importantly, this diversity is positively enriching for our academic communities if institutions are prepared to invest in programmes that support international HEI professionals and doctoral researchers to integrate into the research community. Mentoring partnerships have much to offer in this respect, as highlighted in this chapter.

Central to any institutional mentoring programme to support cultural awareness and adaptation must be training designed to encourage both mentees and mentors to reflect on their own culturally-derived expectations, values and assumptions. As well as the guidance offered earlier in this chapter and in Appendix B, we offer some suggestions as to what such a programme might consist of.

If your institution already runs a mentoring programme or buddy scheme, you might wish to ensure that any questionnaire you send to potential mentors/buddies asks if they would be prepared to mentor someone in need of support in adapting to their new culture. You would also need to provide some information on the common types of support needed for cultural adaptation, so that potential mentors can gauge whether they have the necessary experience and insights to be an effective mentor for an international mentee. Reflection Point 5.1 provides useful information on this and so could be used as the basis of any material you might design for this purpose.

Another way of promoting greater awareness of cultural diversity in your institution is to design and incorporate a cultural awareness session into any supervisor training or line management training programme currently offered. A good starting point for such a session is Hofstede's (1984) framework for cross-cultural communication. Although much work has been done since on cross-cultural understanding, we like to refer to this framework, not just because it has been pivotal in the field for a considerable number of years, but also precisely because of its age; so much has changed in the world since 1984 that a really good starting point for any discussion on diversity in, and across, cultures is to critique Hofstede's own framework from the perspective of the 21st century. This helps to drive home the point that culture is not fixed and static.

Within that session, you can encourage participants to discuss cultural differences by presenting them with a case study or two (such as Case Study 5.1

in this chapter) that illustrate how relationships can break down if there is inadequate awareness of potential differences between cultures. Having one case study that illustrates a breakdown in communication between a line manager and junior and one between a supervisor and supervisee can lead to some interesting observations and comments from participants as they attempt to interpret the culturally-based misunderstandings that lie at the root of the breakdown.

The most effective sessions will be those with a good mix of supervisors and/ or line managers from diverse cultures. Ensuring that the session is as interactive as possible will help to make the session informative and engaging, and so it is best to allow plenty of time for discussion. You might find that Activity 5.1 is useful if you are designing a session to fit into a larger supervisor training programme. It will also be useful as part of a larger induction programme for doctoral researchers.

Activity 5.1

Cultural awareness questionnaire for supervisors and Doctoral researchers

Step 1: Ensure that the discussion group consists of as culturally diverse a group of individuals as possible.

Step 2: As part of the introduction to the session, ask individuals to state which country they were educated in and what culture they feel they identify with most naturally.

Step 3: Choose *Questionnaire A* if the session participants are supervisors and *Questionnaire B* if they are doctoral researchers.

Questionnaire A: What do you expect from your doctoral researchers?

Decide how strongly you agree or disagree with the statements below about expectations of your supervisors. Score each statement with one of the following:

1 = strongly disagree; 2 = disagree; 3 = neither disagree nor agree; 4 = agree; 5 = strongly agree

1. I expect my doctoral researchers to closely follow my directions for their research at all stages.
2. I expect my doctoral researchers to accept that I will manage their projects and them.
3. I expect my doctoral researchers to regard me as their friend.
4. I expect my researchers to want me to help them direct their research.

(Continued)

5. I expect my researchers to see me whenever they feel the need.
6. I expect my researchers to be fully responsible for directing their own research and to come to me for suggestions only.
7. I expect my researchers to want feedback on their work, nothing else.
8. I expect my researchers to come to me for the research gap or problem they should focus on.
9. I expect my researchers to sort themselves out when they go wrong in their research.
10. I expect my researchers to come to me before they make mistakes, so that I can put them on the right track before it's too late.

Questionnaire B: What do you expect of your supervisors?

Decide how strongly you agree or disagree with the statements below about expectations of your supervisors. Score each statement with one of the following:

1 = strongly disagree; 2 = disagree; 3 = neither disagree nor agree; 4 = agree; 5 = strongly agree

1. I expect my supervisor to tell me what to do at each stage of my research.
2. I expect my supervisor to manage me and my research project.
3. I expect my supervisor to be a friend to me.
4. I expect my supervisor to help me to direct my research.
5. I expect my supervisor to be available for me whenever I need to see them.
6. I expect my supervisor just to make suggestions, not to direct my project.
7. I expect my supervisor just to give me feedback on my work, nothing else.
8. I expect my supervisor to be clear about the research gap or problem I should focus on.
9. I expect my supervisor to tell me when I have gone wrong in my research.
10. I expect my supervisor to stop me from making mistakes in my research.

Step 4: Invite participants to respond to the questions on the questionnaire.

Step 5: Arrange participants in culturally mixed groups (4–6 per group) and invite each group to discuss with each other their responses to the questionnaire. Select a spokesperson for each group and ask them to make a note of the questions that generated the greatest disagreement and agreement among the group.

Step 6: Invite each group spokesperson to provide feedback to the session and encourage session discussion around the questionnaire.

Step 7: If the aim of the session is to help international researchers/supervisors to settle into the host culture's academic expectations, you could invite an academic from the host culture to join in the discussion to give the new researchers/supervisors a better sense of the expectations of the host culture. Alternatively, you, as the facilitator for the session, could take on that role.

For a group of 15–20 participants, this exercise will probably take around 35–50 minutes, depending on how culturally diverse the group is. The greater the diversity in the room, the richer the discussion!

Alternatively, you could suggest that this questionnaire is used in an initial supervisory meeting as the basis for discussion about expectations. This would be particularly useful if both parties decide to adopt mentoring principles in the supervisory relationship, which we discuss in greater depth in Chapter 11.

Chapter summary

In this chapter, we have highlighted the importance of mentoring initiatives for the current internationalisation agenda in HEIs of promoting greater inter-cultural understanding. We have also illustrated how useful cultural awareness mentoring partnerships can be in helping newly-arrived internationals settle in to their new positions. We have also suggested that sometimes relationship breakdowns in an international context can result from poor communication between two parties. Building on this point, in the next chapter, we consider how valuable mentoring partnerships can be in helping researchers to develop effective spoken communication skills.

Further reading

Deeks, M. (2004) *Cross-Cultural Team Working within the Cochrane Collaboration.* https://training.cochrane.org/sites/training.cochrane.org/files/public/uploads/resources/downloadable_resources/English/crossculturalteamwork_000.pdf

Denicolo, P., Reeves, J. and Duke, D. (2017) *Success in Research: Fulfilling the Potential of your Doctoral Experience.* London: SAGE.

Hofstede, G. (1984) *Culture's Consequences.* Thousand Oaks, CA: SAGE.

House, R.J., Hanges, P., Javidan, M., Dorfman, P. and Gupta, V. (eds) (2004) *Culture, leadership, and Organizations: The GLOBE Study of 62 Societies.* Thousand Oaks, CA: SAGE.

Osula, B. and Irvin, S.M. (2009) Cultural awareness in intercultural mentoring: a model for enhancing mentoring relationships. *International Journal of Leadership Studies*, 5(1).

Reeves, J., Starbuck, S., and Yeung, A. (2020) *Success in Research: Inspiring Collaboration and Engagement.* London: SAGE.

Spencer-Oatey, H. and Dauber, D. (2015) How internationalised is your university? Moving beyond structural indicators towards social integration. Briefing paper: *Going Global Event 2015*, London, UK.

Vitae (n.d.) Website. www.vitae.ac.uk/doing-research/doing-a-doctorate/completing-your-doctorate/your-viva/viva-checklist

6

Mentoring for the transition out of academia

In this chapter, we consider:

- The value of mentoring for the transition out of academia for the mentor, mentee and institution
- How to establish a mentoring relationship if you are a researcher or a possible mentor working outside academia
- Ways to nurture the mentoring relationship
- How the institution can facilitate mentoring for the transition out of academia

Introduction

Increasingly, doctoral graduates are looking for jobs out of academia. For example, in the UK, the number of doctoral graduates is increasing (108,470 in 2012/13 to 112,520 in 2016/17 (HESA, 2018)) with only half eventually going into full-time academic jobs, depending on discipline. This means that many doctoral graduates will leave the HEI and look for a job outside academia, possibly without the skills and experience that the wider job market requires. The Vitae report 'What do researchers do?' found the percentage of doctoral graduates finding jobs outside academia to range from 41% for social sciences to 70% for physical sciences and engineering, with the percentage for those from arts, humanities and biosciences lying somewhere between these figures (Careers Research and Advisory Centre, 2018). In the 2017 Postgraduate Researcher Experience Survey (PRES), which polls current doctoral researchers, only 39% of respondents were looking for an academic career in higher education and 11% wanted a research career in higher education (Slight, 2017). While the traditional approach to the training of doctoral researchers has focused on developing skills linked to research techniques, critical thinking, writing, project management, people management and skills that may be transferrable to non-academic careers, it does not often expose them directly to industry or business.

Many researchers will have a plan or a goal for after their doctorate or post-doc, but others will be uninformed about the options available to them or their feasibility. It is therefore incumbent on HEIs to provide the training and developmental opportunities to prepare researchers (both doctoral researchers and ECRs) for a career move out of academia. There are various schemes, workshops and initiatives in place at institutions that cover the development of researchers for such a move, such as panel events with employers and careers fairs, for example. Through these initiatives, researchers are made aware of the options for beyond their postgraduate study. They are also given the opportunity to learn a broader range of skills other than traditional research-related skills pertaining to the narrow doctorate, and given the knowledge about their chosen option. For example, they might be informed about the norms of the profession in which they are interested, and ideally, this support should start long before the researcher is coming to the end of their time at the HEI. Many of these developmental activities can be carried out by dedicated members of staff at the HEI, for example, researcher developers or careers officers; however, to gain a personal insight into the chosen profession, a mentor who has experience of the field can be invaluable.

Mentoring is a good option for a developmental activity at this transition because it offers bespoke support to the researcher. Through mentoring discussions, a wide range of topics can be discussed, including expectations in the profession of the mentor, the sort of training you as the mentee could undertake alongside your doctorate, advice about the move from academia, and ways to widen your network using the contacts of your mentor.

The value of mentors outside academia

As emphasised in earlier chapters, all mentoring relationships have benefits for the mentor and the mentee. These include the general benefits, discussed in Chapter 1, that all mentoring brings, plus some unique benefits that occur because of the nature of mentoring outside academia. These are captured in Table 6.1.

Table 6.1 The value of mentoring for both mentor and mentee

For the mentee	For the mentor
A mentor can be a valuable contact to discuss your current work and your plans for your future, and who will view your situation from a different perspective.	Mentoring may be considered part of your continuing professional development.
You will enhance your communication skills, in this case communicating with a different audience, as your mentor will be a non-academic or will have made the transition out of academia.	By helping your mentee, you will gain a sense of well-being that you may not get from your day-to-day work.
You will also find out how your research is viewed outside academia, which can inform your research plans or the way you present your research to different audiences.	You may meet potential job applicants or collaborators through your mentee.
A mentor will give you connections to views, opinions and networks that you would not normally have access to.	You will feel like you are giving something back to the next generation of researchers, your discipline and possibly your *alma mater*.
Having a mentor in an institution or company that you are interested in working for can help you decide if it is the right choice for you. It will also allow you to see the differences between working as a researcher within academia and working outside.	Increasing your network beyond those whom you would normally come into contact with can expose you to new ideas and different ways of thinking.
If you are thinking of moving out of academia, then someone who has already made the move can act as a role model and advisor and talk about their personal experience.	You are likely to find out about cutting-edge research, issues, opportunities and projects in the institution of your mentee, which you may be able to link to.

Before deciding to seek a mentoring partnership, you might wish to reflect on how you are likely to benefit from mentoring at your current career stage. For example, as an ECR, you might be concerned about the short-term contracts that are widespread throughout academia and be thinking about options for finding a permanent position. As a doctoral researcher, you may love the research but not enjoy teaching and so be considering that a permanent academic position may not be right for you. As a mentor, you may wish to increase your network beyond your current industry and converse with people outside your usual circle.

In Voice of Experience 6.1, a researcher has written an account of their mentoring experience. This researcher, who was on their second postdoc role, chose mentoring because it would be support that was tailored to them rather than a generic training course. They were uncertain of their next career step and wanted help to plan. They were concerned about the short-term contracts that seemed to persist in academia and wished to explore how they could use the skills they had gained within their academic roles outside academia.

Voice of Experience 6.1

My mentor helped me apply for a job outside academia

After five months with my mentor I came across an advert for my dream job – it was the first time I'd applied for a job outside higher education and I was concerned about making the skills I'd learned through my PhD and postdoctoral work relevant to this role. My mentor read through my application form and gave excellent constructive criticism, highlighting areas where I wasn't playing to my strengths and praising what was well-written. Our discussion raised questions about the role that I don't think I would have considered on my own, and I planned to use these if I were successful at getting an interview.

I did get an interview, which went exceedingly well, although I ended up coming second to someone with more relevant experience. While disappointed with this, the practice was incredibly beneficial, because I now have an excellent application and supporting statements I can use as the basis for future applications.

I stopped mentoring after this interview: I felt I had reached the point where my mentor had done a lot for me in encouraging me to think beyond boundaries that I had built for myself, and the application process had shown me my skills are transferrable and there are non-higher education roles out in the wider world. It's now down to me to take what my mentor has taught me, what she has developed in me, and use that to my advantage – wherever that takes me.

A researcher with a mentor from outside academia

The account in Voice of Experience 6.1 illustrates the impact the mentor had on the mentee. However, while the mentor may not always be aware of the impact they have had on their mentee, they do tend to be much more aware of the value of the experience for them as mentors, as illustrated in the short excerpt provided as Voice of Experience 6.2 from an experienced mentor based outside academia.

Voice of Experience 6.2

My experience of being a mentor to researchers and the benefits I have seen

I offered to be a mentor mainly to put something back into the profession that I've done very well out of and to re-establish contact with my old university. The two mentees I have worked with so far have both wanted help with getting their next job. We discussed the types of employment available (start-up, small company, large company, research institution, etc.) and the pros and cons of each, what sort of salaries and benefits to expect, organisations I knew to be hiring, how their skill sets matched up to employers' requirements, as well as reviewing their CVs and covering letters. I hope I was able to give them a taste of what to expect in the outside world and help them with their first steps getting into it. I've enjoyed working with my mentees; it's been a useful experience for me, and I feel that I have been able to 'put something back'.

Dr Tim Mitchell, CEO, Sareum Ltd

How to find a mentoring relationship

A good starting point for getting involved in mentoring either as a mentee researcher within academia or a mentor outside academia is to contact the central services team within an HEI. These teams all have slightly different names, but tend to be part of a staff development, researcher development or careers department. If you wish to become a mentor for researchers, you could contact the institution where you did your degree or further study or the one local to you now. They will often have programmes that you can get involved in. If you are a researcher who would like a mentor outside academia, you might approach the researcher development and careers departments in your institution to enquire if they could find a mentor for you. Alternatively, you could ask them for possible contacts for you to approach directly. When looking for a mentor outside academia, it pays to be imaginative in your search. For example, some academics have collaborations with industries, or alternatively, university departments may have contacts in businesses where undergraduates find work placements. You may be able to find a mentor or mentee through one of these contacts.

Another option is to use links through your institution. You could use an online networking tool such as LinkedIn to create a profile. If you choose this option, you should ensure that your profile is complete with a good quality formal picture of you and a clear summary of what you do. From your LinkedIn profile, you can then join groups that are relevant to your interests along with alumni groups from your current and past institutions. A sensible strategy to use when approaching people in this way to be your mentor is to find someone you know to introduce you, virtually if necessary. However, this is not always possible, and if you cannot be introduced first, then link with the person you wish to approach by introducing yourself via email, outlining very clearly and concisely why you are looking for a mentor, why you feel that they would be a good mentor for you, and how much time you think they would need to invest in the mentoring partnership should they decide to become your mentor.

Alternative ways to find a mentor or mentee are by linking in with other initiatives at the institution, such as a networking event in a department or the wider institution or an event with an invited speaker. You might be lucky enough to secure the mentoring services of the speaker if you approach them. Another great source of mentoring relationships could be a conference where the focus is not solely academic. Many disciplines have 'cross-over' conferences where people from commerce, industry or the professions as well as academics are invited to talk about topics from their respective perspectives. Examples of this could be medical doctors and professionals from the pharmaceutical industry attending a biosciences conference or policy makers and government representatives attending a sociology conference.

Joining a professional body or **learned society** will offer a wealth of networking opportunities that could lead to a mentoring relationship. There are various steps you can take to raise your visibility in these networks, such as volunteering to sit on a committee or, better still, taking a leading role on it. You could also get involved with organising conferences and sessions for the society. A good strategy for building your network is to offer to organise a panel at a conference because you will make connections not just with invited panel members, but also with the conference organisers and audience members on the day. In essence, building your professional network will increase the chances of you finding a suitable mentor or mentee and so it is important to seize every opportunity to do this. For more detailed guidance on useful strategies for building your network, see Chapter 9.

Advice for mentoring sessions

Top Tips 6.1 offers suggestions for maintaining a productive mentoring relationship that are specific to mentoring beyond academia. For general guidelines on how to care for your mentoring relationship, see Appendix B.

Top Tips 6.1

What to do when you have found a mentoring partner

1. As mentee, remember that your mentor is volunteering from outside your institution and fitting your meetings into their workday. This means that you should make the best use of their time by being punctual and perhaps willing to meet outside core office hours. Before your first meeting, think about some of the topics you wish to discuss with your mentor, one of which will be your respective expectations of the mentoring relationship and the topics that you both wish to cover.

2. Discuss how to contact one another. This mentoring may well take place online or by phone as the mentor may not be near the mentee's institution. Mentoring online can be just as effective as mentoring in person, and there are steps you can take to make sure it runs smoothly, such as testing any video-conferencing equipment you need to use before your call. If you are in different countries when you book your meeting, consider the time zones that you are both in and find a suitable time for you both.

3. If it is not possible to meet physically or through video-conferencing, you could consider using email for your mentoring partnership. If you do choose this option, it is important, if possible, to meet up face-to-face at least once. The meeting does not need to be long, but having an initial face-to-face conversation is important in establishing rapport between you. Be imaginative in how you have this meeting – perhaps at an airport if either party is travelling and the airport would be easy for the other to get to, or at a café midway between your respective places of work, etc.

4. It is sensible to discuss confidentiality when talking about the mentee's research. As a mentor, if your mentee does not highlight confidentiality, then initiate the discussion. As a mentee, do not be embarrassed to discuss confidentiality in the first meeting. It is important to know where you both stand. This is a professional stance that your mentor will expect and respect.

This type of mentoring is likely to cover a broad range of topics. Below we outline five common topics that are likely to be discussed within the mentoring partnership, some of which are relatively obvious for the situation whereas others may be more surprising. Each topic is presented from the perspective of mentor and mentee, with some suggestions as to how to shape the discussion when it arises.

1. **Experience outside academia**. Some researchers within academia will have had experience outside. However, some may have spent all their working life within academia and so will want to know how working outside is different. As a mentee, you may be seeking guidance on how to make the step and what the similarities and differences are. The guidance you are looking for might range

from working culture to what a job interview would be like. As a mentor, it is useful to reflect on when you made the step and openly discuss the process you went through and what you have found to be different in your current profession from your academic experience.

2. **Goals for the future**. Any mentoring conversation is likely to discuss the mentee's future goals. A mentoring partnership that supports the stepping out of academia is an opportunity for you, as a mentee, to get feedback on your goals from a specialist either in a certain industry or with a specific lifestyle if that is what you aspire to. For example, the owner of a start-up company will have a unique perspective on setting goals if you also want to start a company. As a mentor in this partnership, it would be useful to unpick these goals with your outside knowledge and give your non-academic perspective on how feasible and realistic these goals are.

3. **Networking outside academia**. While HEIs often run training on how to network, these sessions usually focus on networking within academia (considered in Chapter 9). All businesses and industries will have slightly different norms around networking and so, as a mentee, knowing these before making contact can be invaluable if you wish to form good connections. As a mentor, you might talk about what is expected within your working environment. The mentoring relationship itself may lead to you both increasing your network by meeting people that your mentoring partner knows who may be interesting or useful to you.

4. **Work environment**. The work environment covers the physical working space and also the workplace culture. As a mentee, you may not have any experience of a workplace outside academia and your mentor will be able to help with this by discussing the differences between an academic department and their workplace, and letting you see how life is in a different environment. As a mentor, this may involve physically showing them your workspace or it may be that in your conversations you talk about the norms and expectations of people in your industry. This is valuable as it gives the mentee an insight into your world and will help them make an informed choice about whether it is right for them. These discussions will also boost your mentee's confidence to feel more 'at home' in a potential new workplace.

5. **Feedback from a non-academic perspective**. It can be difficult for a researcher within academia to get a non-academic perspective on their research, ideas or plans. This can be about how research is viewed by non-academics or it can be providing a different perspective on topics about career development, relationship management, work–life balance or any number of topics that occur in regular mentoring relationships. The value here is that the mentor brings an external perspective.

As with all mentoring relationships, it is important to keep reviewing your relationship to make sure that it is still productive. This is especially true of mentoring outside academia because such mentoring is likely to be intended for a very specific outcome. If the scheme lasts for a year, as many institutional mentoring schemes do, then having a review at six months to check that the relationship is still useful and to review the targets will allow both mentor and mentee to ensure that both partners' time is not being wasted. It is important that your mentoring relationship has an agreed endpoint, which should be discussed at the first meeting. As a mentor or mentee, you may notice when the meetings are either no longer mentoring or no longer productive, and, at this point, you should discuss officially discontinuing your mentoring relationship. This is not to say that you must cut all contact; you may well become friends, colleagues or collaborators in the future.

What the institution can do to support development of mentoring for their researchers

It is important to design the mentoring programme that suits your specific institution. For general advice and guidance on establishing a mentoring programme see Appendix A. Below are some guidelines on how to establish a mentoring scheme where the mentors are from outside the institution. These have been summarised in Figure 6.1 into five steps.

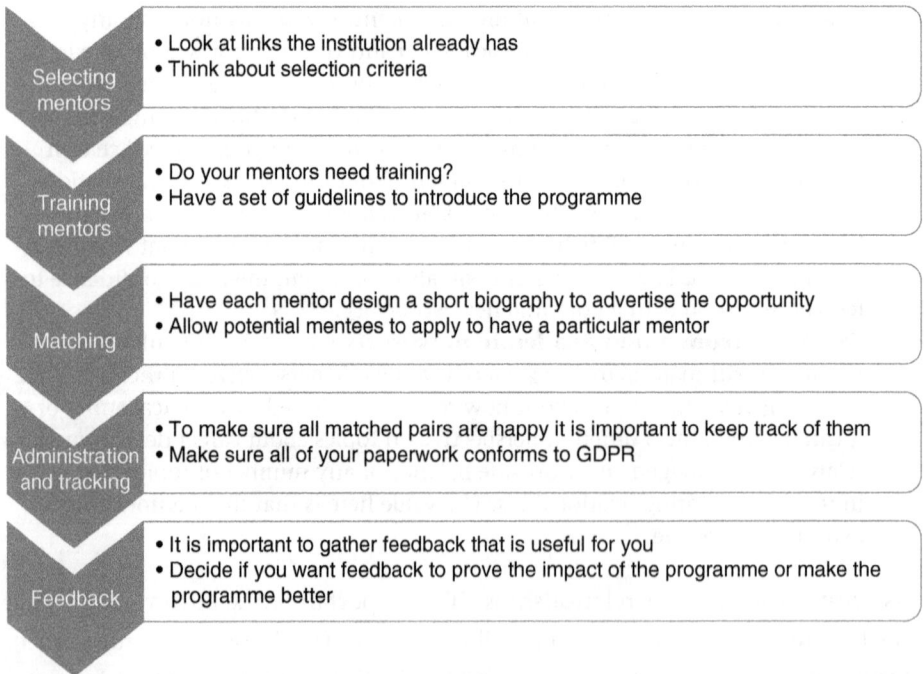

Selecting mentors	• Look at links the institution already has • Think about selection criteria
Training mentors	• Do your mentors need training? • Have a set of guidelines to introduce the programme
Matching	• Have each mentor design a short biography to advertise the opportunity • Allow potential mentees to apply to have a particular mentor
Administration and tracking	• To make sure all matched pairs are happy it is important to keep track of them • Make sure all of your paperwork conforms to GDPR
Feedback	• It is important to gather feedback that is useful for you • Decide if you want feedback to prove the impact of the programme or make the programme better

Figure 6.1 The five steps of establishing a mentoring programme with mentors outside academia

Selecting mentors

Recruiting mentors outside your institution can be challenging. However, there are various ways of recruiting by using the alumni network to ask people who have been at the HEI to offer some time to be a mentor. Be explicit about what the programme can achieve and flexible about what the mentors can offer. For example, allow each mentor to outline what they can help with and how much time they can give to the mentee. You can then broaden the pool of mentors using personal contacts, local networks and recent mentees of the programme who have moved on from academia. One interesting source of mentors is the university itself, where many staff work in non-academic roles and are well placed to offer mentoring to researchers at the institution. An example of this would be a member of staff within the research services department who has a PhD and now works as an ethics specialist or intellectual property expert. It is also highly likely that your institution will have industrial partners or staff who have a split academic/external professional role, perhaps within engineering, sciences, technology, education, nursing, architecture or a business school, and they may be appropriate mentors.

Training mentors

The nature of this programme means that the mentors are distributed throughout the world and so a training session could be logistically difficult and an imposition on these volunteers' time. It is useful to write guidelines or online resources and offer training if the mentor feels it is required. Training can then be carried out on a one-to-one basis, as appropriate. We suggest that within the guidelines you cover:

- the rationale for the programme
- the type of researchers who will be mentees
- basic rules of the relationship
- boundaries of the mentoring relationship
- some straightforward coaching techniques
- the mentoring processes.

After each pairing, we suggest that you collect feedback (discussed later in this chapter). The feedback you get from each mentee will provide an indication about whether they were paired with an effective mentor. You can then make a judgement about whether you will offer that mentor to other researchers.

Matching

It is easiest and achieves the best results if the mentee chooses the mentor for a programme like this. In other mentoring programmes it may be better to adopt a formal approach where the match is done by a third party. However, in a scheme involving external mentors, this is not easy to accomplish because the mentors are gathered in an ad-hoc manner, so the scheme coordinator has little influence over the types of mentor they will get. It is then problematic to ask potential mentees what they want in a mentor and then try to find them a suitable match. Instead, what works well is to have each mentor create a short biography detailing their experience, current position and what they are willing to help with. Then, potential mentees can look at the mentors on offer and select one based on what they want a mentor for.

Allowing mentees to choose their mentors in this fashion has some disadvantages. First, mentees will often be quite narrow in their thinking, and if they want to pursue a career in a certain company, for example, they may not see the use of a mentor who has never worked in that company. Second, sometimes when the scheme coordinator meets with potential mentees it becomes apparent that they want a mentor for a different reason from the one stated, and this only becomes evident through a conversation with them (we explore this further in Chapter 4).

When a researcher contacts you, having identified a suitable mentor, meet with them to discuss the programme and what to expect from the mentor. This expectation-setting conversation is important for the relationship to start smoothly and to make sure that the onus is put on the researcher to drive the mentoring process forward. For example, it is important, in order to maximise the use of the mentor's time, to emphasise to the mentee that it is their responsibility to arrange mentoring meetings and follow up on actions.

Administration and tracking

To begin, send an email to introduce the mentoring pair and within that email state that the mentee should contact the mentor and arrange the first meeting. To that first email attach a form that the pair must fill in during their first meeting. The form checks that they have discussed specific aspects of the relationship, including time allotted, contact and confidentiality. (See Appendix A for an example of a generic mentoring contract proforma.)

It is up to you how frequently you contact your mentoring pairs; however, it is important to keep in contact with them. In our experience, an email after one month and then every three months is not too frequent to be a burden on the mentor or mentee. The email should just check that the pair are still meeting, are happy with the relationship and plan to carry on meeting. Responses to these emails need to be tracked and noted.

Feedback

You may wish to collect some feedback from the people involved in your programme. Before you start, consider the following:

1. What is the feedback for?
    a. to improve the scheme
    b. to prove the worth of the scheme
    c. to allow the participants time to reflect on their experience
    d. to inform you if the mentor is good

2. Who will see the feedback?
3. How will you collect the feedback?
    a. online
    b. email
    c. paper

4. Will you ask the mentor and mentee?
5. Will you keep feedback anonymous?

Your answers to these questions should guide you in the kind of feedback you solicit and in what form.

Chapter summary

As most researchers will ultimately work outside academia, having an external mentor can be a powerful developmental exercise and can benefit the mentor and mentee. This may be true for all the mentoring relationships that we discuss within this book, but mentoring outside academia for researchers allows mentors to link back to the institution and mentees to gain experience, role models and networks beyond their current institution in a one-to-one relationship. Establishing the mentoring relationship can take some effort on all sides, but ultimately it pays dividends in valuable insights and experience about an area that is often a closed book to the other person in the mentoring partnership.

Further reading

Careers Research and Advisory Centre (2018) *Career Destinations by Discipline Infographics, Vitae.* Available at: www.vitae.ac.uk/impact-and-evaluation/what-do-researchers-do/career-destinations-by-discipline-infographics-1 (accessed 19/12/2018).

Denicolo, P. and Reeves, J. (2014) How can researchers make a successful transition to another employment? Chapter 12 in *Success in Research: Developing Transferable Skills, Enhancing your Employment Potential.* London: SAGE.

HESA (2018) *HE Student Enrolments by Level of Study.* Cheltenham: Higher Education Statistics Agency. Available at: www.hesa.ac.uk/data-and-analysis/sfr247/figure-3.

Slight, C. (2017) *Postgraduate Research Experience Survey 2017: Experiences and Personal Outlook of Postgraduate Researchers.* Available at: www.heacademy.ac.uk/system/files/hub/download/pres_2017_report_0.pdf.

Whitmore, J. (2009) *Coaching for Performance: GROWing Human Potential and Purpose. The Principles and Practice of Coaching and Leadership* (4th edition). London: Nicholas Brealey.

PART II

Mentoring for skills development

Overview

Having explored the value of mentoring partnerships at different transition points commonly experienced by researchers throughout their careers in the previous section, in this section, consisting of Chapters 7–10, we consider mentoring partnerships to support skills development. Far from the clichéd notion of sitting in an 'ivory tower' to conduct research, today's successful academic is adept at engaging with diverse audiences. Some of these audiences include funding bodies that need to be persuaded of the innovation and contribution to wider society of a research project; potential collaborative partners from industry, commerce or the third sector; and, of course, specialists within academia. To engage effectively with such diverse audiences, researchers need an extensive array of skills at their disposal, clarity about their purpose in engaging, and real understanding of what each audience needs and expects for their purpose to be achieved.

In Chapter 7, we focus on mentoring to support publication skills. Here, we acknowledge the importance of a strong publication record for a successful academic career and illustrate how mentoring partnerships help those with relatively little experience of preparing a manuscript for publication. We highlight that a mentor can help an inexperienced author to make the most of each step in the process of publication, from planning to honing the manuscript, and how the mentor can also benefit. We then address issues common among more experienced academics, principally finding time and mental space to write publications. We show how mentoring initiatives, such as writing retreats, virtual writing communities and writing buddy schemes, help busy researchers find the time and motivation needed to produce polished publications.

In Chapter 8, we switch focus to mentoring partnerships that can support the skills necessary for a compelling grant submission. We acknowledge the inescapable reality that grant writing over a career is likely to include a high number of rejections but demonstrate just how effective mentoring partnerships can be in developing coping mechanisms and turning negative emotional responses into more positive outcomes. We then explore how an experienced mentor can equip a less experienced grant application writer with numerous effective strategies for pinpointing the best funding body for their project, preparing a meticulous application, actively seeking feedback on the application prior to submitting and remaining positive in the face of negative comments.

Chapter 9 addresses the key research skill of networking. We show how mentoring partnerships can help researchers not just to build their networks, but to use them effectively. We acknowledge the reticence that some researchers feel to build their networks, but emphasise just how fundamental to a successful academic career these networks are. The chapter illustrates how mentoring conversations about networking can help a mentee to be strategic when building their network. It also highlights that networks do more than provide professional contacts; they can also be a source of friendship, which makes the process of networking that much more satisfying and enjoyable.

Finally, in Chapter 10, we focus on the value of mentoring partnerships in supporting spoken communication skills. Here, we reflect on the impact of internationalisation and emphasis on respect for diversity in the workplace, demonstrating how mentoring partnerships can help us to become more finely attuned to the potential sensitivities of others in our daily interactions with colleagues, juniors, seniors and students. We also highlight how mentoring can help international researchers who are working and teaching in a language that is not their first to develop their spoken skills, which, in turn, can positively impact on student satisfaction levels.

At the end of each of these chapters, we provide specific guidance and suggestions for those responsible for mentoring provision on how to best facilitate and support mentoring partnerships to support skills development.

7
Mentoring to support publication

In this chapter, we consider:

- How a mentoring partnership can support the planning and drafting stages of writing for publication
- The value of mentoring events in providing physical and mental space for writing
- The benefits of mentoring to support publication for mentee, mentor and the institution

Introduction

In today's academic world, having a strong publication record is crucial for academic success and progression. If you are relatively inexperienced in writing for publication, you are likely to need considerable guidance on how to choose the right journal or publishing house, and how to produce a polished, convincing manuscript. Even if you have some experience of publication, you may well struggle to find the time and space (both physical and mental) to think, write and produce the written outputs expected of you as an academic. Irrespective of your career stage, building a strong publication track record demands sophisticated writing skills, an understanding of what publication houses are looking for, clarity about your objectives for getting published and the personal motivation, time and space to produce a polished manuscript.

Mentoring partnerships that help mentees to develop their publication record offer benefits to mentee, mentor and the institution, as detailed in Table 7.1.

Table 7.1 Benefits of mentoring partnerships to support publication

Benefits for the mentee	Benefits for the mentor	Benefits for the institution
Having a mentor who can offer feedback on an early draft before you submit a formal report or paper can be a real boost to your confidence.	By commenting on the writing of others, you hone your own writing skills.	Mentoring partnerships for publication help to create a culture of support and community for researchers who often feel daunted by the challenges of having to write high-quality publications.
Your mentor may be able to link you up with writing groups if you are looking for one to join.	As a mentor, you become a role model for your mentee, and that is strong motivation for disciplining yourself not to get into sloppy writing habits. The same applies if you are mentoring less experienced academics in their grant applications, which we cover in Chapter 8.	In mentoring partnerships, mentees tend to look to their mentors as role models. This prompts the mentor to be more aware of their own writing practices and is likely to encourage their desire to adopt good writing practices themselves. This can lead to a general institutional culture of good writing practice, which is likely to positively impact publication outputs.
The right writing mentor may be able to offer culture-related support if you are an international researcher used to a very different academic writing style (discussed more in Chapter 5).	Adding mentoring to your CV adds value to your job application as mentoring initiatives are highly valued in industry, commerce, the third sector and academia. It is also listed on promotion criteria for senior academic positions, such as professor.	Supporting writing skills development through mentoring increases the quality of the academic writing outputs of your institution, which in turn boosts its reputation and enhances metrics submitted for the Research Excellence Framework (REF).
Having a mentor to whom you declare a specific writing target or talk through a specific writing block will motivate you to meet that target or to find ways to overcome the block.	If your mentee is a junior colleague in a different but related discipline, there are potential collaborations that could stem from your partnership.	As writing mentors do not necessarily need to be from the same discipline as the mentee, these writing initiatives can help to break down the silo attitude often found in research institutions. As a result, they promote cross-disciplinary networking and collaboration.
If you are based off campus, abroad or work part-time, having a mentor to whom you can send writing or from whom you can receive feedback helps you to feel part of the academic community, which can often be missing when you are not based on campus.	Supporting the writing development of a more junior colleague allows you to reflect on how far you yourself have developed in your academic career. This can be satisfying and confidence-boosting.	Providing writing support for researchers and staff members based off campus can be a vital lifeline for them as individuals, which is likely to boost their writing outputs for the institution.

Benefits for the mentee	Benefits for the mentor	Benefits for the institution
A mentor is often someone who can share your pain when the writing becomes a little challenging, and this happens to us all irrespective of our stage on the academic ladder. Sometimes all you will need to rekindle your energy for writing is a quick coffee and chat.		

In the rest of this chapter, we identify how mentoring partnerships can support three important aspects of the publication process: planning, drafting and redrafting for successful publication; finding and maintaining motivation to write; and creating time and space to write. There is considerable discussion that we could have on strategies for writing publications, but as our focus is on the ways that mentoring can support publication, it is beyond the scope of this chapter to consider these in depth. You will, however, find extensive discussion of these strategies and other aspects of academic publishing in a sister book, *Success in Research: Publishing for Impact* (Duke et al., 2020), included in the Further Reading section at the end of this chapter.

Mentoring to support planning, drafting and redrafting

Preparing a manuscript for publication is a complex process and requires careful planning, drafting and considerable redrafting in response to feedback from others before the manuscript is ready for submitting. Although this process is time- and energy-consuming, finally getting your manuscript accepted and published is immensely satisfying. A mentoring partnership where the mentor has extensive experience of publications can help to smooth the process from planning to submission, making it a positive learning experience.

To find a mentor with appropriate experience, you have various options: many senior academics are themselves often involved with publishing houses, either as peer reviewers for book proposals or as editors or assistant editors for academic journals. You might, therefore, consider approaching a senior colleague to be your mentor. Alternatively, you could ask them for any contacts within publishing houses, such as professional editors or those responsible for commissioning books, who might be willing to become a mentor. A third option is to seek a mentor through your institution's mentoring programme, if it runs one, as they may have a mentoring for publication support strand that you can access.

At the planning stage of a publication, mentoring conversations are likely to focus on factors to clarify before the process of writing starts. For a journal paper, an important consideration is which journal to target; for a book proposal, if the book has not yet been commissioned, which publisher to target. As a mentor, you can help your mentee to choose their journal or publisher, or at least to narrow down their choice, by encouraging them to reflect on three important considerations: their objective in writing the manuscript; the specific focus of the paper or book; and their timescale for writing.

Planning a journal paper

Before choosing a journal, it is important to be clear about the objective of writing the paper in the first place as this will help to determine the most appropriate type of journal to aim for. A mentoring partnership provides a valuable reflective space for the mentee to clarify their purpose in writing a publication, and there are many possible reasons for wanting to be published. For example, as a mentee, if you have never published before, your objective may simply be to gain experience of the publishing process. If so, you will probably be able to get that experience by choosing a journal that is not as competitive as those commonly targeted by more established and experienced writers.

On the other hand, if your objective is to start to build your publication track record, then you are likely to need to target a relatively high-ranking journal. As a mentor, your understanding of journal rankings will help your mentee to gauge just how high up the rankings to aim. You might signpost your mentee to portals such as Scimago (www.scimagojr.com) and encourage your mentee to explore the journal rankings and other metrics available there, to help them get a feel for the way academics use journals to develop their academic careers. Alternatively, you could suggest that your mentee books an appointment with your institution's bibliometrician, usually based in the Library, for guidance on the significance of the different metrics.

Reflection Point 7.1 may be a useful conversation focus to help clarify the mentee's overarching objective in writing a publication.

Reflection Point 7.1

Identifying reasons for wanting to write a journal publication

Below are some common objectives in writing a journal publication. If you are a mentee, use the statements below to reflect on your own objective. Is it one of these or is it something else? Then consider what steps you can take next to choose the most appropriate journal. If you are a mentor, use the statements below to reflect on what advice you would give for finding a suitable journal for each scenario.

1. I have never published before, so I want to write a manuscript to get experience of the process.
2. To be awarded my doctorate, I must have at least (x) publication/s either submitted for publication or already published by the time of my viva.
3. I have published in my own language but never in English, and I need an English publication because most of the **high-impact journals** in my field are published in English.
4. I have published in non-peer-reviewed journals but never in peer-reviewed ones.
5. I only have low-impact journal publications and for my CV I need to have some high-impact ones.
6. Research in my field moves very fast, and as I have some very good findings from my current project, my supervisor is encouraging me to write a paper for publication.

An important consideration at the planning stage is whether the paper is going to be co-authored or single-authored, and a mentoring conversation around the advantages and drawbacks of each is helpful. A good starting point for such a conversation would be working through Reflection Point 7.1 together to ascertain your reason, as a mentee, for seeking a publication as this may influence your decision about whether to produce a co-authored or single-authored paper. For example, as a mentee, if you wish to boost your CV by having a high-impact journal publication, you might consider co-authoring with authors more established in the field, whose experience of manuscript writing for high-impact journals you can learn from. However, you would also need to reflect on the potential pitfalls of that option, such as whether working with a team of authors who are well respected in your discipline would minimise your contribution to the paper, so that you would get little credit for the paper and your name would feature low down in the list of authors.

Generally, author order is determined by the level of contribution of each author. However, in some disciplines, such as the physical sciences, where there are often many contributors to a single paper, alphabetical order rather than contribution order is followed (Conroy, 2018). As a mentor, you might be able to advise your mentee about which convention is preferred in their discipline. You could also consult the author guidelines of the journal that your mentee opts for to clarify which convention it follows – alphabetical order or contribution order. A useful additional activity you could suggest doing together next is to draw up a table of the advantages and disadvantages of being a single author and being a co-author, once your mentee is clear about their purpose in writing a publication.

Deciding on the focus of the manuscript is another factor to be discussed with your mentoring partner. As a mentee, you should consider who you will be writing for, that is, the readership of the target journal. The first readership, of course, will be the editorial team because if your manuscript does not appeal to them, it will not even get to the peer-review stage. This means that you need to do your homework to gauge the topics and style the editorial team seems to favour. This will involve reading the journal website, particularly the author guidelines, any special issue calls, and some papers already published in the journal. As a mentor, you could point out general differences in types of journal, such as those that prefer review papers or favour papers on qualitative research over quantitative or vice versa. In our experience, this is an area of which those relatively new to publishing are frequently unaware.

A third factor to discuss is the time frame for the manuscript. As a mentor, encouraging your mentee to investigate the timescales for journals that they are considering will help them to find a good match for their own timescale. This is useful because your mentee might not necessarily be aware of the considerable variation in turn-around times from journal to journal. In fast-moving disciplines, such as telecommunications and satellite systems, the publication process, including peer review, can be four to six months; in contrast, particularly in slower-moving disciplines such as English literature or theology, the process can take up to two years. This variation, though, is not necessarily so discipline-specific, being dependent on other factors, such as popularity (there may be a large backlog of excellent articles awaiting publication).

Drafting and redrafting a journal paper

As well as supporting the planning aspects of a journal paper, a mentoring partnership can provide considerable guidance on the drafting and redrafting aspects of writing for publication. Mentoring is particularly useful in supporting less experienced authors who wish to author a paper for a high-impact journal, the pressure for which is now considerable in today's academic climate. There are many facets of a high-quality academic publication, which of course include the rigour of the research undertaken, its contribution beyond academia and its authority. However, inexperienced authors often lose the sense of the quality and rigour of the study in the redrafting process, largely because they lack the writing strategies that seasoned authors of high-impact journals use. As a mentor, you may wish to share with your mentee some of the strategies for writing that you have accrued in the process of building your publishing track record, for example, how to polish a manuscript, so that the quality of the research discussed in the paper is matched by the quality of the writing you use to talk about your research. Reflection Point 7.2 may provide a useful focus for a mentoring conversation around useful strategies for producing a polished manuscript.

Reflection Point 7.2

Strategies for producing a polished journal manuscript

Below we list three important features of a polished journal manuscript – focus, consistency and readability – and offer suggestions for strategies that you can use for each. In your mentoring partnership, reflect on other strategies that can be used to give a manuscript focus, consistency and readability and add them to the lists.

1. Focus
   - Have one main focus or argument in the manuscript. There may be four or five sub-focuses or arguments to support the main argument, but you should ensure that the relevance of those sub-points to the main focus is clear to the reader.

2. Consistency
   - Discuss each sub-focus/sub-argument in equal depth
   - Ensure that writing style is consistent throughout the paper

3. Readability
   - Ensure that the main point of each paragraph is stated at the beginning of the paragraph, not at the end.
   - Use title words throughout the manuscript, preferably using at least one in each paragraph. The introduction section should contain as many of the title words as possible, so that the reader can get an early orientation about the direction of the paper.

Another aspect of redrafting that a mentoring partnership can really support is responding to peer-review feedback. Inexperienced authors frequently underestimate the number of redrafts they will have to do and the level of detailed comments they are likely to receive through peer review. As a mentee, you may find this level of feedback overwhelming on occasion. One way your mentor will probably reassure you is by telling you how normal this is. As a mentor, it is also worth highlighting that peer reviewers act as a bridge between the journal and an author; for example, one of their functions is to ensure that all aspects of the manuscript – the research it presents, the coherence of the document and its authority and persuasiveness – are all the standard and quality required by the journal's editorial team. It is also worth pointing out to your mentee that if the reviewers cannot understand something they have written, it is likely the journal readership will not either. Therefore, they should view the feedback as helping them to produce a clearer manuscript for the ultimate readership.

Feedback from reviewers can also sometimes feel rather negative, which as an author can be demoralising and painful to receive. As a mentor, you may again be able to offer reassurance and ways of coping if your mentee has received negative feedback. For example, you can emphasise the importance of letting negative emotional reactions to feedback settle before responding to the comments. You might also direct them to Voices of Experience 8.2 (p. 115) and 8.3 (p. 116) in the next chapter, where two experienced academics reflect on how they deal with rejection and negative feedback. Although they focus on research grant applications, the strategies they describe for coping with rejection and negative comments apply equally to journal articles.

Planning a book

In terms of authoring a book, there are various options to consider. For example, you may decide to write a monograph – a book written on a single, specialist subject, usually, but not always, by a single author – or, if you prefer a collaborative project, a co-authored book. A mentoring partnership with a mentor who has considerable experience of book authoring or even experience within a publishing house can help you to decide which option will be best for you. As a mentor, you will be able to indicate some of the advantages and drawbacks of being a single author or part of a team. One advantage of a single-authored monograph is that the book will be fully credited to you. However, writing a weighty tome single-handedly can be extremely time-consuming and a lonely experience. Co-authoring a book has the advantage of sharing ideas with colleagues, which is a great way to stimulate new ideas. For a new author, it is also far less daunting than being solely responsible for an entire book. Indeed, as a mentee, you might even be able to draw upon one of your co-authors to mentor you through the entire process.

At the same time, co-authoring can present a few logistical challenges, such as working to deadlines when each author has different work commitments and coordinating diaries for important author meetings. There are other potential challenges too, such as the tensions that can result from the different working patterns of members of the team. For example, an author who likes to work well ahead of deadlines may be irritated or stressed by a team member who prefers to work right up to the deadline. Discussion about these issues within your mentoring partnership will help the mentee to make an informed decision about whether to opt for single- or co-authorship.

Irrespective of the type of book, if the book has not actually been commissioned by a publishing house, a book proposal will need to be submitted to seek a commission. As the proposal must be concise, clear and convincing for the publishing house, a mentor who has written numerous proposals and has been successfully commissioned will provide essential guidance on how to tailor a proposal to appeal specifically to the publishing house targeted. Top Tips 7.1 may be a useful reference in any mentoring conversation you might have about how to tailor proposals for a particular publishing house.

Top Tips 7.1

Tailoring a book proposal for a publishing house

1. As a mentee, do your homework and thoroughly research the publishing house before submitting your proposal. Find out the type of books they publish. How many monographs/multi-authored books have they published? Do they seem to have a preference? What topics or disciplines do they publish? What types of book do they favour, for example, textbooks and supplementary materials for educational courses, books on theory, narratives, etc.? Who is their target readership? Do they have a favoured writing style? (Read a few pages of various books already published to find this out.) How technical/specialist do their books tend to be? What seems to be the range in book length?

2. As a mentor, encourage your mentee to reflect on their ideal publishing house for their monograph/multi-authored book by raising questions such as: Who do you want to read your monograph? What is the unique selling point (USP) of your monograph? What types of publisher do you think will find your monograph

(Continued)

appealing? What is it about your book that will make it stand out for Publisher XXX? Which book category currently offered by Publisher XXX will your book fall into? These questions will help them to decide whether the publishing house they are considering is the best choice for their manuscript.

Drafting and redrafting a book

As with journal articles, producing a book requires many cycles of drafting and redrafting in response to feedback. The advice on dealing with peer-review comments that we gave in that section very much applies to books as well, and a mentoring partnership can help an inexperienced author to understand the value of this process. For example, as a mentor, with your extensive experience of publication, you will be only too aware of the level of polishing that is necessary to ensure that the book is a coherent document. You might even be able to recall occasions when you have lost sight of the focus of a chapter you were writing, which is very normal in early drafting, and the way review comments helped you to get back on track. Sharing your own experiences will reassure your mentee that losing focus is not a failing but is largely inevitable when writing a large manuscript, such as a book.

As a mentee, having a mentor who is also co-authoring the book with you will be a wonderful opportunity for you to learn that the peer-review process also occurs among the co-authors; it is very normal for each chapter written by one author to be reviewed by the others. Inexperienced authors often feel uncomfortable with their writing being reviewed by fellow authors and may view any comments designed to be constructive in a more negative way. They might even regard them as personal attacks on their writing. As a mentor, you can help your mentee to alleviate those feelings by explaining that a key purpose of the feedback is to ensure that the final book has one collective voice. You can also point out that it is far better to resolve any issues in the chapters in the redrafting stage rather than having to make changes once it has been submitted for external peer review, which tends to be the case when a new book title has been written by a team with whom the publishing house has not worked before.

Mentoring to aid motivation to write

As mentioned earlier, writing for publication is time- and energy-consuming due to the amount of thought and reflection that needs to be invested in a manuscript.

For these reasons, maintaining the motivation to complete the manuscript can often be challenging. Mentoring partnerships and events designed specifically to support writing can be wonderful vehicles for rekindling lapsed enthusiasm or energy for a manuscript, or for providing space – both physical and mental – to write. Mentoring initiatives such as writing buddy schemes and writing retreats can forge strong mentoring partnerships that help you to focus on the writing that you may well have put on the back burner due to more pressing deadlines. We explore each of these next.

Writing buddy schemes

Writing buddy schemes are based on peer mentoring where one researcher or professional is paired with another, who is either at the same stage of their career or one slightly more experienced. The purpose of the pairing is to encourage both partners to maintain their motivation for writing. One way to do this is to declare writing targets to each other, sharing writing issues with each other and meeting regularly to check that targets are being met.

Whether you are an early-stage doctoral researcher writing your first report or a seasoned academic putting together a journal paper or book, writing buddy schemes can really help you to focus on, commit to and produce your piece of writing. For example, if you have developed a writing block over a section of the paper or a book chapter, then having a writing buddy with whom you can talk over the block, and who is able to make suggestions for changes to the piece, will be a real aid to overcoming the block.

Formal writing buddy schemes often run within specific departments, particularly where collaborative writing projects are common, such as collaborative journal papers. Here the partnerships will share the same discipline. Other schemes are run centrally, perhaps from the institution's Researcher Development Programme or Graduate School, and will be able to pair up buddies from different disciplines if that is needed.

However, you do not necessarily need a formal scheme to find a writing buddy. If you are working on a collaborative writing project, your fellow authors may well provide you with the motivational support that you need. Certainly, in our experience of writing this book, each of us has drawn tremendous energy from the others at different stages of the project. Of course, for that to happen, there needs to be a basic rapport among the authors, and not all authoring teams will necessarily get on with each other. So, one important aspect of a writing buddy partnership, which you should bear in mind if you decide to find your own buddy, is to choose someone that you will get on with. For example, you could advertise for one in your department, or distribute flyers at events, or you could engage in conversations at networking events, conferences or special interest groups, either within your institution or outside it, to find your buddy. Top Tips 7.2 below may help you to find a suitable writing buddy to keep you motivated to complete your project.

Another consideration is finding a buddy who is writing to a similar time frame as you; the purpose of the writing buddy partnership is to keep both parties motivated to complete a specific publication, and motivation will be highest if both have deadlines that are reasonably close to each other. It is also worth being open-minded about the discipline in which you find a buddy; the person to whom you declare your writing targets does not necessarily have to be a specialist in your subject area, so by considering potential buddies from other disciplines, you increase the likelihood of finding someone working to a similar time frame as you.

Writing retreats and 'Shut Up and Write!' events

Writing retreats are mentoring events that normally span one, two, three or more days with the purpose of creating a space, both physical and mental, for researchers at any stage of career to focus exclusively on writing. They are common practice in many research institutions and are enormously valuable for boosting your writing productivity. They may be an institution-wide event or organised at the school or department level. They can be held on campus, at an off-site venue, such as a country house or hotel with conference facilities, or a youth hostel in a tranquil environment. Such venues are costly though, so may not be affordable if the event is self-funded or being funded by your school or department. Retreats can even run online as a virtual writing retreat.

As a mentee, writing retreats often involve you teaming up with a writing mentor for the duration of the event. You will usually be asked to set writing targets for the retreat, which then get divided up into very specific targets for each day or half-day. Your mentor's role is first to help you to set realistic targets for the time available, then to motivate you throughout the retreat to keep you on target, and finally to hold you to account at the end of each day if you have not met your target.

As a mentor on a retreat, your work is very much about helping your mentee to find the motivation and time to produce their piece of writing. An effective way to help them to do this is to ensure that they are working within clearly defined time parameters for very specific targets. For a mentee, there is nothing more motivating than achieving their first target fully within the time they themselves set. For this reason, in a good writing retreat mentoring partnership, you should help your mentee to learn to gauge what is realistic and what is not within a specific time frame.

An event similar, though not identical, to a writing retreat is a 'Shut Up and Write!' session, which provides a wonderful motivational space and opportunity to meet potential future writing buddies. The concept, originating among creative writers in the San Francisco area in the USA (www.shutupwrite.com/), is for those wishing to write to find motivation by joining others in a relaxed environment – a café – to do their writing. The concept has been widely adopted by many HEIs and is popular among researchers at any stage of career who need to find time and mental space to focus on a specific piece of writing. These events are often organised by Researcher Development teams, who structure the event around a sequence of writing sessions and breaks, frequently based on the Pomodoro Technique created by Francesco Cirillo in the late 1980s (https://francescocirillo. com/pages/pomodoro-technique). In this technique, the writer sets a kitchen timer (a pomodoro) to 25 minutes and must write for that time-span without any interruption. This is a great technique for maintaining focus on a writing task and is a useful way to find out just how much writing you can realistically achieve in 25 minutes.

Top Tips 7.2 may be useful in a mentoring conversation around setting achievable writing targets, which will help to make writing retreats and 'Shut Up and Write!' sessions as productive as possible.

Top Tips 7.2

Achieving writing targets

1. As a mentor, encourage your mentee to be as specific as possible when setting a writing target and to set a time against it for completion. For example, if the target is 'complete first draft of paper', then that needs to be broken down into more specific targets, such as 'Finish drafting Section 1 by 11.00; draft Section 2 by 14.30', etc. This makes a specific target time-bound, which will then help them to see if the original target of completing the first draft of the paper is achievable in the time available.
2. As a mentee, be honest about the amount of time on each day of the writing retreat that you can realistically set aside to write. Having a daily target is good for developing regular writing patterns. Remember to factor in break times and perhaps work in short 20–30-minute blocks; sitting down in front of your computer for two

(Continued)

hours at a time does not necessarily mean that you are writing productively! Also consider your body clock. For example, be aware of when you tend to be more productive and set more ambitious targets for that time of day.

3. If you are a mentee and are struggling to keep motivated, ask your mentor to arrange to see you or to email or text you at a specified time during the retreat to see how you are progressing.

4. As a mentor, if you see that your mentee is struggling to manage their time, you could suggest they follow the Pomodoro Technique, mentioned above.

5. Ensure that both mentor and mentee agree on the nature of the writing required over the time period, for instance whether it is a rough draft or a polished piece. Often a mentee trying to produce a perfected script when only a draft is required results in missed targets, disappointment and demotivation.

Before we end this section, we should also mention the motivational value of Academic Writing Month (AcWriMo) (www.phd2published.com/acwri-2/acbowrimo/about/), an online writing community that seeks to support individuals who wish to produce a writing output in the month of November. AcWriMo was set up in 2011 by Charlotte Frost to provide an academic version of NaNoWriMo (National Novel Writing Month), a non-profit event designed to inspire young writers to find their voices.

Participants sign up to AcWriMo at the start of the month by making an online pledge to the rest of the AcWriMo community to complete a specified piece of writing by 30 November. Each day throughout that month, online events and blogs are released and physical writing events at individual institutions can be run, such as writing retreats that coordinate with the AcWriMo event or writing workshops.

The mentoring takes various forms, such as inspirational blogs from well-known academics or other writers, providing a form of writing role model for participants; online writing tips which offer advice to participants; and chat rooms, where members of this virtual community can share their writing successes, concerns, advice and support with each other. In this respect, for the month of November, AcWriMo provides a community of many writing buddies, who pledge their targets to one another at the start of the month, and who, through the various virtual activities available, build a sense of belonging to that community. This, in turn, motivates participants to meet their targets and to share their success with each other when they achieve them.

One of the great benefits of participating in online communities such as AcWriMo is the network of researchers at all career stages across an enormous range of disciplines throughout the world that participants can build. As such, it offers much in terms of potential collaborative projects. We discuss networking in greater depth in Chapter 9. AcWriMo can attract many participants, which makes this virtual mentoring initiative enormously motivational and energising.

Advice for those responsible for providing institutional publication mentoring

As evident from earlier discussion in this chapter, there is considerable diversity in the type of support that might be needed for publication. For this reason, your programme for mentoring support for publication really needs to be tailored to the specific needs of individual mentees. This, in turn, means that you will need to ensure that your pool of mentors covers as broad a range of publication experience, writing skill and disciplines as possible. It also means that, to ensure a good match between mentee and mentor, you should gather as much information as possible from potential mentees and mentors. Top Tips 7.3 may help you to gather the information you need to find appropriate matches for your mentees and mentors.

Top Tips 7.3

Building a comprehensive profile of your mentors' experience

1. If you use a generic application form (an example of which is provided in Appendix A), ensure that potential mentors complete an additional form specifically for mentoring to support publication, which provides the following information about the publication writing background of each mentor. Your form should include information relating to the following themes:

    - Types of publication they have produced (for example, journal papers, books)
    - Authoring experience (for example, single-authored or co-authored manuscripts or both)
    - Peer review experience (for example, of what – paper or book or book proposal? For whom?)
    - Editing experience (for example, what type of editing – for a publishing house, for the informal support of peers, or something else?)
    - Experience of book proposal writing
    - Summary statement from the mentor about aspects of publication writing that they feel they are sufficiently experienced to give good advice on

These themes can be adapted for a similar form to be completed by mentees to ensure that you have a comprehensive profile of their specific needs for publication support.

Writing retreats

Having run many writing retreats over the years, we have found that the best format is to break attendees down into small groups led by mentors. The role of the mentor is to help each attendee to produce clear writing targets: an overall writing target for the entire retreat and smaller targets for each half-day. Mentors should check that the target appears reasonable and achievable within the time frame. They then check in with each mentee at regular intervals to keep them on target. At our retreats, specialists – in writing skills and in particular subjects – join the retreat for a few hours, so that delegates can talk through issues relating to writing or subject with the appropriate specialist. To aid concentration, we divide the day(s) into writing blocks of approximately two hours, which are punctuated with short 30-minute workshops. The workshops cover writing-related themes, such as 'Getting started', a great freewriting activity that helps to trigger the flow of ideas at the start of the retreat, 'Editing and proofreading your work', or 'Knowing when to stop' – advice on how to know when a piece of writing does not need any more work.

If you are considering running a writing retreat, Top Tips 7.4 may help you to ensure that your event is successful.

Top Tips 7.4

Running successful writing retreats

1. **Be clear about your target participants**. This will determine when, and how long, your retreat is. For example, busy academics may only be able to spare a day or even half a day for a writing retreat.
2. **Choose the best time and space for most people**. If you are targeting academic staff, avoid heavy teaching periods in the calendar. A writing retreat based on campus is more accessible than one off campus if most participants are staff; however, if the majority are remotely-based researchers, perhaps an off-site retreat with accommodation would be preferable. Before you opt for this, though, do consider whether you have enough budget to cover this cost and whether delegates might have childcare issues if the retreat is off-site. Another challenge for physical retreats is finding enough specialists to attend the retreat at appropriate times. Here careful thought about the best time of year for the retreat is important. For example, October to December is a bad time for UK institutions as this tends to be the busiest time of the year for many academic staff. You also need to avoid times that clash with school holidays in your area.

Chapter summary

In this chapter, we have considered various mentoring initiatives designed to support publication. We have looked at mentoring that helps less experienced researchers to effectively plan, draft and redraft a journal manuscript or book. We have also highlighted the value of mentoring initiatives designed to motivate and provide time and space for writing, which are particularly valuable for seasoned academics, whose needs are often related to mental space and time as well as motivation to write outputs. In the next chapter, we shift focus to mentoring to support grant success.

Further reading

AcWriMo, www.phd2published.com/acwri-2/acbowrimo/about/

Cirillo, F. (n.d.) *Pomodoro Technique*. https://francescocirillo.com/pages/pomodoro-technique

Conroy, G. (2018) The A–Z of paper authorship: it's bad news for Z but A is AOK for authors listed alphabetically. *NatureINDEX*, 21 August. Available at: www.natureindex.com/news-blog/a-to-z-of-paper-authorship.

Duke, D., Henslee, E. and Denicolo, P. (2020) *Success in Research: Publishing for Impact*. London: SAGE.

Morss, K. and Murray, R. (2001) Researching academic writing within a structured programme: insights and outcomes. *Studies in Higher Education*, 26(1): 35–52.

Mullen, C.A. (2001) The need for a curricular writing model for graduate students. *Journal of Further Education*, 25(1): 117–126. doi: 10.1080/03098770020030551.

Royal Literary Fund, www.rlf.org.uk

Scimago, www.scimagojr.com/

Shut Up and Write!, www.shutupwrite.com/

8

Mentoring to support grant success

In this chapter, we consider:

- Where to access sources of advice, mentoring and feedback to ensure the greatest chance of grant success
- How mentors can help researchers to identify appropriate funders
- What is good practice for mentors and those giving critical feedback on bids
- How mentors can help deal with reviewers' comments and rejection
- How institutions can best support mentoring for grant success

Applying for grant funding: a key part of a researcher's life

In this chapter, we consider how those new to grant bid writing, most commonly ECRs or junior academic staff, may be mentored by senior academic staff who have grant-writing experience and have already had some research grant success. The mentors might in some, but not all, cases work in a similar research area to the mentee, and therefore might also act as a co-applicant on the grant.

Mentoring for this activity is extremely important because successful researchers are continually honing a never-ending succession of bids and mentoring help can significantly increase the chances of success for those new to the process. Without funding, it is generally not possible to do research or, at best, only do it on a very limited scale. Being able to demonstrate a record of success in winning grant funding is also often a requirement when applying for academic jobs, especially at more senior levels, and appears in academic promotion criteria (considered in Chapter 4 on p. 50). Therefore, applying for grants is an activity that those aspiring to a career in research or academia need to do, and to do successfully.

Mentoring can be critical for those new to bidding for research funds to develop and maintain a realistic and positive attitude to grant bidding. It is a depressing fact that most grant proposals are unsuccessful: around 26% of applications to UK Research Councils are funded, compared to around 20% for the National Institutes of Health in the USA and around 15% for the European Research Council. Without mentoring support, many fledgling researchers simply give up in the face of early rejection. The experience of a senior and successful academic sharing their stories of failure as well as success can, on the other hand, mean that they view the situation much more realistically and philosophically. The value of mentoring to a researcher working on their first bid is exemplified by Voice of Experience 8.1, in which a postdoctoral researcher describes the mentoring help that he received.

Voice of Experience 8.1

My grant-writing mentors gave me their time and good advice

My line manager was very supportive and allowed me to use 'research time' during the first year of my postdoc to develop and write a grant proposal. She was very aware of the need for postdocs to gain independent funding at the first opportunity. She was also willing to spend her own time helping me to develop the proposal to a level where it was ready to be submitted. She highlighted struggles that she had faced, and even provided me with a draft of a previous grant she had applied for so that I was able to understand the nuances of grant writing. Equally important was her reminder that I should not despair if I did not get the grant, which in the end was the case. She admitted that her first few grant applications were also unsuccessful and that ultimately only by practising writing proposals do you gain the experience and skills needed for future successful applications.

Jacques Deere, postdoctoral researcher, University of Amsterdam

Mentoring by an experienced academic can markedly enhance the quality of those early bids, significantly increasing their chance of being funded. We all improve with experience and, once the researcher supported by their mentor has won their first grant(s), the chances of future success swell as they build a track record of both winning funding and, equally critically, delivering on what they said that they would do.

It is clearly of significant benefit to the institution, as well as to the researchers themselves, that staff are supported to write, and write successful, grant bids. Such benefits include:

- Greater grant income to the institution
- Increased research outputs (journal articles, conference proceedings, impact, etc.)
- Increased potential for knowledge exchange and commercialisation of research
- Enhanced Research Excellence Framework (REF) performance
- Heightened institutional prestige and esteem
- Ability to attract and retain the best researchers

In the following sections, we consider how mentoring can support the grant-bidding process, from beginning to end.

Identifying sources of potential funding

Research grants range from small sums to cover, for example, travel to a conference, an archive or a collaborative visit, to very large multi-centre grants employing several staff for several years and with the associated running costs, and everything in between. Sources of potential funding are numerous and diverse, including the small internal grants that HEIs sometimes offer to support travel or a sabbatical, or to 'pump prime' a research project, global and European sources, UK Research Councils, charities and industry. The Vitae web resource 'Where to find sources of academic research funding' (www.vitae.ac.uk/) provides a helpful guide to sources, including links to many funders. Many institutions subscribe to 'Research Professional' (www.researchprofessional.com), which details a wide range of academic research funding opportunities and allows you to set up tailored email alerts to fit your own criteria. EURAXESS (https://euraxess.ec.europa.eu/) is a free-to-use web resource that hosts lists of funding opportunities across Europe, as well as job opportunities and career resources.

If you are new to grant bidding and are interested in applying for research funding but not sure what is available, you may find that your department or institution has a Grants Officer (or equivalent), whose job it is to help identify sources of funding for researchers. They may be able to provide some informal mentoring support during these early stages. For example, you could work together to identify a short list of which sources of potential funding might be most appropriate to you and your research, together with their deadlines for bids. They may also be able to advise you about which other staff members have had grant success with specific funders, and who may, therefore, be appropriate mentors for you during the next stages in the process, which we consider below.

Establishing a grant-writing mentoring partnership

When you have gathered information about the range of potential funders, then, if you are new to grant applications, teaming up with a mentor can make a positive difference to your chances of success. This mentoring partnership can be very rewarding. In Table 8.1, we consider different sources of grant-writing mentors and the advantages to both parties of the mentoring partnership.

Table 8.1 Mentoring for grant writing: sources of mentoring help and benefits to each party

Where to look for a mentor	Benefits of the relationship to both mentor and mentee
You could look for a senior figure in your direct research area who has had grant success (perhaps with one or more of the funders you are considering applying to). It helps if you already have a good personal relationship with them and will feel comfortable sharing your ideas with, and receiving critical feedback from, them. They might be your supervisor from your doctorate, your current line manager or a senior academic in your department.	You already know each other and enjoy a good relationship which you can build on. This is an opportunity to both partners for further collaboration. Because your research interests are closely aligned, you can be co-applicants on the bid. You will both then be committed to making it as strong as possible. The application may be viewed more favourably by the funder because it involves an applicant who already has a positive track record. You will both profit from its success by sharing the funding, working together on the proposed research and sharing the outputs from it.
You could consider someone you do not yet know personally but whose name you know from the literature and whose work complements your own, or someone in your research field whom you have been impressed by, for example, when you have seen them speak at a conference.	This is an excellent opportunity to form a new research collaboration. As above, because your research interests are closely aligned, you can be co-applicants on the bid with all the advantages that brings. The application may be viewed more favourably by the funder because it involves partners from different institutions, with different strengths, facilities and expertise, working together.
You might approach someone who does not work in your immediate research area, but who does have considerable experience of writing successful grant applications, or who sits on grant panels for the funder(s) you are considering. You might be able to identify them through contacts in your department or through a formal institutional mentoring scheme.	The topic of the research falls outside the mentor's immediate area of interest and therefore you will not be co-applicants on the bid, but nor are you likely to be in competition. Nevertheless, during discussions, new ideas or themes will arise, and you will become more aware of the funding landscape. You can build on this in future bids, either individually or together. As a mentor, you will have the opportunity to reflect on your own skills in bid writing, and possibly improve them as a result. Your wider experience will be invaluable and you will be unbiased because you do not know your mentee or their research area, which will strengthen the bid. Working together may add an interdisciplinary dimension to your thinking and planning, which many funders look favourably upon.

If you are new to grant writing, once you have identified a potential mentor, you can approach them with your preliminary ideas and ask if they would be willing to work with you. If the individual is someone you already know well and have worked with before, this should be unproblematic. However, we would advise a note of caution when discussing your research ideas with a stranger. While, of course, most academics are entirely honourable and, as described above, forming a new collaborative relationship through this type of mentoring can be highly rewarding for both parties, it is not unknown for the occasional unscrupulous person to steal another's ideas.

Mentoring to understand and address the funder's requirements and priorities

Once you have established a mentoring partnership, as a mentee, the wider experience of your mentor can be invaluable in clarifying the internal processes, systems and timelines for bidding in your institution, and in supporting you during the preparation of the bid itself. One of the first discussions that you might have as a grant-writing partnership is to agree on which funding scheme to apply to. As a mentee, if you have taken our advice above, you will already have some ideas. As a mentor, you may, from your own experience, be able to guide your mentee in this. Alternatively, you can work together as a mentoring partnership to research what the options are and to discuss which funder best suits the mentee's needs.

As a piece of general advice, we would suggest that if you are new to grant bidding, it is a good idea to start small, gain experience with the support of your mentor and establish something of a track record before attempting to apply for a more ambitious project. Working together, it is critical that you ensure that the planned research is a very close 'fit' for the funding criteria. If it is not, because funders can only fund a very small proportion of the bids that they receive and therefore need to be highly selective, the application simply will not be supported. Activity 8.1 may be a useful framework for you to work together to find out as much as you can about the funder's requirements, priorities and remit.

Activity 8.1

Researching the funder's requirements, priorities and remit

All information that you need to carry out this activity will be available on the funder's website and in the accompanying literature to the call for application or on the application form itself.

Work together to make notes on how your potential funder's priorities and requirements align with your proposed research. You might, for example, make a note of or highlight words or phrases that the funder uses often, and statements that closely align with what it is that you want to do. You might find it helpful to work through the following questions as a guide:

- What is the funder's mission statement? What do they state are their principal interests and aims?
- Do they have priority areas for funding or overarching themes for work that they wish to support?
- Are there any areas they state that they do not support?
- What sort of grant schemes do they have? Do they invite proposals at any time or are there specific calls at certain times of the year? If so, when are the deadlines for applications?
- What types of research have they supported recently? Are there any specific approaches or methodologies or areas that they favour? Do they make publicly available examples of successful proposals that you can learn from?
- What does the application form or process look like? For example, how long is the application form? What types of information are they asking for? Is it electronic with restricted word counts or hard copy with type size restrictions, for instance?
- How many proposals do they fund? What is the success rate of proposals submitted in previous funding rounds?
- What are their selection criteria? Who reviews their proposals? Do they have a Board of Reviewers? Do they ask that the applicant suggests reviewers for their proposal? (Find out more about the work of those who will be judging your proposal and bear them in mind when you are writing your proposal.)

If you have any uncertainties during your discussions, then, as a mentor, you might encourage your mentee to contact the funder directly. Generally, funders are happy to receive such queries because it is in their interest to limit the number of inappropriate applications that they must deal with. If, jointly, you still have concerns, then you can decide together how to move forward: this may involve slightly modifying the focus of the research or angling it in a slightly different way, which is likely to be relatively straightforward to do. On the other hand, it may involve completely rethinking the project, perhaps doing a serious amount of research into the literature and pondering before producing a fresh plan. Your discussions might include some reflection on how much time and effort the mentee will need to dedicate to this, balanced against the ultimate chance of funding success.

Working together to write a compelling proposal

While the details of what each funder requires in a proposal will differ in terms of application length, the amount of detail required and aspects supplementary to the actual research proposal (such as a statement about the impact of the research, how the findings or outcomes will be disseminated, data management, costings, and so on), there are some aspects that are common to all proposals. For this reason, if you are a mentor who has had previous grant success, your experience can be invaluable in advising your mentee on how to make their bid as strong as possible. You might share examples of successful or unsuccessful bids that you have submitted in the past, plus reviewer comments and feedback, which can be especially helpful if the bid(s) were to the funder that you and your mentee are currently considering. One aspect of your wider experience that will be very practical here is your institutional know-how; you can direct your mentee to the numerous sources of wider support available to you both, such as Research Office staff, who can assist with bid-costing and administration, and HR staff to advise about staff costs, and so on. You both might also work together to investigate the support available for grant writing through your researcher development programme. (At the end of this chapter, we suggest some ideas for researcher developers as to the types of workshop and event that might be of benefit to their researchers.) As a mentee, working with such a mentor will ensure that your bid has the greatest chance of success.

One of the most difficult things to get right as you work together as a mentoring partnership is to skilfully give and to receive critical feedback. As a mentor to someone crafting a grant application, the most important aspect of the support that you give is for your advice to be rigorous and honest. Some of the least helpful feedback a mentee can receive is 'it looks fine to me'. Taking the time to read the draft carefully and to provide constructive suggestions for improvement will ensure that your mentee can make the most of your experience and wisdom. However, reflecting on how you phrase feedback – either verbally or in writing – is also important. We all know from our own experience that we feel far more (negative) impact from a single unfavourable comment than we do from a similarly weighted piece of praise. So, as a mentor, balance the negative comments with at least as many encouraging ones, and phrase the negatives constructively as concrete suggestions for improvement. Some examples of how you might do this are given in Activity 8.2. As a mentee, when receiving feedback, keep in mind that your mentor really is on your side and is trying to be helpful, not destructive, and carefully consider how you can improve your writing in response to their suggestions.

Activity 8.2

Critical comment or positive suggestion for improvement?

Below are some examples of some criticisms that a mentor might make of a draft application, phrased in a way that is either negative or unhelpful. As a mentee, discuss with your mentor how you would react if you received this comment on your writing. As a mentor, think about how you might make the same comments in a more positive, constructive and helpful way. We have done the first one as an example.

Critical comment	Put more positively
Your literature review is out of date and the references you have chosen are not appropriate.	The reviewers will need to be convinced that this is an important and topical area for study. To make a strong case, make sure that you are citing the most up-to-date work in this field, as well as the really key references.
Your research question makes no sense.	
Your project proposal is not logical. I cannot follow what you are planning to do, or why.	
This methodology is not appropriate.	
What you are planning does not sound exciting enough.	

Many academics will have heard of the 'slap sandwich' (sometimes called the 'hamburger technique') for giving feedback. Academic staff are often advised to use it when providing feedback to students on their work, and it is recommended as a model for managers giving appraisal to junior colleagues or for mentors giving mentoring advice to mentees. Each piece of criticism – or, put more positively, suggestion for improvement (the 'slap') – should be 'sandwiched' between two positive comments. This has two benefits. First, as a mentee, the criticism is softened by the positive comments and is therefore easier for you to hear. Second, as a mentor, you feel more comfortable being critical when the discussion begins and ends on a positive note. An example of this might be: 'I really like the research area you are proposing; it comes over as innovative and topical ('the top slice of bread'). However, I wonder if you could reformulate your research question so that it is clearer to the reader exactly what it is you are going to investigate (the 'slap'). Your idea of using a mixed methods approach comes over really well ('the bottom slice of bread').'

Another technique that, as a mentor, you can use to help your mentee develop the application is, during mentoring discussions, to ask directed, open questions around areas of the proposal you feel need more work. Open questions are those that cannot be answered with a single word and often start with 'what', 'how' or 'why'. For example, in the mentoring conversation above, asking 'How can you reformulate your research question so that it is clearer to the reader?' can open a discussion between you both; and, as a mentee, you might, after reflection, formulate the research question in a different way. These ideas are also explored in Chapter 11 on p.169, where we present an activity about creating opportunities for reflection by turning assertive comments into open-ended questions.

Obtaining mentoring help through grants panels and peer feedback

Once you have created a fair draft of your bid, a vital next step is that, as a mentoring partnership, you obtain and respond to as much additional critical feedback from others as you can. At its simplest, this can be asking someone – who does not need to know the details of the research – to proofread or to provide feedback on whether the parts of the application that are meant to be understandable to a non-specialist audience really are clear. You might also solicit the mentoring advice of other academics who work outside the immediate topic area of the bid but who are experienced in winning research funding. Most academic departments have mechanisms to assist here, and many researcher development programmes also offer such support. One example might be pairing the mentee, or the grant-writing pair if the mentor is also a co-applicant, with another experienced academic who can provide independent critical commentary and suggestions for improvement. In other places, there may be more of an open peer review process where the applicants pitch their idea or share a draft proposal with a college of peers who can all give advice and mentoring support.

Although it can feel quite intimidating to share your partly-formed ideas with colleagues, it is far better to receive criticism at this stage when you can work to improve your bid than to hear those comments for the first time in the rejection letter from the funder. Having received the feedback, the original mentoring pair can work together to address any points that were raised and further improve the bid before submission.

Mentoring support to deal with reviewers' comments and rejection

Grant bidding is highly competitive, and there are far more (often highly rated) applications submitted to any funder than monies available for distribution.

Your mentoring partnership can play a significant role in lessening the inevitable emotional response that follows from negative reviewer comments and the bid not being funded. As a mentor, your experience of being in a similar situation, and how you dealt with it, means that you are ideally positioned to support your mentee in this, and can play a significant role in supporting them to deal with rejection in a philosophical and positive way.

Handling these conversations skilfully, and with empathy, can make the difference between, on the one hand, a junior researcher understanding that this is 'business as usual' in academia, learning from experience and going forwards to future success and, on the other hand, feeling so disappointed that they are reluctant to repeat the experience and give up. As a mentee, it can be hugely reassuring to hear from a more senior and successful academic that they too have experienced many disappointments, and you can plan together the best way to move forward. In Voice of Experience 8.2, Tom Crook, who has a great deal of experience in grant writing, reflects on how he tries to take a positive stance when faced with rejection.

Voice of Experience 8.2

Dealing with rejection and moving on

It can feel like a real kick in the teeth getting turned down for a grant application, not least because you will have worked incredibly hard on it, and for some time. But remember that it is not wasted work; far from it. For one thing, it might be that you receive useful feedback on the application, which can then help you to refine your ideas, or indeed prepare for another application. And, unsuccessful bids, or parts of them, can be 'recycled', perhaps to other external funding bodies, but also to in-house competitions hosted by your own university. Finally, writing grants involves confronting a series of very important questions, for example: What makes my work original? What are its 'unique selling points'? How might the public benefit from my work? So, do not get too down when you hear that your bid has been unsuccessful. Instead, think: right, where next?

Dr Tom Crook, Senior Lecturer in Modern British History

Our advice upon first receiving a rejection letter would be to read it through once and take in the essence of the reasons for your bid not being funded. Then put it away and let the disappointment sink in for a day or two before going back and considering the comments in more detail with the support of your mentor. As a mentor, your wider experience will be invaluable in helping your mentee to realise that 'failing', if that is how they view it, is no reason to be embarrassed, and that this is something that happens to virtually everyone who applies for funding. The mentoring process can be hugely powerful here because, as you worked together on the bid and, hopefully, involved others in commenting on the draft and providing feedback, the rejection is a shared one that you can both learn from. In Voice of Experience 8.3, Professor Rajat Gupta, who has enjoyed a great deal of grant success, but also inevitably some failures, exemplifies this point in the matter-of-fact way that he deals with rejection and moves forward.

Voice of Experience 8.3

Dealing with rejection and learning from the feedback

Over the last 15 years as a researcher, I have had a lot of grant success, but also rejections. It is important to be realistic and realise that most grant bids, even some of those rated as 'excellent' by reviewers, are sometimes not funded due to budgetary constraints. This can be very dispiriting because each bid takes a great deal of time and effort and emotional involvement. What I have learned is to carefully consider the feedback from reviewers, improve the bid if necessary, and then target other appropriate funding bodies.

Rajat Gupta, Professor of Sustainable Architecture and Climate Change

---

In Table 8.2, we list some common reasons for grant bids being rejected and how, in a mentoring discussion, you might plan together how to move forward. You might work together to have a thoughtful discussion about the specific reasons for your bid not being supported, and which points you can address in a revised application, perhaps to a different funder. Although both Tom Crook and Rajat Gupta recommend considering where to submit the revised bid, remember that it will also have to be adjusted in several ways to match the interests and requirements of the new funder.

Table 8.2 Some common reasons for grant applications being rejected and how to move forward

Reason for rejection	Moving forward – things to explore in mentoring discussions
Proposal does not fit with funder's strategic priorities or remit.	What can we learn from this? Should we have checked more carefully before applying? Would it be best to revise the research plan or to look for another, more appropriate funder?
Application was rated as 'excellent' but owing to limited funds, even the best-ranked bids were not all supported.	There is nothing that we can do about this, and it is positive that the funders rated the application so highly. What other funders can we send a (revised so that it fits their remit) version to? This was so nearly successful that it is only a matter of time before a bid is successful.

Reason for rejection	Moving forward – things to explore in mentoring discussions
What you plan to do is not sufficiently topical or exciting or cutting-edge or interesting or high priority.	Are they right? If so, can we go back to the literature and identify new directions in which to take the work? Can we look together at projects that the funder has supported to try to better understand what they consider to be exciting, topical and worth funding? On the other hand, are they mistaken? Have we not 'sold' the project well enough? Can we revise the bid to send to another funder, making sure that we really explain why it is something that they should be supporting?
Methods are inappropriate for the topic or mundane or out of date or beyond your capability to carry out.	Do they have a point? Can we go to the literature and uncover how others are addressing similar questions? What are the most cutting-edge methods? Do we have the expertise to carry them out here? Can we identify a new co-applicant who has a strong history of working with this methodology or is the methodology in the bid already appropriate? If so, how can we rewrite the bid so that it will convince the reviewers, perhaps with more reference to the literature, that this is the case?
Budget is unrealistic or does not represent good value for money.	Have we not given enough thought to the costings or have we proposed an approach which is unnecessarily extravagant? Can we revisit the project plan and research how much it is realistically going to cost? Can we consult the literature and similar, successful bids that have been funded? Can we think of ways to achieve the same aims in a different, more economical way? Have we undercut our costs so that the research might flounder?
The bid was in some way incomplete, biased, unsubstantiated, poorly argued or badly written.	Even though we might disagree, the reviewers thought it was and we need to take that seriously. How can we revise the application to address any specific criticisms that they make? How can we work more effectively together on drafts to make sure that all arguments are well expressed and substantiated? Can we identify additional sources of feedback to improve the writing in our next bid?

Throughout this chapter, we repeatedly make the point that all successful researchers and academics receive their fair share of grant disappointment. This will be true for both mentor and mentee. What is important for both is that you learn from the experience, do not become disheartened and positively plan within your mentoring partnership how to go forward.

Where to find mentoring help when you are successful

If you are new to grant bid writing, it may not occur to you that hearing that you have been successful can be anything but a cause for joy. However, it is a common experience that researchers feel some trepidation when they receive the news. As one of our colleagues put it, 'I thought "Oh, shoot, now I actually have to do it!"'. This unease comes from both a concern about being able to deliver on the promises that you made in the proposal, and from anxiety around the practicalities of managing a grant when you have never done that before. The issues are multiplied if you have secured funding to employ someone, such as a research assistant or technician, to work with you, because suddenly you become a line manager, which means you need to learn quickly about recruitment and selection procedures and how to manage staff.

Of course, it is in your institution's interest that those, like you, who have won grant funding are well supported. To that end, you will find that there is a wealth of mentoring support and practical help available. Examples include:

- Your Research Office (or equivalent), which will have staff whose job it is to guide you through the procedures for monitoring your progress on the grant, and will probably have handbooks or online resources.
- Your HR department if you need to recruit staff. Again, they will have staff and guidance materials to lead you through the necessary procedures.
- Workshops or seminars to outline procedures and practices run by your institution. (At the end of this chapter we provide some suggestions for researcher developers about useful workshop content.)

Finally, of course, having the mentorship of a more experienced academic who has had experience of running a project will be of huge benefit to you. If your original grant-writing mentor also acted as a co-applicant on the bid, then you will be working together to carry out the research that you proposed, and the mentoring relationship will continue quite naturally. If your mentor was a senior academic from outside your field who did not act as co-applicant, they may still be willing to provide mentoring support going forward. If this is not the case, we would recommend that you seek a new mentor – perhaps an experienced colleague within your department – even if it is for informal, occasional mentoring conversations as the project progresses.

Ways the institution can support researchers with grant-writing success: information for researcher developers

One way in which, as an institution, you can support inexperienced bid writers (most commonly ECRs or junior academic staff) is to match them with experienced and successful grant-winning mentors (typically mid-career or senior academic/research staff) as part of a formal institutional programme. This can be part of a broad mentoring programme where, as one of many options, mentees can request a grant-writing mentor, or it can be part of a programme specifically set up for this purpose. As an example, the University of Surrey runs a 'First Funding

Programme', which includes a tailored plan of support for those who are planning their first funding bid. As a part of this, mentees are matched with mentors who have experience of bidding to the funder that the mentee is applying to or have experience of bidding for a similar scheme (for example, an early career fellowship). If you are involved in researcher development and are interested in setting up a mentoring scheme such as this, detailed guidance is given in Appendix A.

In addition, there are many opportunities to support the process through overseeing, organising and running workshops and sharing good practice. These initiatives will inevitably contain a mentoring element or support researchers to work with their mentors to develop more effective proposals.

Some ideas for initiatives you might consider are given below:

- Running seminars, perhaps as part of an induction programme for those new to research, to encourage researchers to apply for funding and to introduce the range of support available. These seminars might include a presentation by someone influential, such as the Pro-Vice Chancellor for Research or similar, explaining why both research and researchers are valued by the institution. Other seminar content could include metrics about grant income, rankings in league tables, REF results, etc.
- Supporting departments or schools to run 'grants panels', where experienced, research-active academic staff review and give mentoring feedback on either initial project ideas or on draft applications, or both, prior to submission.
- Publicising a handbook or guide for grant application processes, either physically or as an online resource.
- Workshops supporting the grant application process, including institutional checks and processes, timelines and a review of the support available. This might include individuals who can support the mentor and mentee during the grant-writing process, such as grants officers, research managers, research office staff, impact officers, and so on.
- Directing grant-winners and their mentors to appropriate post-award support, both in terms of written guides and staff to support the processes.
- Workshops where successful grant-winners and those involved in the professional support of grant writing and administration can share their experience and provide mentoring help to those new to the game. This might include a question-and-answer panel featuring research/academic staff who have been (more or less) successful in winning grant funding in different subject disciplines, plus non-academic staff who have experience of supporting the process.

Chapter summary

We end this chapter where we began it, with the observation that for most successful researchers and academics, grant bid writing is a continuous and ongoing cycle. As soon as one application has been submitted, and sometimes before, they begin plotting out ideas and planning the next one. This is both necessary if, considering the odds against success, research funds are going to continue to come in, but also an effective insulation against critical reviewer comments and rejection. By the time the rejection letter is received, your thoughts and enthusiasm are already buzzing with your next great idea. In this chapter, we have focused on how, for the novice grant bid writer, having the help and support of a mentor who is experienced in grant bidding, and has had their fair share of success and disappointment, can markedly improve the chances of grant success and cushion the disappointment of rejection. However, for even the most experienced grant writer, ongoing engagement with critical feedback and the advice of co-applicants, colleagues and the professional staff whose job it is to support the process, as exemplified throughout this chapter, can make this career-long process more enjoyable, collaborative, rewarding and ultimately successful.

Further reading

Aldridge, J. and Derrington, A. (2012) *The Research Funding Toolkit: How to Plan and Write Successful Grant Applications.* London: SAGE.

Denicolo, P. and Becker, L. (2012) *Success in Research: Developing Research Proposals.* London: SAGE.

ESRC (Economic and Social Research Council) (n.d.) *How to Write a Good Research Grant Proposal.* https://esrc.ukri.org/funding/guidance-for-applicants/how-to-write-a-good-research-grant-proposal/

EURAXESS, https://euraxess.ec.europa.eu/

Hackshaw, A. (2011) *How to Write a Grant Application.* Chichester: Wiley Blackwell/BMJ Books.

Holloway, B.R. (2013) *Proposal Writing across the Disciplines.* Upper Saddle River, NJ: Prentice-Hall.

Research Professional, www.researchprofessional.com

Spencely, C., Acuña-Riviera, M. and Denicolo, P. (2020) *Success in Research: Navigating Research Funding with Confidence.* London: SAGE.

Vitae (n.d.) Where to Find Sources of Academic Research Funding. www.vitae.ac.uk/

9

Mentoring to support networking

In this chapter, we consider:

- The benefits of having a strong network
- Various opportunities for building an effective professional network
- How mentoring can help mentees overcome shyness and feeling uncomfortable about networking
- Mentoring to support effective networking at conferences and symposia, through learned societies and special interest groups, in the virtual world and nearer to home
- How mentors can support researchers to network strategically as a long-term project and to avoid the pitfalls of networking

Introduction

Effective networking is an essential skill for a researcher and can contribute considerably to your career success whether you choose to stay within academia or seek a career in another field. Networking is making, sustaining, and ultimately benefiting from formal and informal connections with others within and outside your immediate field. However, networking is a professional skill that does not come easily to many, and engaging mentoring support can be key to a researcher skilfully developing a successful professional network.

The importance of networking has long been realised in business and industry where employees are encouraged and trained to network, often considering it a crucial aspect of their job. This is because there are clear benefits in having a well-developed professional network which apply equally to researchers and academics at all career stages. For example, your network provides you with a framework for accessing, sharing and creating information and knowledge; it also increases your visibility and profile as well as those of others in your network. You can benefit materially and psychologically through the advice, mentoring and practical help that your network offers. The informal routes that you build through your network can also be extremely useful when searching for a new job, promotion or a new publication.

There are also benefits for the institution; researchers who are well supported and well connected with broad professional networks are likely to be more productive and to enjoy greater work satisfaction through the benefits of collaboration, enhanced external profile and professional esteem that their network can help them to foster. This, in turn, will have positive impacts on research publication rates and grant-winning success, contributing to enhanced metrics and profile for the institution.

Establishing a mentoring relationship to support effective networking

While most universities and research institutes support dedicated mentoring programmes, the most natural and effective mentoring for successful networking is likely to happen outside formal mentoring programmes and between individuals who already have a close professional relationship. The most obvious relationships here are between fledgling researchers, such as doctoral researchers or early career researchers (ECRs) and their supervisor or principal investigator (PI). However, not all academics are effective networkers, and not all effective networkers are good mentors; so if, as a junior researcher, you are seeking mentoring help outside a formal mentoring programme and your supervisor or PI does not seem to be appropriate for you, then it would be worth approaching another academic whose networking skills you aspire to emulate.

In common with other skills, the more you practise networking, the more proficient you become and the easier it gets. Similarly, each contact you make helps your network to grow exponentially. For this reason, if you are an experienced academic and are willing to share the strategies that you have developed for effective networking, you will be an extremely valuable mentor for someone with less experience. As a mentee, it is important to consider the qualities that you are looking for in your mentor. For example, you need to decide whether you will gain more from sharing the experience of a mentor who is a natural extrovert, or someone who is naturally introvert but has developed successful coping mechanisms in networking situations. Consider whether you will benefit from someone who has a similar character and background to you, so that they can empathise with your situation and outlook, or someone who possesses qualities that you lack, so that you can learn from their different perspective.

Mentoring to overcome social unease around networking

There is considerable diversity around the world in terms of cultural values, expectations and norms, which we focus on in Chapter 5, and which will impact on attitudes towards networking. In UK culture, for example, many people have an underlying feeling that there is something morally suspect about contacting someone for our own benefit, which is the essence of networking. A mentoring partnership can be an excellent space to reflect on any unease that the mentee may feel and to consider strategies to help alleviate that unease. For example, if, as a mentee, you are lacking networking experience and feel daunted by it, thinking about networking framed using different language may help you to feel more interested in, and more comfortable with, the prospect.

Reflection Point 9.1 provides you and your mentoring partner with the opportunity to consider how using different terminology for networking may help to alleviate any feelings of unease you might have.

Reflection Point 9.1

How do you feel about networking?

Describe to your mentoring partner how you feel about 'networking'. Now, describe to your mentoring partner how you feel about 'making new professional friends'.

Importantly, the different emphasis that this alternative terminology offers will also highlight for you that networking is reciprocal – a mutual provision of support, help and assistance in relation to career development or work-related issues. The most successful networks are made up of people who like and want to support each other. Viewed in this light, networking is no more dubious than going to a party and hoping that you might meet some new friends.

Working together to network strategically

As a mentor, when reflecting on the individuals who have had the greatest influence on your career, you will probably realise that many of them were originally chance contacts with whom you happened to form a positive relationship. While this will undoubtedly be true for your mentee too as they progress through their career, it is still good practice to think strategically about your professional network and work actively to build it into a form that will help you to achieve your goals.

In your mentoring discussions, it may be illuminating to both parties to consider the current shape of your respective networks, and how you can build them further strategically. For example, you can discuss why you want to develop an effective professional network, what benefits it may bring to you and what your goals are – for example, publishing, getting a job in academia or business, keeping up to date with your subject, promotion.

Having considered the value of having a strong network, as a mentoring pair it may be illuminating to do Activity 9.1 together, in which you carry out a 'gap analysis' on the state of each of your current professional networks and then draw up an action plan for strategically developing them further.

Activity 9.1

Strategically building your network – a gap analysis and action plan

Gap analysis

- Map out your current professional network – as a table, a list, a spider diagram, whatever makes the most sense to you.
- Where do most of your relationships lie? Which are the strongest/most influential relationships? Which people are personal friends as well as professional contacts? Which relationships are least helpful? Weakest? You could colour-code the different categories.
- Where are the gaps? Where do you need to develop new relationships or strengthen existing ones? Why? What will you achieve by doing so?

Action plan

- Identify barriers or problems you foresee in filling the gaps that you have identified. Consider how you might overcome these obstacles.
- Research your organisation. Find out who is who from organisational charts, newsletters, conversations with colleagues. List who you want to add to your network.

- Research outside your organisation. Find out who is influential in your field. Who might help you to achieve your goals? List who you want to add to your network.
- Consider how your existing contacts might facilitate further strategic introductions or act as formal or informal networking mentors themselves. Are there contacts in either of your networks that will be of benefit to your mentoring partner?
- Prioritise which people on your new 'wish list' of contacts you want to get to know first. Devise ways to engineer opportunities to meet each one.
- Plan for the next year to begin to strategically strengthen your professional network.

Once you have devised a plan, the next step is to put it into action. One of the most common questions asked of their mentors by junior researchers who have been told that they should 'network' is 'Yes, but how do I actually go about it?' In the following sections, we will consider the different opportunities for networking, consider practical ways of successfully and strategically building an effective professional network, and identify how mentors can support the networking efforts of their mentees.

How mentoring can support researchers to network effectively

Networking at conferences and symposia

Possibly the most productive environments for making new contacts and adding to a professional network are conferences and symposia. If you are a junior researcher, whatever your subject area, there will be numerous conferences to choose from, ranging from small-scale, one-day events, which are close to home and inexpensive to attend, to large, expensive, international congresses abroad. Attending as many of these events as possible is generally a good networking strategy. If you are an experienced academic, your mentoring advice on which events to attend and your support in helping your junior colleagues to secure funding – either internal funding from within the institution or from external agencies (considered in greater depth in Chapter 8) – to enable attendance can be invaluable.

To make the most of these opportunities, mentee and mentor can do some homework together beforehand. If you look at the delegate list as a mentee, you can identify people attending whom you will especially like to meet and plan how you will meet them. As a mentor, if you will be attending the conference with your mentee, you can make the introductions. Otherwise, as a mentee, send an email and introduce yourself, saying that you will be at the conference and that you hope you will have the opportunity to meet. If you have a specific reason for wishing to speak with a new contact – for example, to ask for advice or discuss a research idea – ask if it is possible to arrange to meet, perhaps during a specific refreshment break. Say why and you are likely to find that they will be flattered and agree. As a mentor, working through these ideas with your mentee will mean that you reflect on your own networking strategies and by doing so become a more effective networker yourself. If you are attending the conference with your mentee, you too are likely to make the most of the networking opportunities afforded by it. Top Tips 9.1 provides further practical information.

Top Tips 9.1

Making contacts at conferences

1. Coffee, lunch and drinks receptions are opportunities to talk to new people. Greet the person next to you in the queue, offer to fill their glass or coffee cup, ask how they are enjoying the conference.
2. Take your seat in the conference session a few minutes early, just as the room is filling up. Sit near the front where the more important and confident people choose to sit. Find a row that is partially full but still has some spaces and ask 'Is anyone sitting here? Can I join you?' Enquire what presentation they are especially interested in and say which one you are most looking forward to.
3. If you see anyone standing alone, or in a twosome, go over, smile, say hello, introduce yourself. You can have a question ready such as 'Is this your first time at this conference? I don't know many people, do you?', 'What did you think of the first keynote presentation?'
4. Make the most of opportunities to talk to important people – the key speaker in your field, for example – and think about what you are going to say. If you have enjoyed their talk, then say so, but follow it up with a well-thought out question.

Mentoring can be valuable in supporting a mentee to increase their professional visibility by giving an oral or poster presentation at a conference. Most conferences have calls for submitted abstracts, and many have oral or poster sessions specifically for doctoral students and ECRs. Here, as a mentor, you can encourage your mentee to apply, help them to craft an effective submission, and possibly act as co-author to give it authority if that is appropriate in your subject area.

If you are a junior researcher, remember that, while giving a conference talk can be a nerve-wracking experience, it does mean that you stand out; those in the audience see you, hear about your work, feel that they know you, and have a reason to come and talk to you afterwards. It is good for your CV, confidence and development too. Because spoken communication is such an important skill, mentoring for speaking skills is the subject of Chapter 10.

Generally, poster sessions are a less stressful alternative to oral presentations and are also an effective way to be seen and to make contacts. In fact, you may talk to more people at a poster session than when you give an oral presentation. If you are a supervisor or PI, your mentoring advice can be invaluable in advising your mentee how to prepare an eye-catching poster. Typically, poster sessions involve the presenter standing by their poster during a scheduled period, often coinciding with a dedicated networking session, and anyone passing by who is interested can stop and talk to you. If you are presenting a poster, make sure that you really do stand next to it, make eye contact with passers-by and be ready to engage them in a friendly chat about your work. Visit other poster displays and talk to the presenters.

Even without presenting work, there are many opportunities to make contacts and network at conferences. Dinners, refreshment breaks, pauses between sessions and trade exhibitions all provide fertile networking ground, as described in Voice of Experience 9.1 by Alistair McGregor, a highly effective professional networker.

Voice of Experience 9.1

Networking at conferences

I have always found conferences to be a great place to network and this has made a vital contribution to my research career. Speaking to other researchers in the coffee breaks, receptions, poster sessions and dinners has not only allowed me to learn more about their latest methods and breakthroughs – beyond the glossy versions presented in talks – but to also get valuable feedback on my own data, and to build new collaborations. In my experience, other researchers, no matter how senior, are always approachable and very willing to talk about their research with you and they will also take an interest in your research.

Alistair McGregor, Professor of Evolutionary Developmental Biology

If you are with colleagues at a conference, it is very tempting, especially if you are a junior researcher, to stay in your friendship group rather than move out of your comfort zone and talk to strangers, and thereby miss out on valuable networking opportunities. Here, as a mentoring pair, you can work together strategically. If you are a mentor, you can support your mentee by introducing yourself to key new contacts before bringing your mentee into the conversation. In this way, you will diversify your own network and raise your professional profile and standing. Even without mentoring help, we would advise junior researchers to be brave and talk to strangers. When you do so, two of the most important things to get right are, first, to remember your new acquaintance's name and, second, to make sure that you introduce yourself in a clear, succinct and memorable way. We consider below how, by working together as a mentoring partnership, you can hone these key skills.

The essentials (1) Remembering your new contact's name

One common pitfall when meeting new acquaintances in these situations is that in the flurry of the moment, you forget their name. Successful networkers use a variety of strategies to ensure that this does not happen. As a mentor, you will have your own tactics that you can share with your mentee, or you too may feel that you are poor at remembering people's names and need to improve. This might be a particularly timely conversation when you are both about to attend a conference or other promising networking opportunity together. In Top Tips 9.2 we offer our techniques for remembering names so that you can discuss them together and practise.

Top Tips 9.2

Remembering people's names

1. If you do not quite catch their name, immediately ask them to repeat it. It is better to do so now than to ask them to repeat it later.
2. If it is an unusual name or one that you have not heard before, do not be embarrassed to say so. Ask them to spell it. You can ask where it comes from or comment on how your own name is very pedestrian or how it too is unusual and people find it hard to remember.
3. Repeat the person's name back to them – 'Oh, hello, Robert, it is nice meet you'. At the end of the conversation, repeat it again, 'Great meeting you, Robert'.
4. Build a mental image that will help you to remember your new acquaintance's name. The more bizarre this is, the more likely you are to remember it. For example, if you have just met someone called Scott, picture him in a furious snow blizzard surrounded by penguins (think 'Scott of the Antarctic'!).

5. If you really have a poor memory for names, write them down – say 'I am going to make a note of that' – or ask for a business card. Think about getting business cards for yourself. Ask your mentor about the institutional processes and standard formats for doing so.

6. Jot down some notes about the person that you have just met so that you do not forget who they are. Carry a small notebook especially for this task.

The essentials (2) Honing your 'elevator pitch'

It is important that we learn to introduce ourselves effectively to new acquaintances in a professional context. Imagine that you get into an elevator with someone that you want to impress, and you have the time that it takes to travel between floors to make a positive impression to ensure that they remember you. What you say must be succinct, direct, easy to understand and memorable. Your **'elevator pitch'** is central to how you introduce yourself in any networking situation, and it is worth exploring this idea – and practising – in mentoring conversations. As a mentor, you can give your mentee your own 'elevator pitch' and help your mentee to practise theirs until they can introduce themselves effectively. Top Tips 9.3 offers our advice for introducing yourself, which you may find helpful as a basis for your discussions.

Top Tips 9.3

Introducing yourself – your 'elevator pitch'

1. Do not give your job title or the title of your project; instead, explain clearly and simply what you do, why it is important or why you enjoy it.
2. Avoid specialist terms; use everyday language.
3. Say something memorable so that you stick in the other's mind.
4. Get the other person's name, email address, business card and make sure that they have yours so that you can reconnect later.

As a mentee, if you are interested in really honing your communication skills to convey the excitement, interest and relevance of your research to a non-specialist audience and within a limited time frame, you might also engage in the 'three-minute thesis' competition, which we describe in Chapter 10.

The networking skills outlined above are, of course, relevant to networking opportunities other than conferences and symposia, and we consider some other productive networking environments in the next sections.

Mentoring to support networking closer to home

Even outside the fertile networking territory of the conference, mentors and mentees can work together to get the most out of opportunities closer to home. For example, most departments have a seminar programme or at least occasional invited speakers. There are also likely to be lectures, seminars, launches and workshops running across your institution and at neighbouring institutions, all of which are fertile networking grounds. As a mentor, you may receive information about local or institution-wide events that your mentee has not seen or has dismissed as not being relevant for them. You can encourage them to go along or invite them to accompany you. As a mentee, you can ask your mentor to let you know if they see any events that they think might be useful networking opportunities for you to attend – either alone or together.

Top Tips 9.4

Effective networking at in-house and local events

1. Go along, even if you are not interested in the subject, as you may learn something useful even if you do not expect to.
2. Ask a question after the talk. It takes a little courage to do this for the first time, but it gets easier with practice. Thank the presenter first, then ask your question or at least say how their talk links with your work or how it gave a different perspective on your work.
3. If there is a networking event afterwards, then do not miss it. If you have asked a question, the speaker and audience members have a reason to talk to you, and you have a good excuse to go and introduce yourself to the speaker and follow up on what you asked. As a mentor, introduce your mentee to the speaker and to other guests.
4. Get involved in organising seminars, postgraduate conferences and guest lectures. As a mentor, if you know the 'nuts and bolts' of how these events are organised and who takes responsibility for them, put your mentee's name forward to be involved. Suggest 'big names' for the event(s) and facilitate introductions. As a mentee, take the opportunity to put forward the names of people you want to meet, contact them to invite them to speak at the event and host them on the day.

Finally, it is important not to neglect the networking opportunities on your doorstep, and we would advise all researchers to make every effort to be sociable with colleagues. Having coffee or lunch with others in your department is effective networking, but as a junior researcher you may worry that this may be seen as time-wasting if you are away from your desk or laboratory. A mentor encouraging you to do this can be very reassuring. Also, try to keep in touch with colleagues from your department who have moved on to other jobs. They may be the influential players of the future and may potentially act as your champion or mentor in circumstances that you cannot possibly predict.

Mentors as leads into learned societies and other professional bodies

If you are a senior academic, you are likely to be a member of and active in one or more 'learned societies', professional bodies or special interest groups, and you will appreciate the networking (and other) benefits of membership. You can help your mentee to develop their network by suggesting which organisations may be most appropriate for them, advising them to join early in their career – ideally, as an undergraduate or doctoral researcher. New members may need someone to propose them, which you can do if you are already a member. You can be instrumental in bringing your mentee to the attention of influential members and getting them involved in the organisation's activities. As a mentee, be aware that the benefits of membership are multiple:

- It is a ready-made subject-specific network.
- They will often organise meetings, conferences, courses and user-groups that you can attend and meet people.
- Many provide travel bursaries for you to attend both their own events and often other unrelated conferences.
- They are usually keen to have members, especially young members, who will be active, involved and help them organise their activities.
- Being involved in organising a conference session, workshop or event is good for your CV generally, but is also an opportunity to make new contacts within the organisation, and with the speaker(s) and participants that are being invited.

Case Study 9.1 illustrates how, through the encouragement and facilitation of her mentor and PI, a junior researcher got involved in the activities of a learned society and benefited from the networking opportunities it afforded in several ways.

Case Study 9.1

A learned society as a fertile ground for networking

In mentoring discussions about how she could improve her professional network, Claire's supervisor suggested that she join a 'learned society' that he was a member of. The Society

(Continued)

organised meetings that they attended together, and they discussed beforehand how she could get the most out of these events. He introduced her to important people whom she wanted to meet, and they reviewed afterwards how things had gone. He mentored her as she prepared to give her first conference talk at one of these events. He was invited to run a workshop for the Society and in a mentoring meeting asked her to help him. As a result, Claire was invited to join one of their committees and got involved in organising more of their activities. Through her mentor supporting her involvement with the Society, she met many people in her field, several of whom turned out to be influential in her professional life, although she would not have predicted it at the time. When she applied for her first academic post, Claire knew someone at the university that she was applying to because she had met them through the Society, and they put in a good word for her. Recently, when she applied for academic promotion, she needed to nominate external reviewers, and Claire chose senior academics whom she knew through the Society.

Mentoring for effective networking in the virtual world

Increasingly, we inhabit a virtual as well as physical world, and our professional online presence is important. The mentoring advice of experienced academics on how to network appropriately in the virtual world can be very useful for those just starting out in their careers, principally because they did not grow up with a familiarity with computer technology, and so have deliberately learnt to build an effective online presence with a greater degree of caution and thoughtfulness than the '**digital native**' millennials with whom they work. This specific type of pairing will also lend itself to reverse mentoring, which is explored in Chapter 13. Here, the experienced academic can draw on the expertise of the millennial for mentoring support on how to use digital media with greater effect. In this way, the mentoring partnership reverses to allow the more junior partner to mentor the more senior one.

Posting blogs to promote research or to talk about ideas is now widespread within the academic community and is a good way to increase your visibility as a researcher. Finding a blogging mentor from the virtual world – someone whose posts you admire or which interest you – can help you to develop your own blogging skills. These platforms are also avenues for acquiring useful networking contacts and mentors in the virtual world, from whom you can ask for professional or career advice. If you are new to blogging and would like to get started, your first step will be to find out if your institution provides support. For example, several UK universities run versions of a '23 things for research' (based on the original programme launched in 2006 by the Public Library of Charlotte and Mecklenburg County, USA: http://plcmcl2-things.blogspot.com/), an online learning programme where participants set up and maintain a blog charting their learning. If your institution does not run this type of programme, you could consider joining AcWriMo, described in Chapter 7, an annual web-based motivational writing event where participants challenge themselves to meet a self-set writing target, such as starting a blog.

There are several professional online communities, such as 'LinkedIn', 'ResearchGate' and 'Mendeley', which senior academics will be familiar with, but which may be new to junior researchers. As a PI or supervisor, you will be aware which are most favoured in your discipline and can advise your mentee which they should engage with, and how best to build a professional profile. As a fledgling researcher, these platforms are valuable in providing a professional virtual space to promote yourself and your research, make contacts and keep abreast with developments in your field. Careers officers can provide one-to-one advice on building an online profile, and many HEIs run workshops for researchers and academic staff on the use of these platforms as part of their researcher development provision.

Many successful academics and researchers are enthusiastic and skilful users of 'Twitter' and are well placed to mentor on its use in building a virtual network. As a junior researcher, asking the advice of a 'Twitter'-savvy senior colleague can provide you with insight into how best to promote your professional profile, for example, by 'tweeting' about the exciting paper that you have just read, the excellent speaker that you have just heard, the big story in your field, the great conference that you are at, or what you are currently doing in your own research. In Voice of Experience 9.2, Anne Osterrieder describes how engaging with online platforms such as 'Twitter' and 'LinkedIn' have enhanced her professional network.

Voice of Experience 9.2

Effective networking in the virtual world

I received a bursary to attend a conference in a new field. I did not know anyone there, but the conference registration asked for our 'Twitter' handle and listed a conference hashtag. I used it to connect to other attendees beforehand and to stay in touch with my new contacts afterwards. Since then, I have used 'Twitter' to make new connections in my academic field. I usually meet several new people at any conference who are already my 'Twitter friends'. I separate my professional and private identity and keep 'Facebook' for friends and family. In recent years, 'LinkedIn' has become more like a 'professional Facebook'. I use it like an electronic business

(Continued)

card organiser, where I add everyone I meet professionally. Lots of people share relevant articles or job ads. Congratulating them on their achievements is an easy way to stay in touch with them. Connections whose interests only slightly overlap with your own day-to-day work can be very important for coming up with innovative ideas or spotting new opportunities. That's why I prefer open networks like 'Twitter' over closed networks like 'ResearchGate' – serendipity and exposing myself to things 'outside the box' that is my academic discipline have been important during my own career journey.

Dr Anne Osterrieder, Senior Lecturer in Biology and Science Communication

It is important to be aware that the ideal professional network includes contacts within and outside your immediate field. The reason for this is that while as many as two-thirds of doctoral students and ECRs aim for a career in research, most researchers ultimately move outside academia (discussed in detail in Chapter 6). The virtual world has the advantage of lacking physical boundaries, which makes this broader networking straightforward. Large companies often routinely 'tweet' about company developments and job opportunities and 'following' them or responding to their 'tweets' can lead you, if you are interested in moving out of academia, to make contacts with like-minded individuals and potential mentors. It will also increase your awareness of the company's ethos and may even get you noticed by their recruitment department.

Finally, as a junior researcher, your mentor can support you to build a professional web presence. Faculties, schools, departments and research groups often have their own web pages where researchers can post their profile. As a mentor, you can advise your mentee how to do so, and potentially facilitate the process. As a junior researcher, if you meet a new acquaintance in the real or virtual world, or contact someone about a job they are advertising, they will want to know more about you, and a simple search should lead them to your web profile. It is therefore important that it is up to date and truly reflects you and your work.

Avoiding the pitfalls of networking

Networking should be a positive experience which, at best, leads you to meet interesting people who may be helpful in your future career, some of whom will become genuine personal friends. At worst, you may spend time with people who ultimately are not helpful to you and with whom you have little in common.

However, as we all need to be aware of the potential pitfalls of networking, it is worth discussing this frankly in mentoring conversations because making mistakes can be career damaging. Top Tips 9.5 may be a useful focus for such a conversation.

Top Tips 9.5

Avoiding common pitfalls when networking

1. Go into any meeting with a new acquaintance with a positive and upbeat attitude. Avoid negativity, and do not gossip or criticise current or past colleagues or your institution.
2. Most people you meet will be genuine and honourable, but there are unscrupulous people too. Be cautious about talking too openly about any unpublished research results that you have, or those of colleagues. If in doubt, as a junior researcher, check with your mentor, PI or supervisor about what is acceptable to talk about and what is not.
3. When attending social networking occasions such as conference dinners or receptions, remember that you are still operating in a professional context and be on your best behaviour, especially if you drink alcohol.
4. Curate your online presence carefully. Keep your personal and professional accounts separate. Remember that whatever you post on either may be seen by colleagues or employers long after you have forgotten the post.

Considering networking as a long-term project

In your mentoring conversations, when you are reviewing a recent networking opportunity – for example, if you have just returned from a conference together – you may find that you have different views of what constituted successful networking. If you are new to professional networking, you may make the common mistake of assuming you have been successful because you have introduced yourself to a few potential contacts, and, if you have followed our advice, also remembered their names! If you are a more seasoned academic, you will realise that networking is not just about initial introductions; it is a long-term project that requires ongoing effort, which means that you need to consolidate those initial introductions. As a mentor, you may wish to share with your mentee your tips for sustaining an effective network. Some of ours are given in Top Tips 9.6.

Top Tips 9.6

Sustaining an effective network

1. Building trust, mutual liking and respect takes time and effort. Follow up on the initial introduction and consolidate the bond over time, building a deeper long-term relationship.
2. At a minimum, email or telephone a short while after the first meeting. If possible, engineer an opportunity to do so – for example, by offering to send your new contact an article on a topic of mutual interest or the contact details of someone you know who might be able to help them.
3. Keep up regular contact through social media, an occasional email or, better still, meeting face-to-face if you are going to be in the same town or attending the same conference.
4. Look for activities that you can do to be helpful, such as email your contacts about a paper or blog that they might find interesting.
5. Use the framework of the social and academic calendar as an excuse to say 'hello'. For example, if appropriate, send a cheery greeting for the holiday season or the end of the academic year.

Like other human relationships, those in both the mentor's and mentee's professional network will range from the polite, professional and distant to the close, supportive and genuinely affectionate; however, all will require maintenance and thoughtfulness, and can repay great dividends.

Information for researcher developers: Ways of supporting the development of effective networking skills in researchers

If you are involved in researcher development, you can incorporate practical activities into your training programmes and workshops that will support your researchers to network more effectively, or to work with their mentors to develop their networking skills. Some suggestions are:

*   The mentors in these types of mentoring relationship are most likely to be PIs (to ECR mentees) and supervisors (to doctoral student mentees). For this reason, you might include consideration of mentoring advice to support networking success, as outlined throughout this chapter, in institutional training programmes for these staff groups, and provide appropriate web resources, worksheets or toolkits to support mentoring for networking within these relationships.

- Organise cross-campus social events designed for doctoral researchers and ECRs to meet others, and where they, as mentees, can safely practise their networking skills with the support of their mentors. For example, you can organise coffee mornings where doctoral researchers and their supervisors, or ECRs and PIs, from across your institution can socialise.
- Fledgling researchers may benefit from the networking wisdom and experience of a range of more experienced academics. Organise a workshop where 'top tips' for networking – for example, at conferences – are discussed, and where senior staff who are successful networkers share their experience as mentors, perhaps in a question-and-answer 'expert panel' session.
- Earlier, we emphasised how important it is for researchers to develop an effective 'elevator pitch'. This can form the basis of a workshop where you organise researchers into lines facing each other, where each researcher stands opposite someone they have not met before and where they are given two minutes to introduce themselves before moving on. At each iteration, you can explore how effective, or otherwise, their introductions are. For example, how many participants remember the other researcher's name? How many can explain what they work on? Through this, they can explore effective strategies for networking. Previously, we suggested that mentors and mentees can practise this together, and you can support their practice by developing online resources that mentors can use with their mentees.
- Set up a 'speed networking' event where researchers have five minutes to introduce themselves to a new acquaintance before moving on to the next potential new contact, collecting business cards or email addresses as they go. Like the 'elevator pitch' workshop, this can work well when there is a mixture of mentors and mentees. You should ensure that there is opportunity for them to discuss afterwards how they felt it went and what they learned.
- Organise a workshop where participants are paired with someone whom they have not previously met. Based on their partner's name only, ask participants to explore what their online presence tells the world about them. You can then explore ways in which participants can improve their virtual profile.

Chapter summary

In this chapter, we demonstrate that developing a broad and effective network of contacts is an essential requirement for professional success. It is common among researchers to feel shy, to a greater or lesser extent, about introducing themselves to strangers and many, especially early in their career, feel uneasy and uncomfortable about the idea of meeting new people with the specific aim of benefiting from knowing them. We have addressed these reservations, and given concrete advice to mentees, mentors and researcher developers about good practice and effective strategies for making new contacts, networking strategically and maintaining a diverse and effective professional network. We have specifically considered networking in conferences and symposia, networking closer to home, the benefit of networking through learned societies and special interest groups, and in the virtual world. Having a strong professional network benefits you as a researcher in a variety of ways; it is a source of collaborations, professional support and advice, a means of raising and broadening your profile and a source of, in the best cases, genuine and ongoing personal friendships that go beyond the workplace.

Further reading

Ansmann, L., Flickinger, T.E., Barello, S., Kunneman, M., Mantwill, S., Quilligan, S., Zanini, C. and Aelbrecht, K. (2014) Career development for early career academics: benefits of networking and the role of professional societies. *Patient Education and Counseling*, 97: 132–134.

Blackford, S. (2018) Minireview – Professional Development: Harnessing the power of communities: career networking strategies for bioscience PhD students and postdoctoral researchers. *FEMS Microbiology Letters*, 365. doi: 10.1093/femsle/fny033.

Forret, M.L. and Dougherty, T.W. (2004) Networking behaviors and career outcomes: differences for men and women? *Journal of Organizational Behavior*, 25(3): 419–437.

Kiefer, Julie C. (2011) Tips for success: networking is not a bad word. *Developmental Dynamics*, 240: 2597–2599.

Public Library of Charlotte and Mecklenburg County, USA (n.d.) Learning 2.0. http://plcmcl2-things.blogspot.com/

Still, L.V. and Guerin, C. (1987) Networking practices of men and women managers compared. *Women in Management Review*, 2(2): 103–109.

Streeter, J. (2104) Networking in academia. *EMBO Reports*, 15(11): 1109–1112.

10

Mentoring to support development of spoken communication skills

In this chapter, we consider:

- The value of mentoring to support effective everyday spoken communication
- The importance of speaking clearly about your research to diverse audiences and the ways that mentoring partnerships can support this
- The role that a mentoring partnership can play in supporting researchers to communicate effectively in public engagement activities
- Mentoring activities and advice for institutions on supporting the development of spoken communication skills

Introduction

The world of academia is increasingly about effective spoken communication and plain speaking. Funding bodies are becoming ever more focused on supporting collaborative research with genuine impact. Consequently, researchers must speak clearly about their research ideas to a wide range of potential collaborative partners, not just within their own institution, but with other institutions, industry, commerce, charitable and non-profit organisations or social enterprises at home and abroad. To do this effectively, researchers need to develop different **storylines** for their project, depending on their audience. By storyline we mean the way a researcher makes sense of their project for their audience; others call it the thread that runs through a project and brings coherence to all the facets of the project being presented. This is an essential skill at every stage of an academic career, from the doctoral researcher who needs to make clear the story of their doctoral project, to the academic seeking to convince potential collaborative partners to join them on an exciting research project.

Effective spoken communication is not only about seeking funding; it is also about having the ability to converse with colleagues, students and other employees who share your workspace on a day-to-day basis. If you have managerial, PI and/or supervisory responsibilities as part of your academic role, then you need the skills necessary to motivate, direct and, on occasion, discipline your juniors without causing offence. This becomes particularly important with today's emphasis on equality and respect for diversity in the workplace and the international nature of HEIs. Never has it been so important to be aware of what we say, how we say it and to whom we say it.

With so many aspects of effective spoken communication to consider, mentoring partnerships can provide valuable bespoke support to researchers at all career stages. As with all the types of mentoring we consider in this book, these partnerships offer benefits to both mentee and mentor, as summarised in Table 10.1.

Table 10.1 Benefits of mentoring to support spoken communication skills to mentee and mentor

Opportunities for mentoring spoken communication	Benefit to mentee	Benefit to mentor
Improving everyday spoken communication For example, (1) avoiding causing offence to others; (2) speaking clearly and effectively in lectures, seminars and classes; and (3) speaking skills for those in management and leadership positions.	• A mentoring partnership is a safe space to share any issues relating to the workplace that may be particularly personal and sensitive for you. • If you are working in a language that is not your first, a mentor can help you deepen your understanding of the subtleties of the language, which will enhance the clarity of your teaching, lecturing and general daily communication in the workplace. • If you are considering promotion to a managerial/ leadership position, a mentor with experience at that level will help you to identify any communication skills training you might need for the new position.	• Supporting everyday communication helps you to reflect on your own style of interacting, teaching and lecturing as your mentee may view you as a role model. • Mentoring an international researcher is likely to increase your sensitivity to the diversity of communication styles around the world (discussed further in Chapter 5) and possibly enhance your own communication with international colleagues. • Working with a mentee may establish links to their researcher network and, consequently, increase your own network (discussed in more depth in Chapter 9).

Opportunities for mentoring spoken communication	Benefit to mentee	Benefit to mentor
Making storylines clear to the audience For example, (1) giving clear and interesting presentations; (2) presenting a doctoral thesis concisely, coherently and clearly; (3) delivering concise and persuasive pitches to potential research project collaborators and funding bodies; and (4) presenting your work profile in interviews.	• You may have opportunities to co-present with your mentor (for example, at a conference), providing you with a role model to learn presenting strategies from. • Working with a mentor to determine the key elements of your thesis storyline will help you to deliver a confident and competent summary of your project in your viva. • You can learn effective pitching strategies from your mentor, which will increase your chances of winning funding or persuading others to collaborate with or employ you.	• Offering your mentee opportunities to co-present with you may create other collaborative opportunities with them. • Helping your mentee to reflect on ambiguities in their storyline can be useful in helping you to spot ambiguities in your own storylines. • Supporting your mentee in their pitching for funding may create funding opportunities for you.
Speaking skills to increase research visibility For example, (1) dealing with confidence issues when speaking publicly; and (2) speaking about research to excite and inform the public.	• You will be better equipped with useful strategies for positioning yourself to make the most of public engagement opportunities when they arise.	• Advising a junior colleague on public engagement, including media activities may lead to further public engagement opportunities for you.

We continue the chapter by considering how mentoring partnerships can help to support everyday communication skills at each stage of an academic career, which is so vital in our current academic environment of internationalisation, diversity and inclusivism. We then switch focus to the ways that mentoring can support storytelling, as mentioned earlier, which is also a crucial skill at any stage of an academic career. Finally, we consider how mentoring can support research visibility, particularly for those in the early stages of an academic career.

Mentoring to support everyday spoken communication

Spoken communication, particularly in everyday interaction, is necessary in today's academic world because, perhaps more than ever before, we need to be finely-tuned to a whole host of potential sensitivities in the workplace. Initiatives such as the Athena SWAN Charter, overseen by Advance HE (www.ecu.ac.uk), have done, and continue to do, excellent work in raising our awareness of equality issues within higher education relating to gender, ethnicity, age and intersectionality. Institutions require their HEI professionals to complete modules on Equality and Diversity, Bullying and Harassment, among others, to ensure that the workplace is rightly harmonious, fair and inclusive for all. Excellent initiatives such as these make clear to us all that to avoid offending people we perceive as being different from us in some way, it is imperative that we think before we speak.

With this increasing emphasis on inclusivism, equality and internationalisation, a mentoring relationship can help you to reflect on your own communication style, whether you are a mentee or a mentor, and provides considerable scope for mutual learning. For example, if you have a senior role in your institution, you may wish to provide communication skills mentoring support to more junior colleagues aspiring to leadership positions. If your mentee is from a group that is under-represented at senior management levels, not only will you be able to guide them, but in the process you may gain deeper insight into the issues that members of that group face. This will provide you with a real opportunity to reflect on your own assumptions about that group and may enhance your own relationships with other members of similar groups.

Speaking skills mentoring for international staff

From the perspective of internationalisation, mentoring relationships can be hugely valuable in developing the communication skills of international HEI professionals working in a non-native language. For example, if you are working in an English-speaking academic context and English is not your first language, you may feel at times that your speaking skills need improvement. In our experience, non-native English speakers tend to feel that if they are having difficulties communicating clearly and effectively to students and colleagues, it is due to poor grammar or vocabulary. However, lack of clarity in spoken communication is frequently the result of a strong non-native accent, or sentence rhythm and stress pattern issues. Finding a mentor with the skills necessary to help you to develop these aspects of speaking skills can be invaluable, as illustrated in Voice of Experience 10.1.

Voice of Experience 10.1

My mentor helped me to teach more effectively

When I first arrived from Bahrain at my current institution in the US, I felt very confident in my spoken communication skills as I had been used to teaching in English in my university back home. I had a high level of proficiency in spoken English, and even had experience of teaching English to Bahrainian secondary school children. But then came an enormous shock. In my appraisal, I learned that some of my students had complained that they couldn't understand me in lectures. Initially, I thought that my grammar was wrong and that I was perhaps using inappropriate vocabulary, but I didn't really know precisely what the problem was to put it right. I was incredibly stressed about it.

A colleague, who had had a similar problem, suggested that I contact the English language support unit at my institution, and that was where I met my mentor. She was very insightful and helped me to recognise that the problem was not my grammar or my vocabulary, but the speed at which I was speaking (too fast apparently) and the way I was not emphasising the words I needed to emphasise in sentences to get my message across clearly. I worked with her for several weeks, and I am delighted to say that, although I have a long way to go yet, I feel that I am much better able to get my message across in lectures. Hopefully, there'll be no more complaints!

Bahrainian lecturer, based in the USA

As illustrated in Voice of Experience 10.1, inadequate spoken communication skills can have a negative impact on your teaching and lecturing. We certainly do not wish to suggest here that this problem is exclusive to international colleagues; poor communication in teaching can be very much an issue for those working in their native language too, and there can be many reasons for this, such as personality, strong regional accents or perhaps more formally diagnosed conditions that lead to poor social skills, such as (but not exclusively) conditions on the autistic spectrum. However, we focus here on international researchers to acknowledge the current emphasis in academia on developing international research communities.

Suitable mentors to help with daily communication skills, including issues of communicating effectively in teaching and lecturing, will tend to be language specialists, often based in your institution's language support unit, with expertise in analysing sentence structure, and stress and intonation patterns as well as experience in identifying pronunciation issues, and so on. If you are such a professional and are approached by someone to mentor them, they will possibly come to you requesting help with what they perceive to be their language problem; however, in your initial meeting with them, you may discover that the problem is not actually what they perceive it to be. Therefore, an important aspect of that initial meeting will be to take time to find out why the mentee has approached you, what they think their issues are and how they have discovered those issues. By probing in this way, you learn about your mentee's expectations; you will also have the opportunity to listen to the way they speak to gain insight into what you feel their issues are.

This does mean, of course, that if you are the mentee, you should come to the initial meeting prepared to talk openly with your mentor about an extremely personal issue which may be causing you considerable stress if the way you speak is actually impacting negatively on your work, as was the case in Voice of Experience 10.1.

Another source of mentoring support that is particularly useful in the lecturing environment is a School of Acting or Theatrical Department, if your institution has one. One of the great strengths of mentoring support from here is that the mentor may be able to provide guidance on non-verbal cues, such as body language, eye contact and facial expression. In contrast to written communication, effective spoken communication in a classroom environment relies on far more than words; the non-verbal cues that accompany those words go a considerable way to conveying meaning. If you are a mentor from an Acting or Theatrical Department, you will probably have expertise in how to use these non-verbal cues to support, rather than contradict or confuse, the words that are spoken. As a mentee, you will also be able to draw on their expertise in holding an audience, which is such a vital aspect of effective lecturing.

Because of the potentially considerable sensitivity around spoken communication issues, confidentiality between both parties is crucial to ensure that mentoring conversations take place in a safe space. Indeed, as we point out throughout this book, creating a safe conversation space is what makes a mentoring partnership such a valuable support. Clear boundaries are part of creating that safe space, and so, as with any formal mentoring partnership, it is wise to draw up an agreement between both parties, a general template for which we provide in Appendix B.

Mentoring to support everyday communication for managers and leaders in HEIs

Another extremely important aspect of spoken communication skills that mentoring partnerships can effectively support relates to management and leadership. Here, the need for mentoring is likely to relate to a career transition, for example from a researcher to a PI or research group leader role, from non-managerial to a managerial position or from a mid-managerial to a senior management/director role. As a manager or leader, you need to be able to direct, motivate, appraise, inspire and, when necessary, discipline staff. At the same time, you must maintain harmonious day-to-day relations with those whom you line manage and others, such as potential stakeholders in a research project, collaborative partners, administrators, other faculty and department heads and academic peers both within and outside your institution. A crucial element to doing all these aspects of your work effectively is highly polished and versatile spoken communication.

Institutions often provide leadership programmes with a mentoring component to them as part of their professional development provision. For example, the University of British Columbia runs a mentoring programme that matches senior faculty members with those in mid-career to support the mentee at key points of transition, such as career promotion or taking on more responsibilities. More information about their programme can be found at: https://academic.ubc.ca/support-resources/professional-development/mentoring. Another programme, again with a mentoring component, which focuses on supporting women academics, is Aurora (for more information, see: www.lfhe.ac.uk/en/programmes-events/equality-and-diversity/aurora/about-aurora/index.cfm).

While formal mentoring programmes are invaluable, they are not the only way to have a productive mentoring partnership. If you are at a career transition and you feel that you would benefit from a senior mentor who could help you develop the spoken communication skills necessary in more senior leadership and managerial positions, you could approach a senior colleague to be your mentor, for example, someone who is an effective, inspiring speaker, or who has a reputation as a good manager. If you are approached as a potential mentor, be clear about what your mentee is looking for, so that you can decide if you have the necessary skills and experience to help them. While formal mentoring programmes normally have mechanisms in place to ensure a good match between mentor and mentee, you will not have such a mechanism if, as a mentee, you have taken the initiative to find a suitable mentor. Activity 10.1 will help you as a mentee to clarify what your specific needs are, and for you as a mentor to ensure that you are the best person to mentor your potential mentee, to ensure that the partnership is productive and successful.

Activity 10.1

Ensuring a good mentor–mentee match to support managers and leaders

Complete the table below. Use the completed table as a focus for discussion in your initial mentoring meeting to establish whether you feel that a mentoring partnership between the two of you will be able to satisfy the mentee's need(s).

(Continued)

For the mentee

Use the list of common areas of communication skills in the table below to reflect on your reasons for seeking a mentor. Rank each skill in the left-hand column using the Likert scale 0–3 (0 = no need at all; 1 = low level of need; 2 = moderate level of need; 3 = high level of need). Use the far right-hand column to make any notes you feel are relevant. For example, you may have considerable experience of chairing meetings at departmental level but need support at faculty level and so wish to make that point clear.

For the mentor

Use the list of common areas of communication skills in the table below to reflect on your level of expertise/experience in each element. Rank each skill in the left-hand column using the Likert scale 0–3 (0 = no expertise/experience at all; 1 = low level of expertise/experience; 2 = moderate level of expertise/experience; 3 = high level of expertise/experience). Use the far right-hand column to make any notes you feel are relevant. For example, you may have considerable experience of chairing meetings at faculty and departmental level but not as much experience at Executive Board level and so wish to make that point clear.

Spoken communication skill	(For mentee) Level of need for support with this skill	(For mentor) Level of expertise/experience in this area	Miscellaneous notes
Job interviewing (e.g. as part of an interview panel)			
All-staff presentations (e.g. departmental, faculty, all-institution level)			
Adjudication panels (e.g. staff disciplinary panel)			
Research project directing			
External presentations (e.g. to secure external funding or for media engagement)			
Chairing meetings (e.g. research group, departmental, faculty, Executive Board levels)			
Appraisal interviews and work reviews			
Conducting negotiations (e.g. negotiating contracts between HEI and commercial partners)			
Other			

Mentoring for effective storytelling

In any context where you are presenting your research, be it at a conference, in a job interview, when pitching for funding or presenting your thesis in your viva, you need a clear storyline. As mentioned earlier, by storyline we mean the way you make sense of your project for your audience. The clearer the story, the more easily your audience will grasp what it is you are working on, what its value is and how others might benefit from what you are doing.

Importantly, storylines change according to the audience and according to what you hope to gain from telling the story. For example, if you are a doctoral researcher, in your viva the story you tell must satisfy your audience – the examiners – that you have conducted quality research that is novel, robust, rigorous and able to withstand critique. Your story may change, though, if you are talking about your project to a group of school children as part of a schools outreach programme (discussed in greater depth in Chapter 11). Similarly, if you are a more experienced academic hoping to attract an industrial partner for a collaborative project, your story must appeal to that potential partner.

The reflective nature of mentoring partnerships makes them ideal spaces for helping tease out an appropriate storyline that will appeal to the target audience. This means that it is important that if you are a mentor, you have experience of the target audience, and that if you are a mentee, you are very clear as to whom you are targeting your story. For example, in the case of a pitch to a potential industrial or commercial partner, you may wish to find someone from the industry to act as your mentor, which we discussed in Chapter 6. If you are a doctoral researcher preparing for your viva, then you may find your supervisor is best positioned to be your mentor, which we consider in Chapter 11. However, for schools outreach, your supervisor may not necessarily make the best mentor; often, a peer who has already got experience may be better.

When looking for a mentor to give you support for the storyline of your conference presentation, bear in mind that the best mentor does not necessarily have to be from your own discipline. In fact, if your conference is non-specialist, a mentor from a different discipline may be in a better position to guide you with respect to clarity of storyline. What you do need, though, is a mentor with considerable experience in presenting at conferences. Researcher Development Programmes are useful ports of call for support for conference presentations as they may be able to link you up with a colleague whom they know to have a successful conference track record. They also often provide oral presentation skills training that includes a mentoring element, where you can deliver your presentation and they will give you feedback on what worked well and what did not work so well.

In terms of thesis storylines, again, your institution's researcher development team is perhaps the most obvious source of support, since they often provide mentoring to support viva presentation skills. Some also offer mentoring support for doctoral researchers wishing to take part in a 'three-minute thesis' (3MT) competition, an annual event that many HEIs now participate in, which was started at the University of Queensland, Australia, in 2008. In the event, doctoral researchers have precisely three minutes to talk about their research in a way that is meaningful and interesting to an audience of intelligent individuals with no specialist understanding of the researcher's field. Each presentation is assessed by a panel of judges and by the audience on the basis of clarity of presentation and the degree of engagement the audience and panel feel with the project. Vitae run this event annually, under the sponsorship of the Taylor and Francis Group, and more information about their event can be found at www.vitae.ac.uk/events/three-minute-thesis-competition. This event, and the mentoring support that many institutions offer in the lead-up to the event, is a wonderful opportunity to develop your thesis storyline and your confidence in being able to speak concisely and clearly about your project to non-specialists.

Being clear and concise in storylines

Within your mentoring partnership, conversations around storyline should address topics such as conciseness, clarity and impact. Speaking about your research project in a long-winded way will not hold your audience's attention, while not underlining the 'so-what?' element of your project – the importance or impact – will lead to a less than convincing presentation. So, if your mentoring partnership is aimed at supporting the mentee to develop a clear storyline for a conference presentation, then your conversations are likely to focus on gauging the needs and expectations of the conference audience, and on sharing ideas as to the best way to present the project to maximise the impact for that audience.

The same need for conciseness, clarity and impact applies to other contexts, such as pitching to potential industrial/commercial partners and funding bodies. Having a mentoring partnership that includes an industry-based mentor can help the mentee to speak the language of industry, which frequently differs quite substantially from that of academia. For example, as a mentee, if you are from an engineering or science background, you may feel that going into detail about the merits of the method you are using in your project will excite your potential industry collaborator. For some projects this may be the case, but for others, highlighting the impact and value of the project for the audience and highlighting its commercial potential will be more meaningful. Within your mentoring partnership, you may, therefore, discuss how this potential can be made clear for the audience, for example, what to cut out and what to accentuate, what terms to avoid and how upbeat to sound.

You may find Reflection Point 10.1 a helpful focus for a mentoring conversation aimed at clarifying audience needs and expectations, and for identifying an impact that will be meaningful to that audience.

Reflection Point 10.1

Clarifying a storyline – gauging the needs and expectations of your audience

- Who will you be presenting/pitching to?
- What is the purpose of your presentation/pitch?
- What does your audience hope to learn from your presentation/pitch?
- What do you hope to achieve from your presentation/pitch?
- Are the members of your audience specialists in your field?
- If they are not specialists in your field, what will they need to know about your project in terms of:

  o Background
  o Problem/opportunity that your project is addressing
  o Details of your project
  o Value to them of what you are doing
  o Costs/risks to them in the project.

- What technical terms can you replace with commonly used terms or phrases?
- If you must use technical terms, how will you explain them?
- In view of your audience, what can you say about your project that will excite them?

Spoken communication mentoring to increase research visibility for early-stage researchers

Mentoring partnerships can be enormously valuable ways of passing on strategies, advice, contacts and ideas for maximising the visibility of your research, which you need to start as early as the doctoral researcher stage and to continue with ever-increasing intensity at all later stages of an academic career. In the early stages of a research career, your focus is likely to be on building your confidence in speaking to diverse audiences about your research. Confidence is an extremely important aspect at this stage because it provides the foundation that you can draw on later when visibility relates to convincing an audience of the authority and contribution of your work to society as well as to academia.

As a mentee, you are likely to be looking for opportunities to speak to diverse audiences, and there are various initiatives that you can use as the focal point in your mentoring conversations in this respect. Top Tips 10.1 will help both parties to explore the opportunities that are open to early-stage researchers at your institution.

Top Tips 10.1

Identifying opportunities to increase visibility for early-stage researchers

1. As a mentee, clarify precisely why you are looking for opportunities to increase the visibility of your research. For example, are you looking for opportunities to build your confidence in communicating with diverse audiences? If not, is your purpose to tell others about the value and contribution of your project? Knowing precisely why you are seeking these opportunities will help your mentor to support you in the best way.

2. As a mentor, do not feel that you must have answers or solutions to your mentee's questions. Your role as a mentor is very often simply to act as a signpost for them. So, once you know precisely what your mentee wants with respect to increasing their visibility and impact, you may simply wish to point out initiatives offered at your institution that will be of value. These may include conference presentations and the networking opportunities that conferences offer (discussed more in Chapter 9), school outreach activities (discussed further in Chapter 11), or media opportunities (discussed next) if your mentee is lucky enough to find their research subject in the media spotlight.

Mentoring to support public engagement through the media

Emphasis on research visibility has spawned a new generation of HEI professionals who engage with the media far more than in previous years. This engagement may be a one-off interview with a local radio station if a topic in your research area hits the news. At the other end of the scale are those academics who are now reaching celebrity status by hosting their own documentary series. This means that today's researcher needs to be multi-skilled as a speaker: to be able to speak articulately to a specialist academic audience but also to speak in a direct, engaging way to non-specialists and non-academics.

To engage well with the public, you need to be confident and good at gauging the needs of that public so that you can construct the story that you tell clearly, concisely and meaningfully to them. Another important ingredient, particularly if you are engaging through media, is excitement, as illustrated by Voice of Experience 10.2, a senior academic who regularly speaks about current science stories on local radio.

Voice of Experience 10.2

Reflections on public engagement

One vitally important skill that every researcher must possess is the ability to explain concisely, and in a way that conveys excitement, when asked, 'So, what is it that you do?' Practise this. Communicate why you do research in a way that doesn't make it sound confusing or, worse, geeky. Leave people thinking, 'Wow, what a worthwhile thing this person does'. I have been lucky to present a weekly science chat on British Broadcasting Corporation (BBC) radio for almost 10 years. It gets easier with experience to talk about research to the public, but it is not a trivial task to render your passion into a clear message. Avoid acronyms that your professional clique bandy about in work conversation and don't be overly concerned if you feel that some nuance of your work hasn't been explained. People will come to respect you and your views if they regularly feel that they understand your message. Above all else, talking about research should be fun, not stressful. Keep at it, the fun comes with experience.

Professor John Runions, Department of Cell and Molecular Biology, Oxford Brookes University

---

Not everyone in academia can have, or indeed would like, a documentary series to their name or a regular spot on the radio. However, there are other media opportunities that a mentoring relationship can really help with. For example, a topic closely related to your research might be picked up by the media and, consequently, you could be asked to give a radio or television interview. If this happens, you are likely to need some useful interview strategies. If you are a mentor with substantial experience of media interview work, your advice will be invaluable if your mentee is about to do their first media interview. You might offer your advice on how they can keep their nerves under control, for example, by doing a short deep breathing exercise for nine breaths immediately before the interview. You might also have strategies for avoiding hesitation devices (such as 'erms' and 'ahs') when responding to questions.

If you are invited to give a radio or TV interview, it is wise to inform the department responsible for public relations in your institution before you do the interview, as they will normally advise on what storyline to present and what not to say during the interview. This department can therefore provide another source of mentoring support.

To make the most of media opportunities, perhaps the best advice that a mentor can give is to be alert to opportunities. For example, you can suggest that your mentee makes a habit of following the news daily so that they can act quickly if a news item related to their field hits the headlines. You may also be able to guide your mentee in techniques for making their research sound newsworthy. For example, you can both have conversations about strategies for making a research project sound exciting and interesting to the public. Activity 10.2 may provide a useful focus for that conversation.

Activity 10.2

What is exciting about your research?

Reflect on the following questions about your research and make notes for future reference in case you want to engage with the public or the media.

1. What is the most exciting aspect of your research?
2. Why does the public need to know about it?
3. How can you tell the public about that exciting aspect without using technical jargon?
4. If you could sum up your project and why it is exciting in one short sentence, what would that sentence be?

Advice for institutions

We hope we have made clear in this chapter that spoken communication skills development is enormously diverse. For this reason, any mentoring programme to support this development needs to ensure that the pool of potential mentors is sufficiently broad to cover the various types of communication skill support needed. It is probably sensible to categorise your mentors into the following key areas of experience:

1. Conference/symposia presenting and/or presenting as guest speaker
2. Pitching for funding bodies

3. Line management/project directing/principal investigator
4. Senior management/leadership
5. Public engagement

It is also wise, at the application stage, to gather as much information as possible from the potential mentor about what specifically they feel are their spoken communication strengths, or what they have substantial experience in. Perhaps the best way to do this is to send each applicant a summary sheet for completion detailing their speaking experience for each of the five categories listed. Example 10.1 provides a possible framework for the summary sheet.

Example 10.1

Summary sheet for mentors wishing to offer spoken communication skills support

Name of applicant:

Current School/Department:

Research discipline:

Current position:

Please summarise your experience in each of the following areas and indicate whether you feel comfortable to provide mentoring support in that area.

1. Conference/symposia presenting and/or presenting as guest speaker
   Summary of experience:

   _____
   _____
   _____
   _____

   I would feel/would not feel* comfortable providing mentoring support in this area.

2. Pitching for funding bodies
   Summary of experience:

   _____
   _____
   _____
   _____

   I would feel/would not feel* comfortable providing mentoring support in this area.

(Continued)

3. Line management/project directing/Principal Investigator
    Summary of experience:

    _____

    _____

    _____

    _____

    I would feel/would not feel* comfortable providing mentoring support in this area.

4. Senior management/leadership
    Summary of experience:

    _____

    _____

    _____

    _____

    I would feel/would not feel* comfortable providing mentoring support in this area.

5. Public engagement
    Summary of experience:

    _____

    _____

    _____

    _____

    I would feel/would not feel* comfortable providing mentoring support in this area.

    (* Delete as appropriate)

In addition to, or as an alternative to, running a formal mentoring programme, you might wish to incorporate signposting into your current workshops and programmes to help those looking for communication skills support to find appropriate help. Table 10.2 lists the common types of support needed to develop spoken communication skills and possible sources of help. You can use this table as a template, adapting it where necessary for your institution, to signpost the available support for speaking skills available to researchers and staff.

Table 10.2 Sources of mentoring help to develop speaking skills

Type of help needed	Possible sources of mentoring help
Informal speaking skills for non-native speakers	• English language support unit • School of International Studies • Senior academics with extensive experience of international collaborations

Type of help needed	Possible sources of mentoring help
Communicating your research to non-specialists, including getting a clear storyline	• Staff Development/Researcher Development Programme • Public Outreach/ Public Engagement Department • English language support unit • Senior academic/Research Group lead with extensive experience of public engagement • Careers Departments with links to industry mentors • Mentors outside academia
Conference presentations and viva preparation	• Researcher Development team • Colleague (not necessarily from your own department) with substantial conference presenting experience • Doctoral supervisor
Establishing rapport with an audience and non-verbal communication	• Staff Development • Acting and Theatrical Studies Department • Department of Higher Education/Teacher Training Department • Teaching fellow, lecturer or tutor with extensive teaching experience • Public Outreach/Public Engagement Department/Public Relations Office
TV or radio interviews	• Public Outreach/Public Engagement Department/Public Relations Office • Senior staff member with strong public profile

Chapter summary

In this chapter, we have acknowledged that current emphasis on internationalisation, equality and respect for diversity in the workplace highlights the importance of becoming conscious of what we say and how it may be conceived by others to ensure that the academic work environment is one that is inclusive, diverse and respectful. We have also highlighted that irrespective of career stage, mentoring that supports spoken communication skills is a valuable way of helping researchers to communicate effectively with a variety of audiences, ranging from academic specialists to the general public. By supporting academics to develop their ability to communicate effectively, mentoring plays its role in developing researchers who are not only capable of producing quality research, but are also able to inspire the next generation of academics through schools outreach programmes and are adept at keeping the public informed through media interviews. Involvement in such activities can lead to increased research visibility and ultimately more successful academic careers.

Further reading

Advance HE, www.ecu.ac.uk

Aurora, www.lfhe.ac.uk/en/programmes-events/equality-and-diversity/aurora/about-aurora/index.cfm

British Columbia Mentoring, https://academic.ubc.ca/support-resources/professional-development/mentoring

Denicolo, P., Reeves, J. and Duke, D. (2018) *Success in Research: Fulfilling the Potential of your Doctorate*. London: SAGE.

Kogler-Hill, S., Hilton Bahnuk, M., Dobos, J. and Rouner, D. (1989) Mentoring and other support in the academic setting. *Group and Organization Studies*, 14(3), September: 355–268.

Spencer-Oatey, H. and Dauber, D. (2015) How internationalised is your university? Moving beyond structural indicators towards social integration. Briefing Paper: *Going Global Event 2015*. London, UK.

Vitae (n.d.) *Three-Minute Thesis Competition*. www.vitae.ac.uk/events/three-minute-thesis-competition.

PART III
Developing everyday mentoring practice

Overview

Having explored mentoring partnerships to support different transition points common in an academic career (Part I), and to support skills development (Part II), we focus in this final section on the value of developing mentoring practice in an everyday context. We believe, and hope we have made clear in our discussion so far, that mentoring partnerships promote the personal and/or skills development of professionals by drawing on several key mentoring principles, which include creating space for reflection, fostering mentee confidence and role modelling. In Part III, we explore how we can develop everyday mentoring practice by embedding these principles into some of our professional relationships, and what the benefits are.

In Chapter 11, we focus on the value to both mentee and mentor of incorporating the mentoring principles summarised above into the relationship between doctoral researcher and supervisor. Here, we acknowledge a key difference between these two relationships: the evaluative element of supervision, which is not a feature of a mentoring partnership. However, despite this important difference, we suggest that there is enough resonance between the supervisory relationship and mentoring partnership for mentoring principles to be applied within supervision. We argue that to do so enriches the relationship for both parties, encouraging the doctoral researcher to be more autonomous, and freeing the supervisor to adopt more of an advisory role. We also show how the supervisor is perfectly positioned to be a role model for the doctoral researcher, which is confidence-boosting for the researcher and helps the supervisor to uphold the standards of best practice.

In Chapter 12, we consider how incorporating mentoring principles into the relationship between a PI and their research staff can help to maintain harmonious and productive working relations among the research team. We explain why this is so important in this context, highlighting that the fixed-term nature of contracts for research staff on research projects can lead to potential conflicts of interest with the PI. Specifically, the PI is solely focused on completing the research project and generating high-quality outputs; in contrast, a researcher on a fixed-term contract will have the same focus but will also need to plan their next career step. We also acknowledge that PIs will often have had no prior line management experience, and so may struggle to know what strategies to use if this potential conflict of interest does arise. We show how, by adopting mentoring principles, a PI can find useful strategies to minimise the risk of potential conflicts of interest arising, and how research staff can facilitate the use of these principles if the PI does not.

In the final chapter (Chapter 13), we focus on a newly-emerging mentoring partnership, known as reverse mentoring (or upward mentoring), which, again, can be of enormous value in daily work practice. We start by explaining what reverse mentoring is: essentially it is a mentoring partnership where the roles of mentor (conventionally, the more senior partner) and mentee (conventionally, the more junior partner) are reversed, so that the more junior partner is the mentor and the more senior is the mentee. We explain why this is necessary, for example, when a more senior academic is lacking skills that a junior colleague, or even a student, has expertise in, such as IT skills. The chapter considers the value of reverse mentoring partnerships, perhaps the greatest being the mutual benefits experienced by both mentoring partners. It also highlights the confidence that a junior colleague can gain from being the mentor for a senior colleague, helping to break down the traditional hierarchies that prevail in institutions. At the same time, the chapter acknowledges some of the challenges that can arise in a reverse mentoring partnership and offers practical guidance on how these can be minimised.

At the end of each of these chapters, we provide specific guidance and suggestions for those responsible for mentoring provision on how to best facilitate and support mentoring partnerships to encourage the development of everyday mentoring practice.

11

Incorporating good mentoring principles into doctoral supervision

In this chapter, we consider:

- The general benefits to supervisor, doctoral researcher and HEI of incorporating the following good mentoring principles into the supervisory relationship: encouraging a researcher-driven relationship, promoting reflection and confidence building, and role modelling
- Strategies for fostering a supervisory relationship that is driven by the doctoral researcher
- Ensuring that the supervisory relationship nurtures critical reflection and self-confidence
- Ways in which the supervisor can be a role model for the doctoral researcher
- Advice for those considering running mentoring training for supervisors and doctoral researchers in HEIs

Introduction

Doctoral supervision is a complex, two-way relationship that evolves over the duration of at least three years of the doctorate and considerably longer if you are a part-time researcher. Supervision is intended to be supportive and stimulating, and very much aimed at equipping the doctoral researcher with the skills necessary to be an effective researcher. If you are a supervisor, you are aiming to support your supervisee as an individual to help them to acquire the skills of an independent researcher. You are also critically assessing the research they do through the lens of the potential contribution to knowledge and academic integrity.

If you are a doctoral researcher, you will expect your supervisor to support you in different ways as you progress through your doctorate. For example, in the early stages of research, you are likely to feel dependent on your supervisor for guidance and direction. In later stages, you may feel less dependent as a doctoral researcher but more in need of critical feedback on thesis chapters, comments on unexpected results, expert suggestions for resolving problems arising in your study as well as advice on career direction after the viva.

There is considerable resonance between doctoral supervision and mentoring. We have noted how, in mentoring, the process of development takes place through the reflective space that such relationships can facilitate. As a good supervisor, you will wish to support your doctoral researcher to grow, develop and mature into a competent, confident and independent researcher. As a doctoral researcher, your supervisor's feedback, critique and expert probing of a project plays a crucial role in developing your ability to critically reflect on yourself and your project, which is also characteristic of doctoral-level research. Finally, just as mentoring can involve the mentor acting as a role model for the mentee, so too is the supervisor ideally positioned to be a model of good research practice for the doctoral researcher. As such, the everyday relationship that develops between you both in supervision is an extremely useful vehicle for sharing and learning the tools of the trade of academic research and for building self-confidence as a researcher.

At the same time, though, mentoring and supervision are not identical. Perhaps the key difference between them is that, if you are a supervisor, you will be required to formally assess your doctoral researchers at various stages along their research journey, which is very much not a feature of a mentoring relationship. As a doctoral researcher, the formal assessments and evaluations made by your supervisor are important markers for you of your progress, which can be enormously confidence-boosting when they are positive. More negative evaluations are challenging when you first receive them, but are also often invaluable in helping you to develop as a researcher in the long run as they show you which aspects of your project, or of your researcher skills development, you need to focus more attention on.

This requirement for assessment may produce a degree of discomfort for both supervisor and doctoral researcher if the boundaries between mentoring and supervision become blurred. For example, if as a supervisor your doctoral researcher behaves unethically or is failing academically, then your supervisory responsibility is very much to be closely allied to the principles and codes of conduct of your HEI, and to maintain a professional distance from your doctoral researcher; again, this is not a feature of a mentoring partnership. In such a situation, as a researcher, you may feel let down by your supervisor if you expected them in their mentoring capacity to support you in such a crisis.

We certainly do not intend in this chapter to suggest that a supervisory relationship should turn into a mentoring one if either of the parties involved would feel uncomfortable. What we do wish to highlight is the way in which mentoring principles incorporated into the supervisory relationship can reap benefits for supervisor, doctoral researcher and institution, if by doing so, the formal requirements of the supervisory relationship, as laid down in the rules and regulations of the HEI, are not jeopardised. These benefits are summarised in Table 11.1.

Table 11.1 Benefits of incorporating good mentoring principles into doctoral supervision

Benefits for doctoral researcher	Benefits for supervisor	Benefits for the institution
You will greatly increase confidence and self-belief in your skills as a doctoral researcher.	You can enhance your own communication skills by using strategies such as open-ended questions to encourage your supervisee to critically reflect on their project.	Mentoring principles foster positive, reflective communication patterns that can lead to more confident doctoral researchers and greater satisfaction levels for supervisors. Such a culture can have a positive spin-off for HEIs in staff and researcher satisfaction surveys.
Having a supervisory relationship that you are encouraged to drive will help you to become more aware of your specific needs at various stages of your project and to articulate them to your supervisor. This in turn will help your supervisor to tailor their guidance to those needs.	Being aware that you are a role model is a great way to keep your own research practices disciplined and based on sound principles.	Institutional support for mentoring training, like any other training that focuses on enhancing relationships in the workplace, enriches the culture of the HEI by helping to promote it as an investor in people as well as in research.
You will have more opportunities to critically reflect on your progress and your project in general – a fundamental research skill.	By being less directive as a supervisor, you encourage your supervisees to become independent researchers, which they will ultimately be tested on in their viva, and which will increase their chances of completing on time. Importantly for you, this will enhance your reputation as an effective supervisor.	Using mentoring principles in supervision can lead to more independent supervisees, which may in turn lead to better completion rates within the permitted time frame, more papers and better completion statistics for the institution.

Fostering a supervisee-driven relationship

Unlike taught programmes of study, doctoral research is very much self-driven. If you are embarking on doctoral research after being on taught courses, the autonomy you are expected to have can come as a culture shock and be rather overwhelming if you expect that your supervisor will be something like a personal tutor who will direct your studies. As a supervisor, you have a role in helping your supervisee to transition from a formal, taught, course-based programme mentality to a more independent research mentality.

A good springboard for this transition is for the supervisory relationship to be driven by the supervisee more than the supervisor. This is a sound mentoring principle that can reap rewards for both parties, particularly if you apply it at the start of your working relationship. As the supervisor, establishing at the outset that your supervisee is responsible for their project sends them an early signal that doctoral research is very much about their taking on the responsibility of making an original contribution to the field. This then frees you to function more as a guide, a reference point and a mentor, rather than as a tutor or teacher. As a doctoral researcher, driving the relationship, for example, by setting agendas and dates for meetings, gives you the opportunity to develop your project management skills if you have never had to manage a project before. Often, if you are a mature doctoral researcher coming back into academia from a commercial, industrial or third sector environment, you are likely to already have project management skills, and so discovering that you have professional skills that are transferrable and valued in your new academic environment can be confidence-building.

Perhaps the best way to establish this basis for the relationship is for you both to discuss your expectations of supervision in your initial meetings. It is sensible for you, as a supervisor, to instigate the conversation around encouraging your supervisee to drive the relationship. You can do this by, for example, suggesting that they set meeting agendas, organise the meeting calendar, etc. You can also encourage them to include within the agenda time in which they reflect on the challenges encountered and progress made since the last meeting and any training or support they feel they will benefit from in the coming weeks. If your supervisee has come straight from a taught programme of study, or perhaps has had a few years out of academia and is feeling out of touch with academic protocol, they are unlikely to be expecting this type of responsibility, although those mature doctoral researchers who have work experience outside academia may expect it. Your initial meetings, therefore, are crucial in establishing this doctoral researcher-driven dynamic to supervision, and Top Tips 11.1 may help you to do that.

Top Tips 11.1

Discussing expectations in the initial supervisory meeting

1. Allow time in your initial meeting to discuss expectations of the supervisory relationship. As a supervisor, lead this conversation and explain what you expect of your supervisee and how you view your responsibilities as a supervisor. As the supervisee, be open about your expectations; do not be tempted simply to pretend that your expectations are the same as your supervisor's if they are not. Honesty is vital in this initial discussion as it can help to iron out any misconceptions at the outset.

2. As a supervisor, encourage your supervisee to set the agenda for future meetings. This will send a clear signal to them that you expect them to drive the relationship, which will allow you to be responsive to their needs. As a supervisee, be open in this initial meeting about any uncertainties you have about your responsibility in driving the relationship. This meeting is about setting the ground rules, which need to be clear for both parties, so be proactive in this meeting and speak up if something is not clear.

3. As a supervisor, encourage your doctoral researcher to speak to others in the research group. You can encourage them to go for lunch as a group regularly to allow for informal mentoring to occur between researchers. They may need to be reassured by you that you will view this as an important element of networking (discussed in Chapter 9), not as time-wasting. As a researcher, ask your supervisor to introduce you to their research group if they have one.

Further discussion of expectation-setting and the value of encouraging a more supervisee-led relationship can be found in our sister book, *Success in Research: Supervising to Inspire Doctoral Researchers* (Denicolo et al., 2020), listed in the Further Reading section at the end of this chapter.

Embedding the mentoring principle of confidence-building into the supervisory relationship

Focusing on confidence-building within the supervisory relationship can go a considerable way to reducing any anxieties that are common among doctoral researchers. Sometimes these anxieties express a deeper sense of not belonging, inadequacy and inability to acknowledge personal achievements, which is known as **imposter syndrome** (Clark et al., 2014). Imposter syndrome is surprisingly common in academia, not just among doctoral researchers, but also among HE professionals at all levels. This is probably due to the nature of academic work (for example, constant deliberation and critical assessment, including self-critique) and because of the personal characteristics of those drawn to academia, especially to research (for example, self-motivation, perfectionism, independence of mind), which can lead to excessive pondering and self-questioning. Kets de Vries (2005) identifies another possible reason: the emphasis in academia on intelligence. This emphasis can frequently lead to our silence in meetings if we are not sure that we have fully understood a point being made or a question raised. This is particularly the case for researchers in the early stages of their academic career, who at times feel surrounded by senior colleagues who seem to be so much more confident and competent.

One effective way for doctoral researchers to keep imposter feelings in check is to take active steps to develop their sense of belonging to the research community. As a supervisor, you can help your supervisee to do this by signposting for them confidence-building opportunities, such as workshops for researchers or researcher cafés, which are often run within a Graduate School, Doctoral College or Researcher Development Programme. These are excellent events for building research networks, which in turn generate a greater sense of belonging to the research community (discussed in greater depth in Chapter 9). Social gatherings such as these also lessen any sense of isolation doctoral researchers might feel, which can occur during doctoral research, especially if they are new to the city or the country. Other confidence-building activities you can encourage your researcher to engage in are symposia and conferences, or being on a conference organising committee, which HEIs often encourage doctoral researchers to do.

Another useful confidence-building activity is **schools outreach**, which is open to doctoral researchers as well as later stage professionals as part of the current HE emphasis on 'widening participation'. While not all supervisors can see the benefit of encouraging their doctoral researchers to get involved in schools outreach activities, since they take time away from their research project, others do clearly see the benefits. In Voice of Experience 11.1, Sam Connolly, a doctoral researcher who was encouraged by his supervisor to get involved, describes how beneficial this kind of activity can be for building self-confidence.

Voice of Experience 11.1

Building self-confidence through schools outreach

Participating in public engagement has been a valuable experience for developing my career as a scientist. My supervisor has been very supportive throughout my PhD, and she has always been very eager for me to get involved. Together, we started the

Antibiotics Unearthed project, which we ran for three consecutive years and aimed to teach school students traditional methods for culturing microbes which were then tested to see if they produced any antibiotics. Getting involved with projects like this has required me to interact with people of all ages, developing my communication skills so that I am able to spread knowledge to the general public in a fun and engaging way. I would recommend that every aspiring researcher participate in some form of outreach because not only are the public less scary than academics, you will learn how to communicate your knowledge to people outside your field!

Sam Connolly, doctoral researcher

Other ways of building researcher confidence and a sense of belonging include teaching and/or demonstrating. HEIs often provide training for doctoral researchers in these skills, and may even offer the opportunity to acquire a formal teaching qualification, such as an Associate Fellowship of the Higher Education Academy (AFHEA) or Fellowship of the Higher Education Academy (FHEA) in the UK (www.heacademy. ac.uk/individuals/fellowship#associate). As we mentioned in Chapter 2, your HEI may well run mentoring programmes where you, as a doctoral researcher, can join as a mentor, for example to support newly-arrived doctoral researchers. Alternatively, there may be opportunities for peer reviewing, joining committees, becoming involved in the Students' Union, or operating as a representative for a special interest group, etc. There are also potential opportunities for reverse mentoring, which we discuss in Chapter 13. For example, perhaps your supervisor has an IT-related problem, such as difficulties producing a graphic for a paper, which you can help with.

Promoting reflection in the supervisory relationship

Another mentoring principle that can help to enhance the supervisory relationship is promoting reflection. The ability to reflect critically on research, on personal development and on future training needs is central to a successful doctoral project and to having a successful career in general. It is also a vital tool in the confidence-building we focused on in the previous section.

As a doctoral researcher, by regularly reflecting on your research ideas, your strengths and weaknesses as a researcher as well as the strengths and weaknesses of your experimentation, methodology, dataset, etc., you are better able to identify areas that need to be improved or adjusted in some way. This in turn gives you a greater sense of direction and control of your project and reduces the likelihood of feeling overwhelmed, which can erode confidence levels.

Such reflection will make you more aware of the skills training you might need to ensure a successful and timely outcome to your project, which again helps to build confidence.

As a supervisor, by encouraging your supervisee to reflect on their project, you gain insight into the best way to guide and support them. Listening to your supervisee reflect on their challenges, uncertainties, evaluations, etc. is also likely to prompt your own reflection on how far you have come as an academic since your own doctoral researcher days, which can be enormously confidence-building for you as well. In this respect, the value of promoting reflection in the supervisory relationship is very much a two-way process.

There are various ways that both parties can encourage reflection as an intrinsic part of the supervisory relationship. Adopting a doctoral researcher-driven meeting agenda for supervisory meetings is a good start, as we emphasised previously; as a doctoral researcher, driving the agenda gives you the opportunity to reflect on what you have done since the last meeting, what you would like to gain from the current meeting, and what your targets are for the next. From the supervisor's perspective, you can encourage your supervisee to reflect on their project and on their progress since the last meeting by asking questions that prompt reflection.

However, we do need to acknowledge here that question-asking does not come naturally to everyone. If your management style is not to be particularly inquisitive, you might prefer to use statements and assertions, such as 'I don't think that is the best method to use'. Assertion has an important role to play when guiding doctoral researchers because it is a common communication style within academia and the workplace in general; however, from a mentoring perspective, too much assertion, particularly in the early stages of doctoral research, might start to erode your supervisee's confidence as it can lead to a defensive response, or even no response at all if they are fearful of appearing foolish.

If you both choose to adopt good mentoring principles in your supervisory meetings, it is useful, if you are the supervisor, to tune into your supervisee's confidence levels, which will fluctuate throughout the project, and to adapt your communication style accordingly. For example, when confidence is low (which can result from disappointing lab results, critical feedback on written work, or simply uncertainty about where the project is heading), a change in your communication style from assertion-heavy statements to more open questions may provide mental space for your supervisee to reflect on the project to identify issues, and this will increase the chances of their regaining a sense of control over their work. Open questions are also less likely to provoke a defensive response from your supervisee. Table11.2 gives examples of open questions that can be made from assertions.

Table 11.2 Creating opportunities for reflection through open questions

Assertion	Possible question
I have various concerns about your experimentation here.	What have you found are the drawbacks of this experimentation?
This formulation is flawed.	Can you take me through the steps that led you to arrive at this formulation?
The sample size here is too small.	Can you talk me through your thinking behind the sample size?
I'm not convinced by your argument here.	What do you think are the weaknesses of your argument here?
I'd rather see you adopt a more quantitative approach.	What are your reasons for not adopting a more quantitative approach?

From the supervisee's perspective, effective question-asking is an important tool for your communication with your supervisor. You may find reflection a challenging process as it requires a level of critical appraisal which, at times, can be uncomfortable. It will also expose your needs as a researcher, perhaps indicating that further training is required in a specific method, presentation skills, time management or IT skills, for example. Being defensive, passive or unresponsive in your supervisory meetings will be counter-productive and will hamper the two-way flow that a healthy relationship will have. It is important to remember that the challenges your supervisor offers you will promote growth and development, and therefore should be embraced, not feared. One advantage of adopting mentoring principles into supervision is that they intensify the nurturing hue of supervision, which should help you, as a supervisor, to reassure your supervisee that even when you challenge them, you do so to help them to develop rather than to be destructive or negative.

Whatever your needs are, the more positively and proactively you structure your request to your supervisor for support, the easier it will be for your supervisor to respond with constructive help and advice. In short, an important ingredient in reflecting on your needs is also taking steps to find solutions to those needs as well as sharing those needs with your supervisors. Table 11.3 illustrates how you can help your supervisor to provide you with the specific help you really need by communicating proactively rather than passively. It may also provide a useful focus, if you are a supervisor, for encouraging your supervisee to be more proactive.

Table 11.3 Passive and proactive ways of communicating research needs

Passive communication	Proactive communication
'I need more training in time management. Where can I find it?'	'I realise that I need training in time management, and so I have been looking into various training programmes offered. This one offers…, while this one provides…. Which do you think would be the best option at my current research stage?'
'I'm not sure of the best method to use here. What would you suggest?'	'I'm not sure of the best method to use here. I have considered X, Y and Z methods, but I decided that X was too…, Y fell short in terms of… and Z is not really…. Can you help me to assess which of these methods would be useful for me?'
'Thank you for being so positive about my results. Do you think I should do anything with them?'	'Thank you for being so positive about my results. I have been thinking that they would make a good journal article. I have noticed that the *Journal of X* and the *International Proceedings of Y* would both be suitable because they take this type of research. *Journal of X* has a lower impact factor but a quicker turnaround time than *International Proceedings of Y*. Can you help me to decide which would be the better option?'

Role modelling

Another mentoring principle that is very much present within the supervisory relationship is role modelling. As a doctoral researcher, you have in your supervisor someone who has successfully navigated the doctoral process and has since accumulated substantial experience as an academic. You also have a long-term professional relationship with them, and for these reasons, you are likely to regard them as your reference point – your role model – for good practice.

As a supervisor, the way you relate to your researcher is likely to be the way that they will relate to their supervisees if they become supervisors. This kind of mirroring is natural in role modelling. This means that in your everyday work, your supervisee is taking role model cues from you about how to supervise, give feedback, write papers, collaborate, teach, set deadlines and how to conduct research with integrity. They are also gaining a sense of the kind of behaviour that is normal within the discipline, such as how networking is done (discussed further in Chapter 9). For this reason, the more aware of this role modelling you are, the more likely you are to wish to maintain best practice in your role as researcher, teacher, project manager and supervisor. Consciously acknowledging this mentoring principle of role modelling helps to promote a positive culture of best practice that will be passed on to your researcher, who, in turn, will be able to become a model of best practice for those they manage in their future career.

Another important aspect of role modelling is the passion you convey for your subject and your research. To be guided by someone who clearly loves their discipline can be inspirational, motivating and confidence-building. Passion brings a proactive energy, which comes across very clearly in Voice of Experience 11.2, an account by a Professor Emerita of how she has inspired a host of colleagues through role modelling.

Voice of Experience 11.2

Inspiring through role modelling

My methodology expertise lies in constructivist psychology which can be used to explore people's attitudes, beliefs and values in any circumstances, making it a useful approach in a wide range of people-focused disciplines. I passionately believe it also cultivates a way of working with people as well as being a general 'psychology for living and being'.

From my research methods classes in several institutions, requests came for more support in these methods so 30 years ago I set up a regional interest group. The doctoral researchers took on lead roles to arrange meetings, select topics for debate, share ideas, give presentations, write together and generally support each other's research. From these, friendship groups emerged that have been sustained and these doctors, in academia and the professions, continue the work with their students and colleagues. And with me. With one group we jointly wrote a well-received book on the subject; with another pair I regularly run workshops for researchers; one is leading another co-authored book on constructivist coaching with me; another five, spread around the globe, are my editorial team for a book series. All of them introduce their own students or peers as collaborators, co-authors and co-presenters. They have sustained me and each other through many professional and personal traumas.

It's a big constructivist family now.

Professor Emerita

From an institutional perspective, the benefit of role modelling is clear; it provides a natural model for passing on the skills of research in a very personal, bespoke way. We do perhaps need to point out here that not all supervisors will necessarily be modelling best practice, and so institutions should bear a degree of responsibility for ensuring that models of best practice are clearly accessible to both supervisors and doctoral researchers. This is often done through supervisor training workshops and doctoral training sessions dedicated to helping researchers maintain positive working relationships with their supervisors, such as 'Managing your Supervisor' sessions. It can also be done in a light-touch way by embedding training in mentoring principles for supervision in larger training initiatives for academic staff, which we invite you to reflect on at the end of this chapter.

Advice for those wishing to establish mentoring training for doctoral supervisors

If you are considering setting up mentoring training for doctoral supervisors in your institution, there are a few points to consider to maximise the success of the training.

First, know who precisely you will target the training at. If you target experienced as well as new supervisors, there may be a degree of resistance from those who have supervised for many years. One way to minimise this is, before you implement the training, to run a short promotional campaign designed to raise awareness of the benefits of mentoring in supervisory relationships. As part of that campaign, you could approach an experienced supervisor who already uses mentoring techniques to write a short post on your internal news bulletin. Alternatively, you could invite experienced supervisors to share their experience and wisdom with junior colleagues. Framing the invitation in this way is perhaps more likely to receive a positive response.

Second, be very clear that mentoring is not synonymous with supervision. As we mentioned earlier in this chapter, a key difference between mentoring and supervision is that the latter has an assessment and evaluative element to it, which is not a feature of a mentoring relationship. Any training should therefore highlight this difference and emphasise that any mentoring principles adopted should only be used if they will enhance, not jeopardise, the broader function of supervision. Thus, the message delivered is likely to be that supervision is a compulsory component of any doctoral programme that must adhere to the rules and regulations of supervision according to your institution's governance. As long as that governance is not jeopardised in any way, embedding good mentoring principles, such as allowing the doctoral researcher to drive the supervisory relationship, fostering opportunities within supervision for reflection and confidence-building, and encouraging the supervisor to function as a role model for the doctoral researcher, can be beneficial to both parties and to the institution, as shown in Table 11.1 above.

Third, the training programme you are considering implementing should also consider the diversity of supervisory styles within any single HEI. Not all styles will lend themselves to adopting the mentoring principles we mentioned above. For example, a supervisor who, as a doctoral researcher, was supervised by an academic who preferred to maintain a power distance may have a natural tendency to adopt a similar style with their researcher. Indeed, if the doctoral researcher comes from a culture characterised by power distance and hierarchy (which we discuss in greater depth in Chapter 5), this type of supervisory relationship will probably be expected and will be extremely productive. For them, the idea, for example, of their supervisor expecting them to drive the relationship may make them feel uncomfortable and may even erode their trust in the relationship, as we explored in Case Study 5.1 in Chapter 5.

For this reason, it is perhaps sensible to adopt a light-touch approach to any mentoring training offered to supervisors. One way to do this is to embed such training within one or more of many larger training initiatives available for doctoral supervisors at your HEI. For example, if your institution runs a supervisor training programme, you might consider embedding a workshop on mentoring principles within that programme. Alternatively, these principles could be included within a broader induction programme for new academics. As training provision for academics varies considerably from institution to institution, we invite you in Reflection Point 11.1 to consider the programmes that run in your HEI in which you could include a light-touch approach to mentoring training for supervisors.

Reflection Point 11.1

Finding opportunities to embed mentoring training for supervisors into larger training initiatives

Investigate the types of training provision offered at your institution that will appeal to doctoral supervisors (for example, supervisor training, cultural awareness programmes, academic staff induction programmes, staff mentoring programmes) and consider where you can best embed a workshop or short module on the value of mentoring principles in supervision.

Chapter summary

In this chapter we have considered the value of fostering key mentoring principles – promoting a doctoral researcher-driven relationship, reflection and confidence building, and role modelling – in the supervisory relationship for both supervisor and doctoral researcher. We have emphasised that to do this effectively requires effort from the researcher as well as the supervisor, reflecting the two-way dynamic of a positive supervisory relationship. We have also highlighted some important considerations if you are intending to set up mentoring training for supervisors in your institution and have underlined the merits of adopting a light-touch approach to communicating principles of best practice. By adopting this light-touch approach, the institution creates a supervisory culture that is both inclusive and based on best practice principles, which in turn is likely to lead to more productive researchers and better doctoral researcher completion rates.

In the next chapter, we focus on principal investigators (PIs) as mentors.

Further reading

Clark, M., Vardeman, K. and Barba, S. (2014) Perceived inadequacy: a study of the imposter phenomenon among college and research librarians. *College and Research Libraries*, 75(3): 255–271.

Denicolo, P., Duke, D. and Reeves, J. (2020) *Success in Research: Supervising to Inspire Doctoral Researchers*. London: SAGE.

Higher Education Academy, www.heacademy.ac.uk/individuals/fellowship#associate

Kets de Vries, M.F.R. (2005) The dangers of feeling like a fake. *Harvard Business Review*, September. https://hbr.org/2005/09/the-dangers-of-feeling-like-a-fake

Parkman, A. (2016) The imposter phenomenon in higher education: incidence and impact. *Journal of Higher Education Theory and Practice*, 16(1): 51–60.

Wood Brooks, A. and John, L.K. (2018) The surprising power of questions. *Harvard Business Review*, May–June. https://hbr.org/2018/05/the-surprising-power-of-questions

12

Incorporating good mentoring principles as a principal investigator

In this chapter, we present:

- The term 'principal investigator' (PI) and what it means in academic settings
- Advice for researchers working with a PI who would like to create a mentoring partnership
- Advice for PIs wishing to take on more of a mentoring role with members of their research team
- Information for staff developers seeking to encourage mentoring by senior staff members in daily practice

Introduction

The term 'principal investigator' (PI) is generally understood in academia as the lead researcher or academic on a funded grant. The focus of the PI is to complete the research project and create some high-impact outputs from it, as these are the overarching measures of success for the project. To do this effectively, the PI will often be able to use part of the funding to employ research staff, who might be early career researchers or individuals with specific technical skills or experience necessary for the project. This means that in addition to leading the project, the PI will also have line management responsibility.

As the PI may have had no previous managerial experience or training in line management, having such responsibility can be challenging. This challenge is rooted in the fact that the research staff employed will be on fixed-term contracts (discussed in Chapter 3), and therefore will need to actively search for their next position at the same time as working on the funded project. For example, they may be using their free time to investigate writing their own funding applications (mentioned in Chapter 8) or applying for jobs. Their split focus – on the project and on the next career move – can lead to a degree of conflict with the PI's focus, which is solely on completion of the project and impressive outputs. If the PI has no previous line management experience, they may struggle to know how best to balance the demands of the project with the researchers' needs to secure their next post.

One way that a PI can manage this potential conflict of interest, which is necessary to do in order to maintain harmonious relations throughout the project, is to apply good mentoring principles when managing the team. Indeed, as we have highlighted in this book, particularly in Part III, incorporating mentoring principles into various day-to-day work contexts does far more than simply manage potential conflict; it can help to build the confidence of members of staff, to motivate them and to empower them to seek responsibility in their work. In these respects, there is much resonance between the features of mentoring and the qualities of an effective PI, two of which, according to Vitae (2018), are to be 'empowering' and 'motivating'.

The value of adopting mentoring principles in the PI/research staff relationship

There are considerable benefits to both mentee and mentor of adopting mentoring within the PI/research staff relationship. For example, stronger and more engaged researchers are likely to contribute to more successful publications, collaborations and research funding bids. We summarise the main benefits in Table 12.1, which has been partly adapted from McCook (2011) and Guccione (2018).

Table 12.1 Benefits of mentoring for the mentee and the mentor

Benefits to mentee	Benefits to mentor
Building a strong relationship between mentor and mentee will increase the likelihood of you collaborating with each other later.	
Being open to the other's ideas facilitates stronger research.	
You will learn problem-solving skills which will make you a better researcher on the current project and future projects.	As your mentee learns problem-solving skills, they will become a better researcher on the current project.
Having a mentor will encourage you to take ownership of your career.	Incorporating mentoring principles into your working relationship with your research staff is likely to make your research group more productive.

Benefits to mentee	Benefits to mentor
You will get an outsider's view on your strengths and weaknesses as you work together on job searches and applications.	The success of your mentees may lead to fresh funding, publication and collaboration opportunities for you (Nature jobs, 2018).
You can gain practical advice and support on topics like interview skills, writing funding proposals and job seeking.	Mentoring more junior researchers will give you confidence which can translate into promotion.
You will gain insights into challenges you are facing or decisions you are taking about a specific topic.	You can transfer your mentoring skills to learning and teaching practices and use them as evidence for applications to bodies such as Advance HE (formerly known as the Higher Education Academy).
If you are an ECR looking for a career in academia, by speaking to your mentor, who has already made the transition to an academic position, you will be able to make a more informed choice.	Being known as a good mentor as well as a good PI will help to attract the best people to the research group when they see the outcomes of previous members of your research staff.
Having a mentor can keep you on track and proactive. This is especially important in a short-term position because your time is limited, and you have to keep moving forward with your career plans. It is all too easy to let things pass.	

Applying mentoring principles in conversations between PI and researcher

Mentoring principles can be applied in two main types of conversation between the PI and researcher: within normal everyday conversations about the research project and in conversations about career steps. In everyday conversations as PI, for example, ensuring that your usual discussions about the project have a reflective element, where you might talk about your own relevant experiences, can help your researcher to broaden their insights into the topic. This, in turn, can build your researcher's confidence and may lead to them being more effective in their work. The value of the PI talking about their own experiences is illustrated in Voice of Experience 12.1.

Voice of Experience 12.1

Empowering researchers by having a PI as a mentor

More than advising, from her own experience my PI will often warn me of things to be aware of. By hearing other people's actual experiences, you have some data, something

(Continued)

concrete, to start from. The advantage with these chats with my PI is that I can keep her up to date with what's going on. She always says that she will back me up whatever I decide, which is one of the bonuses of having a manager as an advisor.

Researcher at a London-based research institute

Another useful technique in everyday conversations between PI and researcher is to ask questions, which is a technique used in coaching as well as mentoring. While we generally consider coaching and mentoring to be distinct (as described in Chapter 1), coaching techniques, such as promoting reflection through questioning, is also a valuable mentoring technique. As a PI, it is easy, especially when you are extremely busy and may be dealing with inexperienced research staff, to offer your own solutions to problems to expedite meetings. In fact, you probably view this as part of your job. However, sometimes a more valuable learning experience for the researcher can be gained from you stepping back and asking questions to help them to find answers for themselves, helping them to develop and gain insights into research problem solving.

This is also a valuable technique if your researcher wishes to have a conversation about their next career steps. Asking them questions about what they are considering with respect to career allows them to reflect on their aspirations, concerns, etc. and helps you to gauge how best you can guide them in their career decisions. We consider this strategy in greater depth in Chapter 11, where we also provide some helpful pointers for asking questions to promote reflection.

Encouraging your research staff to develop their problem-solving skills in this way can be beneficial for you as PI because as they develop their confidence in problem solving, they will be able to relieve you of some of the workload for the project. As a researcher working on a project, if you would like your PI to adopt a more mentoring approach, you could be proactive in encouraging them to do so. One way to do this is, when you encounter a problem linked to the project, to consider possible solutions before presenting the problem to your PI. By doing this, your PI is much more likely to view you as a potential problem-solver, which will encourage them to call on you for your ideas on other problems. You may find that by working on problems together, jointly found solutions are more creative and effective than those found individually.

Another important aspect of PI mentoring that is particularly valuable is role modelling. As a PI, you will know the expectations of how to behave in your department and, more broadly, in your discipline. As these expectations may not be explicit, a new researcher having a PI who acts as a role model can help to bring these expectations to light for you. This will not only benefit you in your current position, but also in your future role, where you may have the opportunity to put into practice what you have learned. This role modelling is even more important if you have moved institution, discipline or country, as norms and expectations can vary considerably. We discuss in more depth the ways that such norms can vary from one country to another in Chapter 5. As a researcher, look to your PI and use them as a role model if you are unsure of how to behave in a situation and, as a PI, you can give friendly advice on how to behave when interacting with colleagues and peers to help the researcher fit in. Role modelling often occurs naturally within these relationships, but it is useful to be mindful of this important aspect of mentoring.

How to create a mentoring environment between PI and researcher

As discussed above, mentoring at this level is likely to be focused around two broad themes: mentoring during everyday interactions on the current research project, and mentoring about the mentee's next career steps and choices. As funded research projects have considerable workload and tight deadlines, any conversations about next career steps are likely to be driven by the researcher rather than the PI, whose focus will be on completion of the project and obtaining high-impact outputs. As a researcher, it is therefore important for you to be clear about what you would like from your PI so that a beneficial mentoring environment and relationship can be created.

The first step to do this is to be clear about why you may want to foster a mentoring relationship with your PI. Reflection Point 12.1 may help you to clarify your reasons.

Reflection Point 12.1

Research staff – reflect on why you may want your PI as your mentor

Consider why you may want to foster a mentoring relationship with your PI. For example, do you:

- Want guidance on your current research project to enhance your problem-solving skills?
- See your PI as well placed to give advice on your next steps after your current contract?

(Continued)

- Wish to tap into your PI's network of colleagues and collaborators?
- See your PI as a role model of how you wish to work, balance your life, make progress?
- Want something else...?

Note down your aims or goals for the mentoring.

Having an informal mentoring conversation

As a member of research staff, you may not feel comfortable asking your PI to act in a mentoring role. If so, there are ways you can be mentored by them without officially labelling it as such. For example, if you would like some mentoring about your next career step and you think your PI would be a good person to talk to, then book a one-off meeting with them and state upfront what you want to talk about. Be clear about what you wish to discuss, investigate your options and demonstrate to them that you are taking the conversation seriously. State the options you are considering and ask your mentor's opinion or ask them to discuss each one. Doing this will allow you to get an outside point of view on your situation and may highlight aspects that you have not considered. An example is given in Reflection Point 12.2. You might consider, if you were a PI, which version of the question would be the most productive start to a conversation.

Reflection Point 12.2

Wording a statement to prompt a constructive response

Consider the difference between the response you are likely to get to the following two statements.

'I just don't know what to do next.'

'I have been thinking about my next steps. I have investigated a fellowship or moving into a research position in business and I would like to discuss how you made the decision to gain any insights into how to make the choice.'

When you feel the mentoring conversation is coming to an end, set some actions that you will take forward. Discuss with your PI what your next steps could be. These might be anything from speaking to someone from another research group to applying for a job or writing a funding application. Whatever the next steps are, outline and agree on the plan with your PI and they can highlight any steps you have missed, contacts they can give you or advice they wish to pass on.

If you are the PI on a project and a member of research staff approaches you with questions like those above, then it is important to consider if you have the time to give to the conversation immediately or if it would be better to book a dedicated time slot to talk. As with all mentoring, having the time to really listen to what your mentee wishes to discuss is vital because this will help you to give appropriate advice and to help your mentee create an effective plan of action for their next steps.

Formalising a mentoring partnership

If you would like a more formal mentoring partnership, then you should explicitly state the fact. As a member of research staff, the simplest way is to ask your PI if they are willing to take on the role. When doing this, be very clear about precisely what you wish to discuss and how often you would like to meet as mentor and mentee, rather than as PI and staff member. You could approach the topic by asking them for support on a specific subject, such as building your career in the long term or juggling a research career with a family. As a PI, if a member of staff approaches you to be their mentor, make sure that you are the best person for the role and that there is no conflict of interest in having the conversation that your mentee wishes to have. You should also be sure that you have the necessary skills and/or experience to provide the support that your mentee is looking for. If not, consider contacting a colleague who could substitute for you in that role.

Once both parties agree to form a mentoring partnership, then, as with all mentoring relationships, it is important that the mentee states the topic for discussion at each meeting. As a mentee, think about what you would like to discuss and send your mentor a summary before the meeting. As a mentor, make a point of asking your mentee to send you the topic before you meet. For your mentoring meetings, it is a good idea to meet in a neutral place outside your normal working environment, for example a meeting room close by or a café that is local for you both. In a neutral space, you are less likely to be interrupted by phone calls or knocks on the door. In addition, the act of moving to a different space sets this conversation apart from your regular research project meetings.

How to have a non-directive conversation

Earlier, we highlighted the value of the PI adopting a more coaching or mentoring, and less directive, stance with their researcher. Here, we consider in more detail how to have a non-directive conversation. As a PI and mentor, you might wish to adopt some of these tools and techniques during your mentoring conversations with research staff. We should point out, though, that it is important that any of the techniques you adopt feel natural. This means employing techniques that feel right for you. If the conversation feels forced or stilted, then the mentoring partnership will feel awkward. At the same time, with practice, these techniques can become second nature and just part of your normal working.

Listening is key to any mentoring that you do. As a busy academic, it is too easy to half listen in a meeting while planning the next part of a paper or the next lecture that is high on your to-do list. Being fully present in the conversation and actively listening to members of your team will maximise the value of the meetings for all parties involved. For active listening, you might wish to try some of these simple techniques (adapted from Samaritans, 2018) in Top Tips 12.1.

Top Tips 12.1

Active listening techniques

1. **Open questions**. Open questions usually begin with 'what', 'how', 'tell me' or 'why' and elicit answers of more than a single word. Take care when asking questions beginning with the word 'why', because sometimes they can sound judgemental or accusatory even if they are not meant to be. For example, although 'Why did you do that?' is an open question that requires more than a one-word answer, it is sometimes used to imply that you do not agree with the way that they have done something, rather than just wishing to know their thinking behind a decision. A good alternative might be 'How did you come to the decision to use that approach?'
2. **Reflective language**. This means using similar language to that used by the person you are speaking with. For example, if they use the word 'cross', then do not use the word 'angry' when asking them to clarify something. The idea is that while you might feel the words 'cross' and 'angry' are synonyms, the person you are speaking to might not. Using the same wording will show empathy and build trust.
3. **Summarising and clarifying**. If your mentee is discussing a challenge or several options they are deciding between, then it can help if you listen to what they are saying and then summarise or ask questions to clarify. This will help you because you will be sure you understand the issue, but it also helps them. Hearing their challenge or options in someone else's words can make the way forward clearer.

4. **Use short words of encouragement (like 'yes' or 'uh-huh'), nod and smile**. If your mentee is having trouble articulating the issue they wish to discuss, this technique can help them to keep talking while signalling that you are actively listening to what they are saying.

Within mentoring conversations, another set of tools which can prove useful are basic coaching techniques, as we have mentioned earlier. Many coaching models have been published, and we have included some of them in the Further Reading section at the end of this chapter if you wish to find out more (Whitmore, 2009; Fletcher and Mullen, 2012). The simple principle of these models is that you structure your conversation to allow the other person to discuss an issue without being interrupted by you with an immediate answer. To use this principle, as a mentor, begin the conversation by asking what your mentee would like to discuss. Then help them to find a few solutions to the particular challenge they have identified. It is important that you do not offer a solution but instead allow them to arrive at their own ideas first. You can then add some of your own. To finish the conversation, you could ask which of the solutions might work best, and why, and then discuss how they could put the solution into practice. As the mentee, it would be difficult to contrive this type of conversation if your mentor is not knowledgeable of coaching techniques. You could always influence the conversation with your mentor by guiding your mentor to discuss several options and then move forward and plan, selecting the option that suits you best, as discussed above.

Information for staff developers and researcher developers

If you are a staff or researcher developer, there are four main ways you can encourage mentoring behaviour between PIs and their research staff: through training, the appraisal or performance review, using guidelines, and setting the expectation of mentoring with all new staff. Below, we focus briefly on each of these.

Training

Most institutions offer training for academics wishing to supervise doctoral students and those wishing to teach. Within this training, you could offer a short introduction to mentoring and coaching techniques. These techniques are not only beneficial for managing staff, but can also be incorporated into everyday practice in teaching and supervising (Guccione, 2018).

There are many ways to approach training. In our experience, it is good to keep the session short and targeted to practical aspects of mentoring, as demonstrated in Example 12.1.

Example 12.1

A sample training session for PIs who wish to mentor

10:00 am: Activity about the nature of mentoring. As a short exercise, ask the group to discuss and write down what they believe is the definition of mentoring. *Make sure everyone knows what is being talked about.*

10:15 am: Video or live talk with an academic at the institution who uses mentoring in their practice about the benefits as they see them. In our experience, a colleague giving their 'stamp of approval' lends credibility to the initiative.

10:20 am: Discussion about why mentoring and coaching are important in managing research staff. Ask how participants think they could use it in their everyday practice.

10:25 am: Activity in active listening. You could build an activity around the advice given by the Samaritans (2018) using the link in the Further Reading section at the end of the chapter. The activity could be an imagined conversation with examples of all the different variations of active listening.

10:40 am: Discussion of a basic coaching model. An example of a simple non-directive model that you could introduce to your PIs is the GROW model (Whitmore, 2009). Of course, you could use any model you preferred; we use this one because it is simple and straightforward.

10:50 am: Practice in pairs with the non-directive coaching model and active listening.

11:15 am: Discussion on how the group think they could use the techniques practised.

11:25 am: Questions and follow-up.

11:30 am: End.

Using the appraisal, performance and development review

One way to foster mentoring relationships is to alter your appraisal process to structure in a mentoring conversation for research staff. This would not have to be a big change to your current process; it could simply be the addition of a few well-written questions. Of course, this change would have to be in collaboration with the HR department that manages the institutional appraisal process. During the appraisal process, the appraisee can reflect on the progress they have made in the last year and their targets for the future. This is the outline for the beginning of a mentoring conversation, so it is not a big step to mentoring. Guide the line manager to explore the answers to these questions further, to help the member of research staff make a plan for the next steps – this is a mentoring conversation. This method will work best if both parties see the usefulness of the appraisal process and do not see it as a box-ticking exercise. If the appraisal is seen as another administrative task, then the rich conversations that could happen will be stifled under deadlines and administrative procedures. The solution to this is greater than the scope of this book but lies in all members of staff valuing the conversations they have during their appraisal and seeing them as important.

Guidelines

Writing a set of guidelines about mentoring may be a more acceptable way to approach the subject with academics who are PIs on projects. These guidelines could be distributed through heads of department and at departmental meetings so each academic can then choose whether to adopt any of the advice.

The guidelines should be adjusted for your own institution but some points to consider are included in Example 12.2.

Example 12.2

Points to cover in guidelines for mentoring relationships between PIs and research staff

- Describe what a mentor is in this context and why it is important to act as a mentor for research staff. Use the sections above to outline what you see as the role of a mentor in this situation. It is important to write these guidelines being mindful that as well as mentor and mentee, the relationship will also be line manager and member of staff.
- Outline how the PI should set expectations with the mentee and how the relationship will work alongside their day-to-day interactions as a line manager and researcher on a project. Consider:
  - o the time available
  - o appropriate topics
  - o the frequency of mentoring

(Continued)

- o   the role of a mentor in this context
- o   confidentiality

- Summarise the benefits as you see them to both the mentor and the mentee. You can use the benefits listed in this chapter (pp176–177) for examples. As you gain feedback, you will be able to add to this list.
- Outline the skills and qualities of a mentor, focusing especially on the skills needed to mentor a member of staff for whom they have line management responsibilities.
- Lay out the practical side of being a mentor to research staff:
  - o   the time necessary to build a strong mentoring relationship
  - o   the space needed for a good mentoring relationship is neutral ground, a meeting room away from the corridor where the mentor and mentee work or a café close by
  - o   how to arrange meetings
  - o   how to end the relationship when the PI feels they have done all they can or the mentee feels they have got all they need. This is especially important if the mentoring has been around career steps when there is still some time before the current project is completed. Of course, if the PI is adopting a mentoring approach to their everyday practice, then this is not an issue.

- Provide some basic coaching and mentoring techniques, such as active listening, coaching models and open question examples.
- Offer a directory of all the support and assistance that is available to staff at the institution and beyond so that the mentor can signpost them. Examples might be well-being services, research support services and library services. It is important to provide this information as sometimes PIs are unaware of the extent of what is available to research staff in support and development opportunities.
- Ask PIs who are already mentoring to write something about how they use it and what they have found to be the benefits to them and their team.

As with any guidelines, not everyone will read and follow them but having them as a reference point for the mentors will be valuable. If you keep them short and practical, then PIs will be more likely to adopt some of the suggestions.

Setting expectations with new staff

The value of encouraging all new staff to act as a mentor is that it is more likely to become a measure of best practice. Further, as people in departmental management see the value in mentoring research staff, then this will filter down to all staff. These expectations could be set out in conjunction with the guidelines for the new staff training and induction. A large part of this will be to demonstrate how mentoring can benefit the mentor as well as the mentee, perhaps by showing case studies of where these relationships have increased productivity or fostered collaboration when the member of research staff moves away from the institution.

Chapter summary

Mentoring as a PI can have benefits not just for those who are being mentored, but also for those who are doing the mentoring. These benefits occur in the more effective day-to-day running of the research project and in the empowering of the mentee to find their next career step after their contract has finished. The skills of being a good PI overlap somewhat with the skills of being a good mentor so that learning how to be a mentor ultimately leads to being a more effective PI. Of course, it is not easy to be a mentor when the academic workload is heavy. Under such pressure, when a researcher asks for help, the default option is to become the immediate problem solver. However, stepping back and thinking about these conversations from a mentoring perspective will benefit the PI, the member of research staff and, in turn, the HEI.

Further reading

Carnell, E., Macdonald, J. and Askew, S. (2006) *Coaching and Mentoring in Higher Education: A Learning-Centred Approach*. London: Institute of Education, University of London.

Fletcher, S.J. and Mullen, C.A. (eds) (2012) *The SAGE Handbook of Mentoring and Coaching in Education*. Los Angeles, CA: SAGE.

Guccione, K. (2018) Aren't they all leaving anyway? What's the value of mentoring early career research staff? Peer reviewed Case Study for Leadership foundation in higher education (1–24).

McCook, A. (2011) Mentoring: On the right path. *Nature*, 474(7353): 667–669. doi: 10.1038/nj7353-667a.

Nature jobs (2018) *Career Toolkit: Mentoring*. Available at: www.nature.com/naturejobs/science/career_toolkit/mentoring (accessed 20/12/2018).

Samaritans (2018) *Active Listening, Samaritans*. Available at: www.samaritans.org/active-listening (accessed 20/12/2018).

Vitae (2018) *Skills and Characteristics of a PI – Vitae Website*. Available at: www.vitae.ac.uk/doing-research/leadership-development-for-principal-investigators-pis/developing-yourself-as-a-pi/skills-and-characteristics-of-a-pi (accessed 20/12/2018).

Whitmore, J. (2009) *Coaching for Performance: GROWing Human Potential and Purpose. The Principles and Practice of Coaching and Leadership* (4th edition). London: Nicholas Brealey.

13

Reverse mentoring

In this chapter, we consider:

- What reverse mentoring is and the range of issues that it can be helpful in addressing
- The benefits of reverse mentoring to the mentee, the mentor and the institution
- How to set up a reverse mentoring scheme and how to get involved in reverse mentoring if your institution does not have a scheme
- How to be an effective mentor and how to get the most out of reverse mentoring as a mentee

Introduction – what is reverse mentoring?

'Learning is ever in the freshness of its youth, even for the old.' Aeschylus, Greek playwright

'Reverse mentoring', or 'upward mentoring', is where (usually) older, senior or more experienced staff are mentored by (usually) younger, more junior colleagues or students. As such, it turns on its head the conventional model of mentoring, where the mentor is typically older and therefore, theoretically at least, wiser. In this chapter, the mentees are most commonly mid-career or senior academic staff and their mentors are undergraduate or doctoral researchers, early career researchers and junior research staff, and early career academics.

This type of mentoring takes advantage of the skills and experience of the young mentors and is most commonly used to support the older mentee in developing competences related to emerging technologies, IT or social media that their younger colleagues often take for granted. It is equally powerful in supporting the mentee to develop cultural awareness about gender, ethnicity or other aspects of workplace diversity. (As cultural awareness is such a critical issue, we address mentoring to support it specifically in Chapter 5.) As with many mentoring initiatives, reverse mentoring began and first became popular in the business world, and it is only more recently that HEIs have begun to appreciate its potential.

There are many examples of reverse mentoring in the business world. One of the best-known is that of Jack Welch, the then Chief Executive Officer (CEO) of the American company, General Electric, who is often credited with setting up the first reverse mentoring scheme (Greengard, 2002). In 1999, he anticipated that the then new technical innovation of the internet would have far-reaching implications, and realised that while his young, technically-astute employees were already engaging with it, his senior team was not. He took a young mentor to help him understand the new computer technologies and instructed his top 500 executives to do the same. Another example is that of the computer giant, IBM, which has a broad portfolio of mentoring programmes. These include reverse mentoring where junior employees mentor senior colleagues, and a programme that pairs heterosexual mentees with lesbian, gay, bisexual, transgender, queer plus (LGBTQ+) colleagues to help them understand the issues that this staff group faces in the workplace.

Reverse mentoring is also becoming popular in academia. An early example (Cotunga and Vickery, 1998) was that of the University of Delaware, Newark, USA, where undergraduate nutrition students, confident in the use of the then emerging technology of the internet, were paired with dietetics professionals who were new to the technology. They designed and facilitated a hands-on workshop and then mentored their partners over the period of a semester. A more current example is the 'social media support group' of Maltepe University, Turkey, where undergraduate students were recruited as mentors to assist staff, including the President, with use of their social media accounts to promote the university and its activities (Gündüz and Akşit, 2018). Oxford Brookes University runs an 'e-pioneer' reverse mentoring scheme (www.brookes.ac.uk/instepp/) that supports undergraduate and postgraduate students to produce reviews of technology-enhanced learning tools and resources, and to present them to staff and other students during a seminar series designed to build a 'community of practice'. It also aims to support them to work with academic staff as equal partners in developing digital teaching resources and course content, both enhancing the academic staff member's digital capabilities and the digital literacies of the students taking their courses.

The reciprocal benefits of reverse mentoring to mentor and mentee and its value to the institution

Throughout this book, we have emphasised that all types of mentoring benefit both mentor and mentee. However, this is especially true of reverse mentoring. It has sometimes been called 'mutual mentoring' because the mentoring is so obviously reciprocal. These shared benefits come from the unusual nature of the partnership where, as a mentor, you are likely to be younger or more junior – perhaps an undergraduate or doctoral researcher or junior researcher/academic – and as a mentee you are likely to be a mid-career or senior academic. Therefore, there is a breakdown of the usual perceived hierarchical barriers between you and your mentoring partner, facilitating freer and more open dialogue, which advantages both of you. This is highlighted in Voice of Experience 13.1, where Jason Okwuonu, an undergraduate student, highlights how positively he felt about being able to communicate on an equal footing with academic staff.

Voice of Experience 13.1

How being a reverse mentor benefited me

I joined the e-pioneer (reverse mentoring) programme as I was looking for an extra-curricular activity to take part in during my time in university and I was quite interested in learning more about the online tools that we use, such as Google's online software and Moodle (the virtual learning environment used for teaching). I was given the task of researching Google slides and how to embed them into Moodle. Once I understood how to do this, I presented to some of the academic staff at an 'expert pool' at lunchtime. It was great to present what I found to a small group of people, and I felt like it prepared me for future presentations I might have to do. Also, doing that presentation and working with others of different ages and from different departments was great. I felt that I was on the same level with them, despite some people having a PhD. Furthermore, I got to learn about software, which I can use to better my productivity in university.

Jason Okwuonu, second-year undergraduate student in Medical Science

Whether you engage in reverse mentoring as a mentor or as a mentee, it can effectively breach the divide in experience, knowledge and understanding between you and others with whom you need to work productively, and to communicate effectively, in your everyday professional life. As an example, if you are an undergraduate or doctoral researcher who is comfortable and skilled in using IT applications and social media, you can, like Jason Okwuonu, share your skills with an older, more senior mentee in a reverse mentoring partnership. If you are a senior academic for whom aspects of the technology are unfamiliar, you can benefit greatly from your mentor's knowledge and experience. In addition to sharing this subject-specific knowledge, you can both form a genuinely friendly relationship across the generations and enjoy an unusually open and honest dialogue. For both of you, this is likely to bring a deeper understanding, empathy and respect for members of a group with whom you are each likely to spend a great deal of time in your professional life, interacting in taught classes or supervision meetings.

The learning is even richer when you and your mentoring partner happen to come from different ethnic, cultural or societal backgrounds, and, as already described, some reverse mentoring programmes are designed with this aim specifically in mind. That improved dialogue and rapport can have significant benefits to many aspects of your daily working life. Some of the more obvious benefits of reverse mentoring are outlined in the Table 13.1.

Table 13.1 Reciprocal benefits of reverse mentoring

Benefits to the mentor	Benefits to the mentee
You have access to your mentee's professional experience and knowledge, and the unusual nature of this mentoring partnership means that you can tap into this very openly.	You can form a genuinely friendly relationship, enjoying open and honest dialogue with your mentor. This may bring you deeper understanding, empathy and respect for members of a group with whom, in your professional life, you are likely to spend a great deal of time.
Your mentee can provide you with insight into a 'take' on the professional world that may be very different from your own. That insight may be helpful to you in your studies and your professional development.	You may receive valuable feedback and insight into how your leadership, management or teaching style is perceived – positively or negatively – by your mentor and their peers.
The usual hierarchical and cultural barriers fall, and you have the opportunity to discuss, debate, ask probing questions and speak much more frankly than otherwise you might.	Your mentor has greater status in this relationship than they will find in any other type of interaction with you, and therefore increased confidence to speak openly. You will thus have access to a degree of honesty that may be difficult to illicit from your mentor in any other professional situation.
You will gain an insight into your mentee's role, perspectives and the issues facing them, and build your confidence when interacting with senior staff or those from different cultural or societal backgrounds in future.	You will gain a deeper insight into the perspective and lived experiences of someone from a different generation, group or viewpoint than your own.

Benefits to the mentor	Benefits to the mentee
Your mentee may act as a role model with whom you can talk frankly and learn from.	The improved dialogue and rapport that you gain from working with your mentor can increase your empathy and understanding of others from a similar background and have significant benefits to diverse aspects of your daily working life.
Working with your mentee may bring you to the attention of staff who may be decision-makers or have an influence on your future within the organisation.	Being seen to be engaged in reverse mentoring may be viewed positively by your colleagues and bring you to the attention of senior management, enhancing your professional reputation.

As well as having benefits for the mentor and the mentee, it also makes strong business sense to ensure that HEIs are as welcoming and inclusive environments as possible, and that all individuals are equally supported to succeed. Reverse mentoring programmes are an effective means to promote cultural awareness, including deeper appreciation of the lived experience of women, those who are working or studying in a culture different from the one in which they were brought up, and BME, LGBTQ+ or disabled staff and students, among others. It can be a powerful means to challenge **unconscious bias** and address equality, diversity and inclusion issues in a highly practical way. On a strictly business-case basis, this makes for stronger student recruitment and attainment, and better scores in the NSS and league tables. It also means that you recruit and retain the best staff and that those who are capable are rewarded fairly through promotion. As well as this being fair and making the institution a more pleasant and more decent place to work in for everyone, it is reflected in the statistics that institutions value and contributes towards accolades, such as Athena SWAN and HR Excellence in Research awards.

Ways to get involved in reverse mentoring

As reverse mentoring becomes increasingly popular, more institutions are likely to have reverse mentoring programmes, such as the 'e-pioneering' scheme, described previously. If you are interested in getting involved in reverse mentoring, the first step is to find out if your institution has such a scheme and, if it does, to apply.

If your institution does not have a programme, it will probably run other mentoring initiatives that you can tap into. For example, if you have a staff mentoring programme that works along more traditional lines of matching junior staff with senior and experienced mentors, you can still apply to it (such schemes are described in Chapters 2, 3 and 4), but specifically request a reverse mentoring partnership. As a potential mentee, being clear about your goal for the mentoring relationship is important. For example, do you want to master 'Twitter' or to better understand the perspectives of BME colleagues? You might add a note clarifying that you would welcome a more junior mentor. As a potential mentor, consider, and be specific about, the skills or experience that you can offer. For example, can you share your IT knowledge or your lived experience of disability? Again, state that you would welcome a more senior mentee. Such requests may even inspire those who run the mentoring scheme to expand it specifically into reverse mentoring.

If these avenues are not open to you, then, as a mentor or a mentee, you will need to seek a mentoring partner for yourself. The way that you can approach this most effectively will depend upon the specific skills you want to share or learn, or your mentoring goal, but two examples are outlined here.

Mentoring for improved IT skills and use of social media

Within HEIs, there are large numbers of individuals, predominantly but not exclusively undergraduate students, doctoral researchers and younger staff members, who are skilled in IT and social media applications. If you wish to be mentored on these topics, there should be a wide choice of potential mentors available to you. However, it is important to think carefully about how you identify and approach your potential mentor(s) and to make sure that both of you are very clear about the boundaries to your mentoring relationship. For example, if you are an academic member of staff, then you will have access to undergraduate students who might have the skills you are looking for. However, you also have a potentially compromising power relationship with them. A junior staff colleague might be a more suitable choice. An example of this is highlighted in Voice of Experience 13.2, where a professor sought mentoring help in use of a software program that she needed to use in her teaching from a younger, recently appointed junior lecturer who was familiar with it. Another example is that if you are interested in learning how to use Twitter, you will probably find that there are interns or junior support staff who, as part of their everyday job, are responsible for the official Twitter feeds, and they might be willing to mentor you on its use. If you possess these types of skills and wish to share them as a mentor, you will need to look for opportunities to work with colleagues who are open to learning from you.

Mentoring for improved cultural awareness

In the case of improving the cultural awareness of individuals who have different backgrounds or lived experiences from yourself, then groups or organisations that support those individuals may be a helpful conduit to mediate mentoring partnerships. As an example, if you want to improve your cultural awareness around LGBTQ+ staff and students, or as an LGBTQ+ individual you want to support others in improving their awareness, then an obvious place to start would be your local LGBTQ+ group. Similar advice applies if you are interested in getting involved in reverse mentoring around improving empathy with BME colleagues and students, with those who are newly-arrived in the UK, with those from specific social backgrounds (for example, those who are the first person in their family to go to university or those who have caring responsibilities), with those who have particular needs (such as individuals with a physical impairment), and with those who have different ways of thinking (such as dyslexia, dyspraxia, Asperger's syndrome and autism).

Voice of Experience 13.2

A junior colleague helped me to get to grips with unfamiliar software

I need to log coursework and examination marks in a master Excel spreadsheet for my undergraduate modules, and eventually upload the final marksheets to the central University systems in the same format. Fortunately, the spreadsheets are usually provided for me with all the clever stuff done behind the scenes and I only have to add the marks; it does all the maths automatically. Recently, I felt stupid when I was asked to help with the assessment of some undergraduate coursework from a new module that I had not been involved in before. The students had done some very simple – to them, at least – calculations using Excel. I had no idea how to assess them so realised that I needed help. I approached the module leader, a young and recently appointed junior lecturer, and asked if he could give me some lessons. He was very helpful and sent me all the workbooks and exercises for the basic introductory classes that he does with the undergraduate students. He suggested that I work through them myself and meet with him when anything did not make sense. I am still no expert, but I feel now that I at least know the basics of Excel, and I can go back to him for advice when I need to set up something more complicated, as I am sure I will need to do in due course.

Lecturer in HEI institution in the UK

How can both mentors and mentees get the most from a reverse mentoring relationship?

In your initial mentoring discussions, mentor and mentee should work together to clarify the parameters of your relationship. As a mentor, it is important to describe your background, skills and experience, and to be honest about what you think you can offer. As with other types of mentoring, agree clear goals for what the mentee wants to get out of the mentoring relationship. For example, as a mentee, be clear about the specific skills you wish to learn. You might work together to carry out a personal SWOT analysis (strengths, weaknesses, opportunities and threats), described in Activity 13.1, to clarify what the mentee wishes to achieve. This can be helpful to you both in understanding your starting point for the mentoring and where the mentee wishes to go.

Activity 13.1

Personal SWOT analysis

Considering this mentoring opportunity, as a mentee, what strengths can you bring to your mentoring goal? What weaknesses can your mentor help you to address? What are the threats in your working life that your mentor can help you to be better prepared to face? What opportunities can they support you to take advantage of?

An example is given below for a mentee who is seeking mentoring on use of social media.

Strengths	Weaknesses
I use computers every day in my working and personal life and feel comfortable and confident with them. Over the years, I have needed to learn new technologies regularly and have generally done so easily.	I have no experience of social media. I do not really understand it. I have a Facebook page, but I never post anything; I use it to keep up to date with what my friends (my real friends in real life, not imaginary ones!) and relatives are doing. I have a Twitter account, but I do not use it. I occasionally read 'tweets' from various famous people that seem to randomly show up, but I do not really know what I am doing.
Opportunities	**Threats**
I see that it is increasingly necessary to have a professional online presence and can imagine that it will be useful in publicising my research; attracting great researchers and students to my lab; and raising the profile of my department (which has got to be good for me too).	I worry that if I post something on social media it is there for ever and can be viewed by people everywhere. I do not want to embarrass myself. I worry about confusing my personal social media with my professional online presence.

The unusual nature of reverse mentoring means that there can sometimes be tensions in the early stages of the relationship, which both mentor and mentee need to work positively together to address. These can arise from a level of discomfort, on the part of either the mentor or mentee, with the traditional roles of the mentor, normally older and more senior, and the mentee, normally younger and more junior, being reversed. If as a mentee, you have sought a mentor to help you to understand the cultural issues experienced by someone whom you perceive as being 'different' from you, the potential awkwardness and scope for misunderstanding in your interactions is magnified. This is especially true because you will probably be anxious not to inadvertently cause offence to your mentor. Top Tips 13.1 offers some practical advice for the mentor and mentee in handling this type of relationship skilfully and starting out in a positive way.

Top Tips 13.1

Having a successful reverse mentoring partnership

1. As a mentee, and the more senior partner, you may need to guide the initial discussions to ensure that from the beginning of your relationship your mentor feels comfortable to talk honestly and freely with you, and to challenge you if necessary, as they would do if the power dynamic were more even.
2. If you find your initial interactions a little uncomfortable because of the age, social, ethnic or cultural differences between you, remember that your partner will probably feel the same way. As a mentor, bear in mind that your mentee requested this relationship, and they genuinely want to learn from you. Try not to feel intimidated; be straightforward with your advice, avoid being patronising and be as helpful as you can.
3. If you are mentoring about IT skills, as a mentor, bear in mind that while your mentee, as a senior academic, may use technology in their everyday work and may be skilled in the use of many applications, they are not a 'digital native' as you are, and probably view technology differently from you.
4. As a mentee, show respect for your mentor's knowledge and be willing to learn.

Going forward, it is good practice to agree on how often you will meet and how you will communicate between meetings and/or arrange them. This can sometimes cause tension when you are communicating with someone from a different age group. The (older) mentee might be more comfortable making arrangements by email or telephone; the (younger) mentor might prefer instant messaging or social media – this can be quite ironic if the goal of your mentoring is for the mentee to become more confident with new technologies!

Finally, it is good practice for you both to take stock periodically and review what you have learnt, how much progress you have made and what you still wish to achieve. As with every other stage in the mentoring process, this should be done honestly, openly and tactfully, with respect for the other and what they can offer.

Taking the opportunity to reflect on and improve your face-to-face communication skills

As we emphasised previously, one positive outcome of interacting with a reverse mentoring partner who comes from a different cultural or social landscape from your own is that it can be a rich learning experience that translates into improved communication with others from diverse backgrounds across your professional and personal life. (We consider the value of cultural understanding in HEIs in greater detail in Chapter 5.)

If such communication is either the principal focus of your mentoring relationship, or if it emerges in your mentoring conversations as an issue that you both feel you would like to explore, then you might find Activity 13.2 helpful in thinking about how you both communicate and in working to improve your skills. You can do this individually or, more revealingly, work through the questions together and compare how you view your own skills with how your mentoring partner perceives them. We also consider mentoring specifically to improve your speaking skills in Chapter 10.

Activity 13.2

How strong are your face-to-face communication skills?

Tick the box that best describes how often you behave in the way described in the statement. Be honest about how you are, not how you believe you should be. Add up your scores to find out how strong your face-to-face communication skills are, and how you might improve them. You can also score your mentoring partner on their communication skills using the same grid (adapted from www.mindtools.com).

Statement	Never (0 points)	Rarely (1 point)	Sometimes (2 points)	Often (3 points)	Usually/ always (4 points)
When I talk to people, I pay careful attention to their body language and facial expressions.					

Statement	Never (0 points)	Rarely (1 point)	Sometimes (2 points)	Often (3 points)	Usually/ always (4 points)
When I talk to people, I pay attention to my own body language and facial expressions.					
If I do not understand something, I immediately ask the person speaking to clarify what they mean and ask further follow-up questions until I am sure that I really get it.					
If I think I have offended someone or that they have misunderstood something, I try to explain at once.					
When I am talking to someone with a different view from my own, I try to see things from their perspective and not to become defensive.					
I think before I speak, making sure that what I am about to say is accurate and that I am conveying what they need to know.					
If I am explaining something complex, I may use diagrams or charts to get my point across.					
I try to be sensitive to cultural differences and potential barriers when I am talking to someone from a different background from my own.					
I try to make sure that the person I am talking to understands the background to and context of what I am saying.					
When someone is talking to me, I focus carefully on what they say and I do not interrupt them.					

(Continued)

0–10 points: You need to work on your face-to-face communication skills. You tend to speak before you think and not take the other person's point of view into consideration. It is likely that you are often misunderstood.

11–20 points: You have good communication skills but sometimes you may misunderstand what others are saying or not get your own point across effectively. Make sure that you listen actively as well as thinking before you speak.

21–40 points: You are an excellent communicator. You think about how you convey your own messages and you listen carefully and make sure that you understand what others are saying to you.

If Activity 13.2 suggests that you may benefit from working to improve your skills, Top Tips 13.2 offers some techniques you can use. You may find some of these challenging if one of you was brought up in a country different from the one in which you now work, as body language and other communication norms can vary significantly between cultures, as we consider in Chapter 5. You can explore such differences with your partner during your discussions, especially if the aim of your reverse mentoring is to increase your understanding of differences in your backgrounds or life experiences.

Top Tips 13.2

Effective face-to-face communication

1. Before you speak, think about what exactly it is that you need to communicate. Stick to the point; saying more will obscure what you are trying to convey.
2. Think about the person you are speaking with and phrase what you say in a way that is appropriate to them, in a way that they will understand.
3. When you have said what you wanted to say, ask the other person if they would like you to clarify anything.
4. If you are the mentor, then your mentee, especially if they are older or more senior than you, may feel sensitive about their ignorance of the topic that you are helping them to understand, so be mindful of this and tactfully encourage them to be honest about what they do and do not understand.
5. When you are listening to the other person, give them your full attention and do so respectfully. Ensure that your body language and facial expressions are open and welcoming. In UK culture, making eye contact is perceived as indicating that you are listening and are engaged, but if your mentoring partner is from another culture, be aware that this is not always the case.

6. Concentrate on what the other person is saying as they speak. Do not interrupt them.
7. When they have finished speaking, check that you have really understood what they meant by rephrasing the key point(s) and repeating it back to them.
8. If you are a mentee, take care that you do not talk down to your mentor and that you show respect for the expertise that they are bringing to your relationship.
9. If you do not understand anything, ask for clarification. Do not feel embarrassed if you have to ask repeated questions before you feel confident that you have really understood.
10. Watch your partner's body language. Try to judge their level of engagement, understanding, agreement, defensiveness and confidence, and adjust your own message accordingly.

Guidelines for setting up an institutional reverse mentoring programme

Generic guidelines for setting up any institutional mentoring programme are given in Appendix A and can be consulted if you are planning to set up a reverse mentoring programme. In addition, below we highlight some considerations specific to these programmes.

1. **Define the purpose.** This can be, for example, to up-skill senior staff regarding IT or to raise cultural awareness around the experience of junior women staff. For institutional buy-in, which is essential if the programme is going to be supported and succeed, this should be based around a proven need. For example, if analysis of staff data across the institution demonstrates that there is a situation where junior BME staff are leaving or not being promoted at the same rate as their white counterparts, a reverse mentoring programme may form part of the solution. It is desirable to have data or metrics to support your case for the programme and to set a goal for it – in this example, to improve the data on BME staff retention with a particular defined target. As well as making a strong case for the need for the programme, demonstrating its effectiveness provides convincing evidence for the need for further support.
2. **Recruit a champion.** Depending on your institution, you may encounter some resistance from senior members of staff to the idea that a more junior mentor has anything to teach them. A good way to counter this, and drive a shift in institutional culture, is to have a reverse mentoring champion – someone in a senior role who acts as sponsor for your programme. Ideally, they will have a personal story to tell about how reverse mentoring has benefited them. They can be a powerful catalyst to recruit your first mentees.

3. **Name the programme**. 'Reverse mentoring programme' may be the perfect title for the programme or it may be off-putting or too hierarchical for some potential mentors and mentees. Think about the goals of your programme and how you can best capture them in its title. This will be important in the publicity materials that you produce to advertise it. Other terms that are used interchangeably with reverse mentoring, such as 'upward mentoring' and 'mutual mentoring', may be better. 'Learning', 'practice sharing' or 'collaboration' may also feature. Previously, we mentioned the Oxford Brookes University initiative, called 'e-pioneers'. Whatever its name, in any publicity materials, emphasise that at its basis there is a requirement for mentors and mentees to approach it with an open mind, and be willing to step outside their comfort zones and put aside their preconceptions and prejudices.

4. **Call for mentees**. It is common for there to be a lot of enthusiasm from potential mentors and, initially at least, less demand from mentees. If the programme is successful, its reputation will grow, and this will gradually change over time. However, to begin with, it is good practice to recruit your mentees – using your reverse mentoring champion to lead the call – and then to open the programme to potential mentors, saying that there is the opportunity for a limited, defined number of matches. It is helpful to have a larger pool of mentors than mentees in order to facilitate as appropriate a pairing as possible for each mentee.

5. **Match mentors with mentees**. Do this carefully. The mentees are likely to have busy timetables and be unwilling to spend time with someone whom they do not respect or who does not have the knowledge, skills or background that they seek. Similarly, mentors will not engage with mentees who are arrogant, dismissive or unwilling to learn. In the application process, mentees should be explicit about what they want to achieve, and mentors need to be honest about what they can offer. A tick-box list for both mentors and mentees will aid matching, especially if it is linked to the goals of the programme. You may want to add space for mentors and mentees to list personal interests which, if they have at least something in common outside work, may oil the wheels of the relationship. Of course, as we mention in our general guidelines in Appendix A, it is important to be compliant with the new **General Data Protection Regulation (GDPR)** rules, so take advice on this. You could allow mentors and mentees to form their own partnerships, described below. It is good practice to have mentor and mentee matches from outside each other's usual line management chain.

6. **Train your mentors and mentees**. You will need to provide at least light-touch training. This can be, at a minimum, a brochure, guidance sheet or webpage. Some ideas are given in Appendix A. A face-to-face workshop or introductory training session is probably most effective. Some training for the unfamiliar roles may be helpful: mentors may benefit from some practical training, practice or role play in how to confront or challenge a potentially intimidating senior colleague in a way that promotes open dialogue and discussion; mentees may benefit from exercises designed

to help them confront their prejudices, biases and assumptions and to encourage potentially timid junior colleagues to be forthcoming and honest with them.

You may want to run an open workshop to which all potential mentors and mentees are invited. Provide an overview of the programme, guidelines for good practice and training and allow mentors and mentees to network and choose their own partnerships. This can work well because the best mentoring relationships are built on both mutual respect and strong personal chemistry. Similarly, disastrous mentoring partnerships happen when the two parties simply do not 'click', and this can only be judged once they have met. Arguably, this is especially important in reverse mentoring, where, by definition, the two parties are from different cultural backgrounds and/or generations.

Chapter summary

Reverse mentoring offers clear, reciprocal benefits for both mentor and mentee. While this is true of all mentoring, it is especially so here. Benefits emerge from participants taking the opportunity to be honest and to express views openly, with respect, to someone with whom they might normally be wary of being so forthcoming, because of the perceived differences between them. As such, it is a powerful framework for bridging the normal boundaries between people of different ages, seniority or culture, in the broadest sense. In return, this leads to an increased understanding of the perspective of the mentoring partner and translates into greater effectiveness, improved empathy and clearer communication when working with students or staff from different backgrounds. This is clearly beneficial to mentor, mentee and the institution for which they work. Moreover, many participants in these types of programme report how enjoyable it is to get to know someone with whom, initially, they felt they had little in common.

Further reading

Clutterbuck, D.C. (2011) *Reverse Mentoring*. www.gpstrategiesltd.com/learning-lab/reverse-mentoring_22.shtml

Cotunga, N. and Vickery, C.E. (1998) Reverse mentoring: a twist to teaching technology. *Research and Professional Briefs*, 98(10): 270–273.

Greengard, S. (2002) Moving forward with reverse mentoring. *Workforce*, 81(3): 15.

Gündüz, S. and Akşit, B. (2018) Student–president reverse mentoring at universities: Maltepel University case. *Yuksekogretim Dergisi*, 8(3): 346–356.

Mindtools (n.d.) *How Good Are Your Communication Skills? Speaking, Listening, Writing, and Reading Effectively.* www.mindtools.com/pages/article/newCS_99. htm (accessed 18/10/2018).

Myers, K.K. and Sadaghiani, K. (2010) Millennials in the workplace: a communication perspective on millennials' organizational relationships and performance. *Journal of Business and Psychology*, 25(2).

Oxford Brookes University e-pioneer programme, www.brookes.ac.uk/instepp/

APPENDIX A

Generic guidelines for setting up an institutional mentoring programme

Here we present generic guidelines for setting up an institutional mentoring programme that can be adapted for different groups of researchers and/or academic staff; for example, for mentoring those entering doctoral education (Chapter 2), ECRs (Chapter 3), for academic progression and promotion (Chapter 4), for publication (Chapter 7) and grant writing (Chapter 8). Directed advice regarding schemes aimed at specific groups of individuals is given in the relevant chapters in this book.

1. **Consider the evidence for a need for the programme and define its remit**

    Throughout this book, we have presented the case for mentoring being an effective tool to empower researchers and academics at different stages in their careers to successfully achieve career goals. You will be much more likely to convince potential mentees, mentors and, crucially, senior management (and those who hold the purse strings) if you can present concrete evidence that there is a need for your programme. This might be, for example, institutional data about the experience of a certain researcher or staff group, or feedback from institutional surveys requesting mentoring support. You might present evidence from other institutions of the effectiveness of their (similar) programmes.

    Having identified a need, you should carefully define the programme's remit. What researcher/staff group(s) is it specifically open to? And what aim(s) does it have? As an example, during institutional analysis of promotion/retention statistics for academic staff for Athena SWAN awards, you might identify that a specific group, for example early-stage female academic or research staff, appear to be performing less well than their male colleagues in terms of publication, grant success and promotion, and are more likely to leave the institution. You might, therefore, propose a mentoring scheme in which these staff members are offered mentoring by more senior, successful academic mentors.

2. **Get support from the top**. Having identified the aim and target audience for your programme, present your evidence-based case to senior management. This might be initially through talking to influential individuals in your research management structure, Human Resources, or whoever has responsibility for the staff group(s) or issue(s) that you are targeting. Ideally, your mentoring programme should be an integral part of an institutional strategic or business plan.

3. **Devise an application form for mentors and mentees**. A generic example is given at the end of this section. You will need to ask for all the information that you will need to effectively match your mentor–mentee pairs. This can be on the basis of an open question such as 'What can you offer as a mentor?', 'What do you want to get from the scheme as a mentee?', or by asking applicants (mentors and mentees) to check different categories, such as 'applying for promotion', 'building professional networks', 'career development advice', etc. You should take advice to make sure that you are compliant with the new GDPR legislation.

   You can also ask mentees if they have anyone in mind as a mentor. We have found that when mentees name a potential mentor who is not currently part of the scheme, if we approach them and tell them that they have been specifically requested as a mentor, they invariably are happy to take part. Another approach is to have mentors listed online, with a brief biography and summary of what they have to offer. Mentee applicants can then choose which mentor(s) they would like to be matched with.

4. **Pilot it**. For example, within a single faculty or staff group, or with a defined, small number of mentor–mentee matches. Getting feedback from your pilot group on their experiences will help you to iron out any issues before a general launch. Getting qualitative data on the impact of a pilot will strengthen your case for requesting resources for a larger-scale programme.

5. **Launch it**. This might be by holding a launch event, ideally including endorsement from high-level 'champions', such as your Pro-Vice Chancellor for Research. Alternatively, or in parallel, spread the word more informally at staff meetings or events.

6. **Call for mentors and mentees**. An email call backed up by posters or flyers outlining the scheme works well. Explain the evidence base for the need for

the scheme, its aim, and what commitment will be required from mentor and mentee. A good model is to say that, as a guide, mentor and mentee should agree to meet for about an hour, about once a month, for no longer than a year, and with a defined goal in mind.

In terms of recruiting mentors, you will need to decide whether to simply hope that appropriately qualified and experienced individuals respond to an open call or whether you will target individuals. For example, if you are setting up a scheme to support the progression or promotion of academic staff, you might specifically invite staff members who have recently been successful in achieving academic promotion to sign up.

Once the scheme is running, you will need to decide if it will remain open to applicants throughout the year, or whether you will have, for example, an annual call. In terms of ongoing monitoring and evaluation, the latter is easier to manage. However, it is important also to consider how support can be offered in a timely manner: waiting for up to a year to be matched with a mentor will be especially unhelpful to research staff and those on short-term contracts who may not be able to make use of a yearly call.

7. **Train the mentors**. This can be a workshop or online training. At its simplest, provide mentors and mentees with written guidance on good practice, either as an attachment to the email confirming their pairing or through a mentoring scheme website. It might include: an outline for the programme; a definition of mentoring; the responsibilities of mentors and mentees; top tips for effective mentoring conversations; proposed topics; limitations; common challenges faced by mentors and mentees and how to address them; where to go for help; some guidance on unconscious bias; and guidelines for mentors and mentees. Some links to established mentoring schemes and their resources are listed at the end of this section and you might find them helpful.

8. **Match mentors with mentees**. Create a system that works for your situation and develop it as you pilot the programme. Some alternatives are given here:

   i.   Simply laying out all the applications on a very large table and matching them according to their stated requirements works well. It works best if the scheme coordinator has a good understanding of the requirements of the mentees and the types of experience offered by the mentors.

   ii. Other institutions have more complex systems, including face-to-face interviews of all applicants, which can allow the manager of the scheme to read between the lines of what the mentee really wants and make a match based not only on what the person writes on their application form but also what they say in conversation. A good example of this from our experience is that ECRs often apply for mentoring about funding, for example, and then, through conversation, it transpires that they would benefit from mentoring on funding but also managing career and family or dealing with an overbearing head of department.

iii. There are commercially available software programs available to assist in matching and to manage mentoring programmes. An example is Sumac (https://sumac.ac.uk) which was developed at University of St Andrews by Jos Finer, a researcher developer with experience of running mentoring programmes there.

iv. In our experience, in the first year(s) of a programme, it is more difficult to match mentees with appropriate mentors because the pool of mentors is necessarily limited to begin with. As the scheme progresses, mentors remain on the database and their numbers grow, thus giving a much broader pool of expertise to choose from. Of course, mentors will be lost if they ask to be removed from your database or can leave the institution. Of course, in some mentoring schemes mentors will, by definition, only be around for a defined time period, for example, if they are doctoral researchers or researchers on a fixed-term contract.

9. **Confirm the matches**. An email confirmation works well, stating:

- The identity of the mentor/mentee match
- The criteria on which the match was made
- That it is the mentee's responsibility to initiate contact if they wish to go ahead
- That if either party wishes to decline the match they can, and can request an alternative pairing
- That if the mentoring relationship does not work out, they can request an alternative pairing

10. **Provide guidelines for mentors and mentees**. These can be adapted for the needs of your specific programme, but some examples of good practice, adapted from Gubbi et al. (2017), are given here.
Mentor and mentee must both have clearly defined expectations of their responsibilities to the mentoring relationship which should be discussed frankly at their first meeting. These include:

- Equal commitment from both parties; mutual respect.
- To remain open-minded and put preconceived ideas and prejudices aside.
- To work to overcome any barriers to understanding and communication.
- To respect the confidentiality of what is discussed.
- To agree to a long-term, but time-limited relationship, for example, a notional one-hour monthly meeting throughout the course of a year.

- To define a goal. It is especially important to do this at the first meeting. As time goes on and the relationship develops, it may be that the focus of the mentoring may broaden or diverge.
- To establish trust as the relationship develops through open, honest and friendly exchange of views.
- The mentee to send a summary email to the mentor after each meeting. This is helpful to ensure that both have clarity on what was discussed/agreed/achieved and is a helpful 'paper trail' to track progress between meetings.
- To discuss honestly what works and what does not, for both mentor and mentee; and to understand that the relationship and how you interact will evolve over time.
- To be honest if things are not working, or if the mentee feels that either the mentoring relationship is not right for them or that everything that can be achieved from it has been achieved.

11. **Provide mentors and mentees with a 'contract'**. This can act as a framework for them to agree strategy, define commitment and boundaries, outline confidentially and clarify their objectives. A generic example is given at the end of this section.

12. **Check how mentoring pairs are working**. Check in with mentor–mentee partners at intervals during the mentoring relationship (for example, by email at three, six and nine months in a year-long programme) to ensure that the partnership is working and is productive. If issues have arisen, depending on the nature and the scale, one-to-one or group coaching to support mentors and mentees to handle their roles effectively may be necessary. Where partnerships have not worked out, re-matching may be required.

13. **Keep careful records**. Many scheme coordinators simply have a series of paper files or an Excel spreadsheet, and we find that works perfectly well. However, as mentioned previously, there is software available that is designed specifically to administer mentoring schemes.

14. **Review and refine**. At the end of the programme, collect formal feedback. This can be quite light touch, for example, a simple questionnaire, and is valuable as a source of information to help you to improve the programme in subsequent iterations. Instead of, or in addition to, a questionnaire, you could collect feedback through a live meeting to which all mentors and, separately, all mentees are invited at about halfway through the programme and at its end. Hold focus groups with mentors and mentees. Such evaluations should explore both the perceptions of mentors and mentees regarding the effectiveness and organisation of the programme, and developmental opportunities through the mentee offering feedback to their mentor on how effective they found the mentoring, and *vice versa*.

Clearly, any generic issues that arise should be addressed in the next iteration for the programme and improvements made over time as the programme evolves. Review should be supported by quantitative evidence of impact, which can only be collected longitudinally over time. For example, if a mentoring scheme was set up in part to address a paucity of women academic staff in more senior positions, data demonstrating an improvement in the statistics or evidence of mentees achieving promotion will be helpful in demonstrating that it is effective.

15. **Celebrate and publicise your success**. Success breeds success, so publish good news stories from your mentoring programme in institutional newsletters, webpages, online and in face-to-face meetings. The more staff hear about the scheme and its effectiveness, the more interest will grow. Many mentoring programmes have a celebratory networking event at the end of the mentoring period, which is an excellent opportunity to invite previous mentees to discuss their career progression since involvement in the scheme and how they feel it helped them, or for mentors to share how they feel that they have benefited. All these factors help build a culture where mentoring is accepted, valued and integrated.

16. **Lobby for your scheme to be integrated into everyday practice**. For example, for mentoring for academic progression to be a standard part of annual appraisal discussions, for mentoring more junior colleagues to be one of the criteria for promotion to senior academic positions, and for staff to receive workload planning allowances to engage in mentoring as mentors or mentees.

Generic application form for a mentoring scheme

Q1 Would you like to be considered as a mentor/mentee/both (delete as appropriate)

Q2 Title/name

Q3 Gender (optional)*

Q4 Department

Q5 Job title

Q6 General area of research/academic discipline

Q7 Would you prefer to be matched with someone of the same gender as yourself – Yes/no/no preference? (delete as appropriate)

Q8 Do you have any other preferences regarding your partner? (Mentees – if you have a specific mentor, or mentors, in mind, name them here)

Q9 Mentors – What can you offer? Mentees – What do you want to achieve?

(Please give as much detail and be as specific as you can – this will *really* help with matching)

It is good practice to add a statement regarding the General Data Protection Regulation (GDPR).

* We explain that we are requesting this information for monitoring purposes, so that we can judge if any group is under-represented by the scheme, and to facilitate matching with a partner of a specific gender, if requested.

Generic mentoring contract proforma

This sample contract can be adapted by individual mentors/mentees and is provided for guidance only. You may wish to change, add or delete sections. It is not essential that you use a contract, but many mentor/mentee partners find it helpful.

- What do we want to achieve? (It may be helpful to summarise in bullet points)
- Practicalities of meeting. How often shall we meet, and for how long? (It is envisioned that this should be approximately once a month, for approximately an hour and for no longer than one year.)
- Should it be at a regular time/day? If so, when would be best for us?
- Where shall we meet? (Shall we sometimes 'meet' by phone, skype, etc., or will it always be face-to-face?)

We agree that:

- We will choose a room that is quiet and we will guard as far as possible against interruption.
- We will be punctual, keep to time and use our time productively.
- We will have a brief agenda for each meeting and we will agree this beforehand (how? email?). (How long beforehand? Who will take responsibility for this?)
- We can both put forward topics for discussion, and while these may be wide-ranging, they will fall within the broad remit of what we agreed under 'What do we want to achieve?', above.
- We will work together to agree actions at the end of every meeting.
- The mentee will note the mentor's feedback and report at the next meeting if, and how, they have acted on that feedback.

Dimensions of the mentor–mentee relationship. We agree that:

- We will have an honest, trusting, supportive and open relationship with the opportunity for two-way constructive criticism.

- If either of us finds the working relationship difficult, or our meetings to be unproductive or unhelpful, then either of us can choose to terminate the meetings at any time.
- The details of what is discussed between us remains confidential unless the health, safety and well-being of the mentee or people around the mentee are at risk.

The above forms the basis upon which we agree to meet and work

Signed.. (Mentor)

Signed.. (Mentee)

Date ....

References and further reading

Gubbi, P., Hubbard, S. and Smith, R. (2017) *How to Create a Successful Reverse Mentoring Program to Promote Gender Diversity*. Society for Human Resource Management. https://blog.shrm.org/blog/how-to-create-a-successful-reverse-mentoring-program-to-promote-gender-dive, 16 February 2017.

Some links to mentoring schemes and their resources

Swansea University mentoring scheme to support academic promotion: www.swansea.ac.uk/personnel/promotions/academicpromotions/mentoring

University of St Andrews teaching research and academic mentoring scheme: www.st-andrews.ac.uk/capod/staff/coachingandmentoring/mentoring/researchstaffmentoring/

University of Glasgow mentoring toolkit: www.gla.ac.uk/myglasgow/humanresources/employeeandorganisational development/toolkitstosupportyourlearning/mentoringtoolkit/

Sumac data management for mentoring and coaching schemes: https://sumac.ac.uk

APPENDIX B
Guidelines for both mentor and mentee on setting up a mentoring relationship

Mentoring is a great development activity, at the core of which is the development of the mentee. The development needs addressed by the mentoring relationship can vary and the focus should be decided by the mentee. The mentee must lead in both identifying issues and, with their mentor's guidance, resolving them. The mentor is not expected to provide instant answers but to guide the mentee towards the right answer for him or her. As mentor, passing on the benefits of your experience is part of the process, but this should be achieved in a non-directive way. You might share any hints and tips or provide some options for your mentee to consider rather than giving instructions for action.

Role of the mentee

As a mentee, you can expect to:

- Take responsibility for the content of your mentoring sessions
- Be open to developing self-awareness, making changes and taking actions
- Be receptive to what your mentor says/their advice. You do not have to agree with it; just receive it, reflect and make your own decision on how to act on it
- Allow time between sessions to think about what has been discussed and to implement the actions agreed
- Behave in a professional manner with respect to timekeeping and how you interact with your mentor.

Role of the mentor

You will be viewed as a more experienced person who is willing and able to pass on the benefit of your experience to someone who is (usually) at an earlier stage of their academic/career journey. Your role is not to 'tell' the mentee what to do, but to act as a sounding board. Aspects of your role when mentoring will include:

- Helping your mentee to set a goal for each session
- Listening to the issues raised
- Questioning your mentee to explore the issues that concern them
- Encouraging your mentee to develop ideas for action
- Offering your feedback on issues raised and proposed actions
- Building rapport and providing non-judgemental support
- Providing a different perspective based on your own background and sharing knowledge and advice.

Skills and qualities of mentors

- **Time**. The length of the mentoring relationship will depend on the situation of each mentoring partner, and the issues that the mentee wishes to address. Sometimes a one-off intervention may be all that is required or mentoring could last for a year or longer. Having a review every few months gives both parties the chance to assess how well the process is going. It is important that, as mentor, you make it clear to your mentee what your time commitment can be at the start of the process so that their expectations are set at the right level. Mentoring sessions typically last 45–60 minutes but can be longer.
- **Listening**. Successful mentoring requires active listening by mentors, where the focus is on understanding what is really being asked/discussed, giving mentees time to express themselves and summarising/reflecting back what you think is being said.
- **Advising**. As the mentoring relationship is led by the mentee, mentors should allow their mentees to reach their own conclusions in their own time rather than offering suggestions or advice too early.

Practicalities of being a mentor

How you choose to mentor will depend on what your mentee needs and what you are able to commit to. You can choose to mentor by:

- Face-to-face meetings
- Telephone or video conferencing calls
- E-mentoring via email

Guidelines for setting up a mentoring relationship

- **Agree when, where and how long the meetings will be.**
- **Agree a method of contact**, for example, by email or telephone. It is a good idea to confirm the details of a meeting/session shortly before it is due to take place. Discuss the importance of punctuality and agree what to do if one of you must cancel a meeting or is running late.
- **Recording progress**. As either mentor or mentee, it may be useful to keep a record of what you discuss within your mentoring meetings and the actions to agree to take between meetings.
- **Define your role**. Make sure that both of you know what the purpose of your relationship is and discuss what skills and experience you are bringing to the relationship as mentor and what your aim or goal is as mentee.
- **Mentors cannot solve all issues**. As mentor, it is important that you make this clear at the outset of the relationship. You can refer your mentee to others who can help.
- **Confidentiality**. Mentees need to be reassured that anything they say in mentoring sessions is confidential and that information will only be disclosed with the mentee's consent or in exceptional circumstances where their safety and the well-being or the safety of others is a concern.
- **Withdrawal/endings**. It is important to formally end the relationship and not allow it to continue when it is no longer useful.

Glossary

Academic culture   Expectations, attitudes to working and style of thinking, writing and speaking typical of individuals educated in specific parts of the world.

Athena SWAN   A charter, established in 2005 and run by Advance HE, to recognise and encourage the advancement of gender equality in academia.

Digital native   An individual who learned to use computers and the internet as a child and so feels very comfortable using digital technology.

Dyadic   Between two people or two parties; for example, mentoring is a dyadic relationship (a relationship between two people).

Early career researcher   An individual holding a fixed-term contract for a postdoctoral position normally in the first four years of research activity.

Elevator pitch   A very succinct, but persuasive and memorable, presentation.

Esteem measures   Indicators of an individual's research reputation. Indicators vary and include the individual's editorial roles, positions on national and international advisory bodies, keynote addresses, highly-esteemed journal publications, etc.

General Data Protection Regulation (GDPR)   Formal regulations relating to the processing, use and storage of data that must be followed by anyone who processes or uses the personal data of others.

High-impact journal   A journal considered to be very influential in its particular field.

HR Excellence in Research awards   The award which recognises an institution's efforts, and success, in taking concrete steps to enhance working conditions for researchers as set out in the European Charter and Code.

Imposter syndrome A sense of not belonging, inadequacy and inability to acknowledge personal achievements.

Learned society A non-profit, subject-specific academic organisation intended to support its members and to maintain/raise standards of excellence within the subject.

Principal Investigator (PI) The holder of an independent grant who is responsible for leading a research project.

Research Excellence Framework (REF) The system used in the UK for assessing the quality of research in higher education institutions.

Schools outreach Programmes and activities run by higher education institutions to encourage and support school students who may not ordinarily consider taking up subjects at a tertiary level.

Storyline The way a researcher makes sense of their project to their audience or readership, also known as the thread that runs through a project and brings coherence to all the facets of the project being presented.

Unconscious bias The making of very quick judgements about people without realising it. These judgements are often shaped by personal experiences, background and culture.

Woman (researcher)/man (researcher) Used throughout this book, as adjectives instead of 'female' and 'male' in response to guidance from Advance HE that 'woman' and 'man', which refer to gender, are more inclusive than 'female' and 'male', which refer specifically to biological sex.

Index

www.ingramcontent.com/pod-product-compliance
Lightning Source LLC
Chambersburg PA
CBHW070922030426
42336CB00014BA/2499